Explorers' Maps

H.M.S. *Racehorse* in the ice north of Spitsbergen, 10 August 1773

From a water-colour by John Cleveley in the British Museum

Explorers' Maps

R A Skelton

Chapters in the
Cartographic Record of
Geographical Discovery

Spring Books
London · New York · Sydney · Toronto

Original edition published 1958 by
Routledge & Kegan Paul Limited

© Copyright R. A. Skelton 1958

This edition published 1970 by
The Hamlyn Publishing Group Limited
London · New York · Sydney · Toronto
Hamlyn House, Feltham, Middlesex, England

Printed in Hong Kong by
Lee Fung Printing Company Limited

SBN 600 01195 x

CONTENTS

FOREWORD

THE ORIGIN of this book will explain its intention and character. It reprints, with suitable revision, a series of fourteen articles written for *The Geographical Magazine* (London) at the desire of its Editor, and published between July 1953 and August 1956. It is designed chiefly as a picture book, and not as a systematic history of exploration. The chapters, which are grouped in a rough regional order, present some episodes and phases in the history of geographical discovery for which the evidence of contemporary maps is specially interesting or accessible. The treatment is therefore selective, and may seem arbitrary; but the dominant themes have not been ignored.

The book may be regarded as a pictorial companion to general histories of exploration (some of which are listed on page 328). The maps used or drawn by explorers describe the borderland between the known and the unknown. Their evidence may tell us what a traveller expected to find or what he in fact discovered. They may have the authority of a prophecy, of a prospectus, or of a chronicle. In early maps information derived from theory and from experience is often inextricably entangled, and for this very reason they are important documents in the history both of geographical ideas and of geographical discovery. They illustrate the always shifting 'relation of observation, theory, and practice' in this field of science.

The recording of an itinerary or a journey is one of the oldest uses which maps have served, but systematic survey and map- or chart-work in connection with voyages of discovery are scarcely found before the 15th century. This is strictly the chronological starting-point of the book. The first chapter, written as a *pièce d'occasion* for the 700th anniversary of Marco Polo's birth, defines some of the motives and objectives by which explorers from the 15th to the 18th centuries were prompted.

The text is planned as a concise summary of geographical ideas and events associated with the maps reproduced. It contains little that is original, and much that will be commonplace to well-informed readers; in the historical background thus presented, it may be hoped that simplification has been achieved without distortion. Each chapter, originating as a separate article of a periodical, has a certain completeness and unity, at the cost of some overlapping; repetitions have, however, been removed so far as possible. The new material added to the articles includes a particular commentary, at the end of each chapter, on the maps reproduced, and notes on the text, amplifying or qualifying details in it or providing references to other chapters and illustrations.

A Note on the Reprint

RE-READING these essays in preparation for their third resurgence in print, I have found little to alter, apart from correction of some minor errors. Since a photo-offset reprint does not allow extensive revision, this conclusion is fortunate. It arises, of course, not from the author's infallibility but from the caution with which, in essays of a general character which are largely compilations from the published work of other students, he has avoided judgments on controversial issues.

There are two matters however on which something more must be said. First, knowledge of early Portuguese cartography has been greatly increased by the studies of Professors A. Cortesão and A. Teixeira da Mota in the magnificent facsimile atlas *Portugaliae Monumenta Cartographica* (1960). The statements in the present book (pp. 33–4, p. 47 n. 12) on the loss of early Portuguese charts must be qualified. At least three such charts are now known from the 15th century: the first signed one is of *c.* 1485, the first dated one of 1492. Second, in the discussion of the erroneous interpretation of Frobisher's discoveries by mapmakers (pp. 133–4), more weight should have been given to the influence of the so-called Zeni map published in 1558. On this, reference may be made to Miller Christy, *The Silver Map of the World* (1900).

January 1969   R. A. S.

ACKNOWLEDGEMENTS

THE BEGETTER of this book is, in a real sense, Mr Michael Huxley, Editor of *The Geographical Magazine*, to whose enthusiasm and craftsmanship the articles from which it is developed owed their birth and form. I wish to express my grateful appreciation of his encouragement and help, and particularly of the editorial skill which he devoted to the selection of the illustrations and to the planning of their layout. In this connection I would also thank Mr Derek Weber, Art Editor of the *Magazine*. I am further indebted to Mr Huxley for permitting the use of the blocks which accompanied the original articles and without which no reprint could have been contemplated. In addition, he has allowed the use of some blocks which illustrated two articles on 'Explorers' Ships', by Mr George Naish and myself, published in *The Geographical Magazine* in December 1956 and January 1957; and Mr Naish has kindly authorized me to incorporate in this book a few short passages from those articles.

My thanks are due to my wife, for her forbearance and candid criticism; to Dr Helen Wallis, for valuable advice; and to many scholars whose works on the history of exploration and of cartography I have consulted with profit.

For permission to reproduce maps in their custody I am indebted to the Trustees of the British Museum, the Deputy Keeper of the Records, the Hydrographer of the Admiralty, the Benchers of the Middle Temple, the Royal Geographical Society, the Hakluyt Society, the School of Oriental and African Studies (London), the Real Academia de la Historia (Madrid), the Duke of Alba, Messrs Martinus Nijhoff (The Hague), the John Carter Brown Library (Providence, R.I.), and the Free Public Library of Philadelphia.

April 1958   R. A. S.

PUBLISHER'S NOTE

The publisher is most grateful to the Editor of *The Geographical Magazine*, for permission to use in this book much material which first appeared there in a series of articles by Mr R. A. Skelton under the same title.

PART ONE

The Way of the East

I

MARCO POLO AND THE MAPMAKERS

*The European discovery of the Far East,
13th to 16th centuries*

◇◇

THE HISTORY of geographical knowledge records no more violent illumination of
a practically unknown continent and civilization than the discovery of Central and
Eastern Asia to European eyes at the end of the 13th century. From Hellenistic
times, indeed, contact between Europe and the Far East had been gradually developed by sea and land. By the 2nd century A.D. Roman merchants were making
voyages with the monsoons from the Red Sea to India, Malaya and up the Chinese
coast, and had travelled by the old silk road overland to markets in the Pamirs,
where they trafficked with Indians and Chinese, and as far as China itself, where in
the 7th century Syrian missionaries introduced Nestorian Christianity. Although
the world map in manuscripts of Ptolemy's *Geographia* (*c.* A.D. 150)[1] showed a
landlocked Indian Ocean, the Greek geographer Cosmas Indicopleustes, writing in
the 6th century, knew that 'Tzinitza' (China), 'the country of silk', could be reached
by a sea voyage first east, then north; but he added that 'one who comes by the
overland route from Tzinitza to Persia makes a very short cut'. There were in fact
two sea routes, starting respectively from the Red Sea and the Persian Gulf; and two
principal land routes, to the north and south of the Caspian Sea.

These lines of communication were abruptly cut by the conquests of the Moslem
Arabs who from the 7th century spread through the Near and Middle East to the
gates of Byzantium; and the curtain which fell between Europe and Asia was not to
be drawn back for six centuries. The opportunity was created by a new political
power in Asia; the immediate instrument was a young Venetian merchant, born in
the year 1254. During the first half of the 13th century the nomadic Mongols, or

3

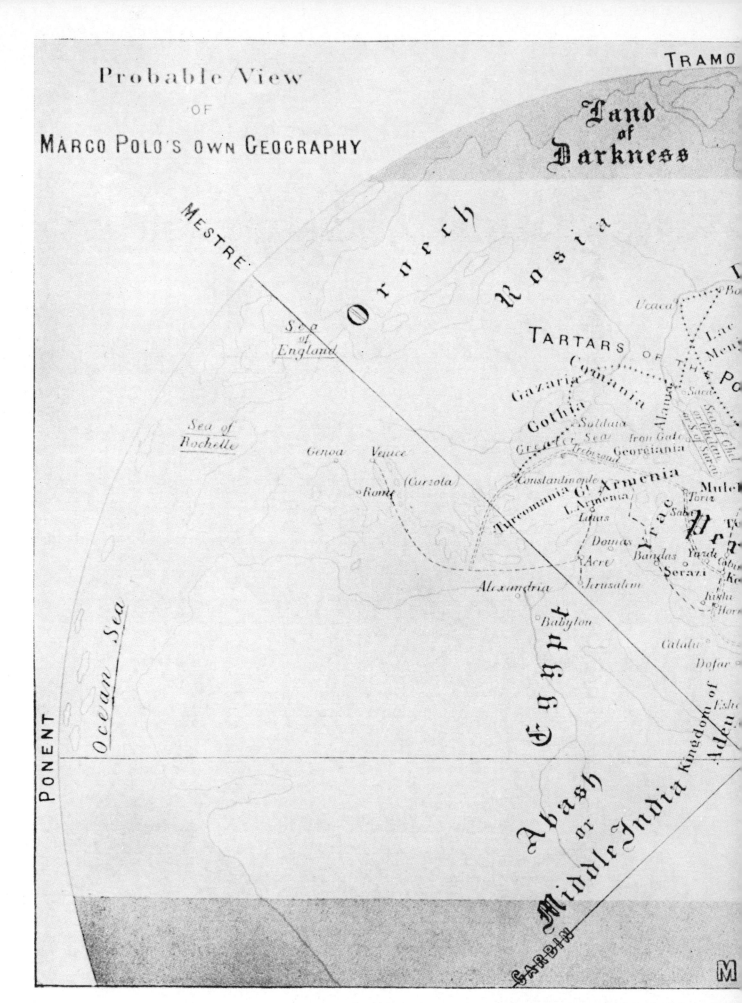

FIG. 1.—The world as known to Marco Polo. Constru…

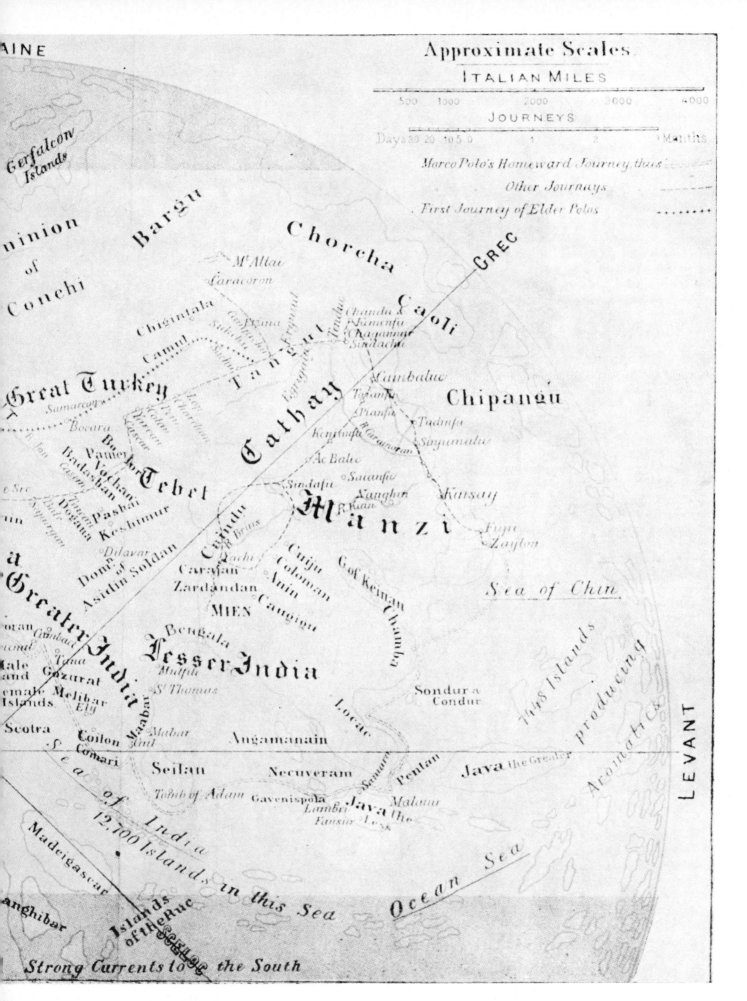

his description of the East by Sir Henry Yule.

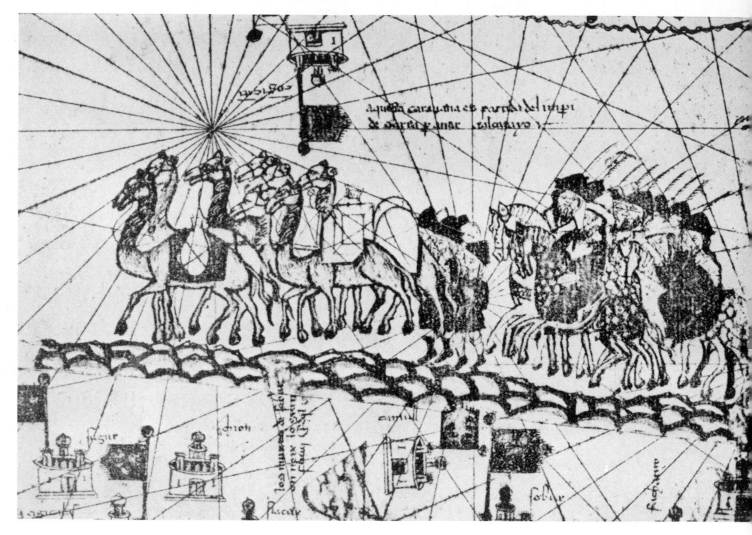

Fig. 2.—Detail from the Catalan Atlas, 1375. The caravan from Bokhara to Peking.

Tartars, under Jenghis Khan and his successors had overrun the Chinese Empire, Central Asia, Persia, and south Russia, and by the date of Marco Polo's birth 'one empire stretched from the Yellow River to the banks of the Danube, and from the Persian Gulf to Siberia'. After 1259 the Mongol dominions became a loose association of four khanates owning a general allegiance to the Great Khan in Peking (Fig. 1). This obliteration of political frontiers not only reopened the natural routes to the Far East, only one of which—that by the Red Sea—remained closed by the Moslem rulers of Egypt. The emergence of sovereigns professing a more tolerant faith than that of Mohammed, suspected indeed of leanings towards Christianity, and willing to promote trade, also encouraged the belief in Europe that Asia was now ripe for conversion to Christianity and for the development of new markets.

The Franciscan missions of John de Piano Carpini (1245–7) and William of Rubrouck (1251–4) brought back frigid and unfavourable replies from the Great

Khan. Meanwhile the Venetian jewel merchants Niccolo and Maffeo Polo, on a trading journey in 1255 to the Mongols on the Volga, had pushed on across the steppes to the south-east and, after staying three years in Bokhara, accompanied a Mongol embassy returning by the northern silk road to the court of the Great Khan, Kublai, at Peking (Fig. 2). Kublai welcomed them and sent them back with letters to the Pope, desiring 'that he should send him some hundred wise men, learned in the law of Christ'; and after a journey taking three years the brothers reached Acre in 1269. They set out for the East once more in 1271, without the hundred missionaries but accompanied by Niccolo's son Marco, then seventeen years old.

Travelling overland to Ormuz, at the mouth of the Persian Gulf, and through Persia, the Venetians took the southern silk road over the Pamirs to Kashgar and Lop Nor (Fig. 1), and in 1275 found Kublai at his summer palace of 'Chandu' (K'ai-p'ing-fu, north-west of Peking). The Great Khan, who needed intelli-gent and uncorrupt civil servants for the administra-tion of his great empire, took

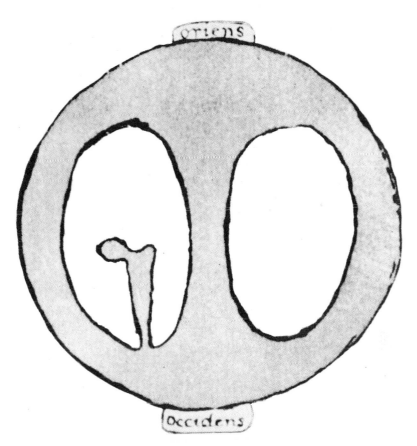

FIG. 3.—*Mappa mundi*, in a manuscript of Marco Polo.

them into his service, in which they were to remain for seventeen years. Marco in particular, showing himself apt at mastering languages and at describing 'the novelties and customs and habits of foreign countries', was entrusted with 'all the important and distant missions'. These (Fig. 1) took him from the Khan's capital of 'Cambaluc' (Peking), in 'Cathay' (northern China), south by the Grand Canal and through the coastal provinces to 'Kinsai' (Hangchow), capital of 'Manji' (south China), 'the noblest and richest city in the world', and on to 'Zayton' (Chuanchow, in Fukien), the great port of Manji and 'one of the two greatest harbours in the world for the amount of its trade'. On a mission to the south-west he travelled as far as Szechwan and Yunnan, skirting Tibet, and into Upper Burma. For three years he was governor of the city of Yangchow.

In 1292 the Polos were permitted by Kublai to return home with the embassy escorting a Mongol princess to the Ilkhan of Persia. The flotilla travelled by sea, sailing south from Zayton, through the Straits of Singapore and Malacca, west by the Nicobars to Cape Comorin, and up the Malabar coast to Ormuz (Fig. 1). The Venetians returned by Persia, the Black Sea and Constantinople to their own city, which they reached in 1295 with (we learn without surprise) 'a smack of the Tartar in their appearance and speech'.

The freshness of Marco Polo's observation and the vitality of his description, which impressed the Great Khan, can still charm us in the Book, describing 'all the great singularities of the vast regions of the East', which was in 1298 written down in Italianate French, at his dictation, by the Pisan romancer Rustichello in their Genoese prison after their capture in a sea-battle between Venice and Genoa. The Khan's capital at Cambaluc and his summer palace at Chandu—Coleridge's Xanadu —marble-built, with its parks and bamboo pavilion, its sorcerers and its herd of white mares; the magnificence of Kublai, who went hunting with 20,000 huntsmen and 10,000 falconers; the imperial administration, with the system of metalled roads radiating from the capital, the post service, the paper money; the markets and ports, especially Zayton which handled a hundred times as many shiploads of pepper as all the ports in Christendom together; the great cities of China and the waterways that linked them, above all Kinsai the 'City of Heaven', 100 miles in circuit, built like Venice on canals, with 12 gates and 12,000 bridges—all these things, in Marco's reports, entered into the imaginative consciousness of Europeans. There too they could read, for the first time, detailed descriptions of Central Asia, its peoples and caravan routes, of Tibet and Burma, of Indo-China and the Archipelago, of Java and Sumatra, of India and the western littoral of the Indian Ocean as far south as Madagascar. Marco Polo has rightly been called 'incomparably the greatest traveller and the most magnificent observer of the Middle Ages'.

The strangeness of his story inevitably called his credibility in question. Robert Burton coupled him with Mandeville (who indeed borrowed from him): 'I would censure all . . . Sir John Mandeville's, Olaus Magnus', Marcus Polus' lies'; and Sir Thomas Browne, combating 'vulgar errors', wrote that 'if any man . . . shall cast a wary eye on Paulus Venetus . . . I think his circumspection is laudable, and he may thereby decline occasion of Error'. In his own day Marco did not escape the scepticism to which he owed the half-mocking, half-affectionate nickname 'Il Milione' —the man who talked in millions. He himself, 'asked by his friends on his death-bed to correct the Book by removing everything that went beyond the facts', asserted 'that he had not told one-half of what he had really seen'. He tells us that on his journeys 'whatever he saw or heard, he always wrote it, and had it in mind to declare to the Great Khan', and he is reported to have written from his prison in Genoa to his father at Venice requesting him 'to send the notes and memoranda which he had brought home with him'. There are certainly some curious omissions from his Book, which contains no reference to the Great Wall, to the Chinese language, or to tea; its chronology cannot in some instances be reconciled with known events; the style of his battle-pieces (perhaps due to Rustichello) recalls romance rather than history; and, after the manner of his age, he fills out his account from hearsay and from such sources of legend as the Romance of Alexander, with the disarming admission 'that which I saw, I declare as I saw it, and that which I knew by others, I declare as I heard it'. Yet Marco's mode of description, concrete (even matter-of-fact), precise, and loaded with detail, compels confidence; and his reports on the countries which he visited have been strikingly confirmed by later travellers and, in this century, by archaeological investigation. A great part of the caravan road by which the Polos reached China was not again trodden by Europeans until the 19th century, and (as a modern editor[2] remarks) 'many of the places visited and localities described remained unvisited again for over 600 years'.

The door which Marco Polo had opened on the Far East was in fact soon to be closed. In the early 14th century many merchants and missionaries followed in his footsteps, and by 1340 a handbook describing the nine-months' trade-route from Tana (on the Sea of Azov) to Peking had been compiled by a Florentine factor. The principal records left by missionary travellers were those of John of Monte Corvino, first Archbishop of Peking, who lived in China from about 1293 to 1328; Friar Odoric of Pordenone, who between 1316 and 1330 visited India, went on by sea to Canton, and, after spending three years in Peking, returned overland through Tibet and Persia; and John Marignolli who was for four years (1342–6) Papal Legate in Peking. In 1368 the Mongols were driven out by the native Ming dynasty; China was once more closed to foreigners; and the western terminals of the road to Cathay were occupied by the Ottoman Turks.

The popularity of Marco Polo's Book is attested by the survival of 138 manuscripts and by its translation, before 1500, into Latin, Italian, German, and Spanish. The only map in any manuscript of the Book is a crude world diagram in the traditional circular form (Fig. 3); and the authenticity of a group of maps supposed to have come down from Marco Polo is not generally admitted. Map-makers were somewhat slow to incorporate his geography of Asia. A world map showing his

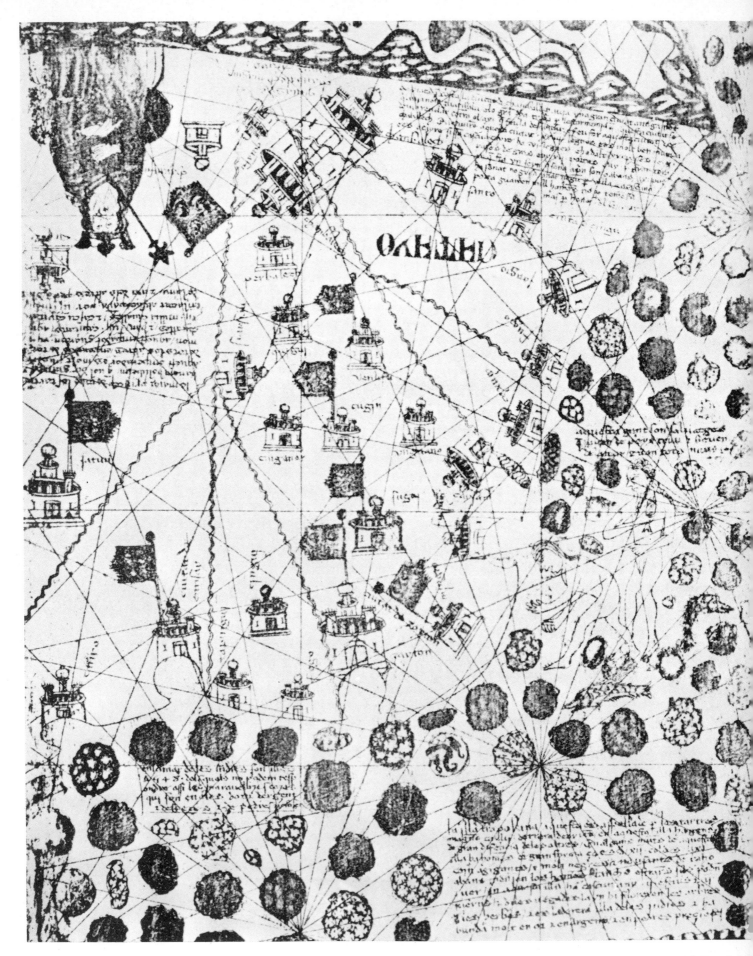

FIG. 4.—China delineated in the Catalan Atlas, 1375. From the descriptions of Marco Polo and Odoric of Pordenc

FIGS. 5, 6.—The Far East in Fra Mauro's map,
1459. *Right:* Zaiton and the island of 'Zimpagu'—
Marco Polo's 'Chipangu', i.e. Japan. *Below:* The
imperial city of 'Chambalech' and summer palace of
'Xandu'.

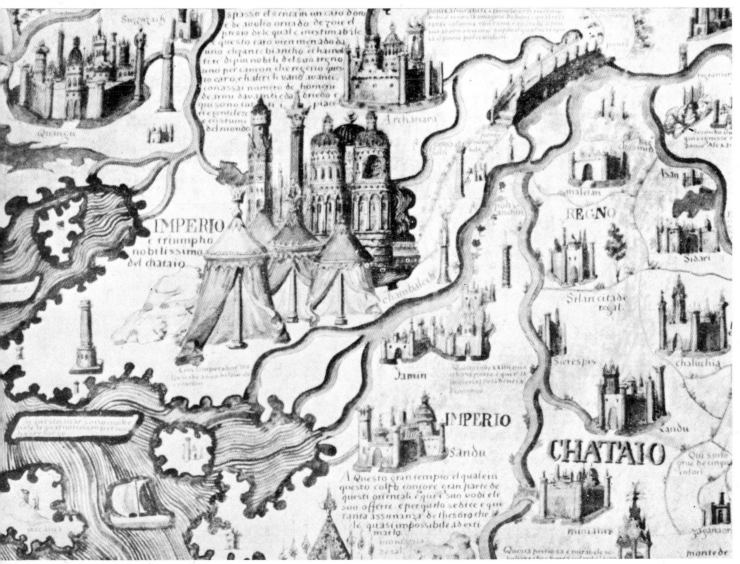

FIG. 7.—Sebastian Münster's map of America and the Far East, 1540.

route was apparently painted on the walls of the Ducal Palace at Venice in the early 14th century. The earliest surviving map to show his influence is the world map on eight panels, now known as the Catalan Atlas, drawn about 1375 by the Majorcan Jew Abraham Cresques, cartographer to the King of Aragon, and presented to King Charles V of France in 1381 (Figs. 2, 4). Besides elements from traditional Christian cosmography and from nautical charts, the geography of Central and Eastern Asia in this map is largely derived from the narratives of Marco Polo and of Odoric. Marco Polo's Book (as Sir Henry Yule, its greatest editor, observed) 'is full of bearings and distances [in days' travel]', and 'on land journeys he usually carries us along a great general traverse line'.[3] On the Catalan map the itineraries of the Polos may be traced in lines of towns; Marco's south-west journey

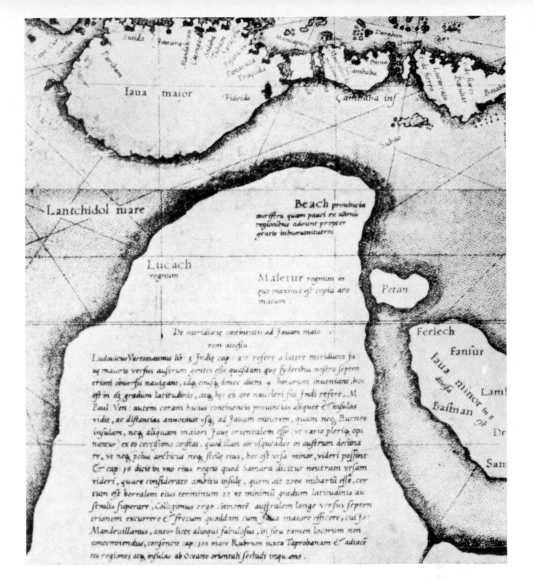

FIGS. 8, 9.—Two maps of the
[six]th century, illustrating mis-
[in]terpretations of Marco Polo. 8,
[ri]ght: Part of the Southern Con-
[ti]nent, from Mercator's world
[ch]art, 1569. 9, below: 'Tartary or
[th]e Kingdom of the Great Khan',
[by] Ortelius, 1570.

to Burma is the source of many names; the great cities of 'Chambalech', 'Cansay', 'Zayton' (all from his Book) and 'Zincalan' (Canton, from Odoric; not visited by Polo) are marked; the trend of the coastline of China is correctly indicated; and the descriptive legends are taken from Marco Polo.

After a lapse of nearly two centuries Fra Mauro (Figs. 5, 6), was also to draw much of his geography of Asia from Marco's Book, with some additions for India and Indo-China from the narrative of Niccolo de' Conti, who between 1419 and 1444 had coasted India and visited Burma, Java, and perhaps south China. Conti, the first European to report on the Spice Islands, may have supplied information personally to Fra Mauro, whose world map completed in 1459 is the earliest to name 'Zimpagu' (Japan)—Marco Polo's 'Chipangu'. The representation of Central and Eastern Asia by mapmakers of the 16th and 17th centuries (Figs. 7, 9–11), often curiously reconciled with new data, continued to be drawn from Marco Polo, whose topography of the mainland of China was not superseded until the Jesuit surveys in the 17th and 18th centuries.[4] In 1561, five years after the publication of Ramusio's Italian edition of Marco's Book,[5] Jacopo Gastaldi made a map of Asia in which he attempted to reproduce all the localities and names mentioned by Polo. Ortelius acknowledged his debt to Marco Polo for the maps of Asia in his atlas of 1570 (Fig. 9).[6] Marco's description of Cathay encouraged English enterprises in search of Northern Passages. In 1577 John Frampton made the first English translation of the Book, 'perswading that it mighte giue greate lighte to our seamen, if ever this nation chaunced to find a passage out of the frozen Zone to the South Seas'; and Mercator, writing in 1580 to Richard Hakluyt 'touching the intended discouerie of the Northeast passage' (i.e. by Pet and Jackman), referred to Cathay in terms derived from Marco Polo.[7]

Mercator himself was responsible for a striking perversion of Marco's geography of south-east Asia, which was to mislead geographers until the 18th century. 'Locac' (Indo-China) was described by Polo as 'a continental province', not subject to the Great Khan, producing ebony, gold, and elephants. In his world chart of 1569 (Fig. 8), Mercator places this name, together with its doublet 'Beach provincia aurifera' and 'Maletur' (Marco's 'Malaiur', Malaya), on a promontory (in about latitude 20° S) of the vast Southern Continent which had already appeared on earlier maps as a coast bounding the Indian and Pacific Oceans to the south. 'That very vast regions exist here' (wrote Mercator in a note on his chart) 'he easily believes who has read Book III . . . of Marcus Paulus Venetus'; and the outline which he gives to 'Lucach' has suggested to some writers an early discovery of the north coast of Australia. The supposed Southern Continent remained on the maps until the voyages of Captain James Cook two hundred years later.[8]

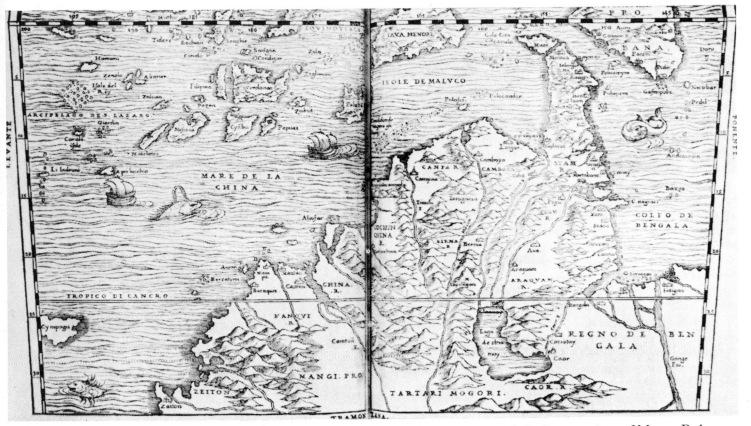

FIG. 10.—South-east Asia and the Philippines, from a map accompanying Ramusio's Italian version of Marco Polo, 1559.

FIG. 11.—Map of China, in Mendoza's account of China, 1585.

From the 14th century the trade routes across Central Asia were closed to European traffic by the growing Turkish power in the Near East, and merchandise from China reached Mediterranean markets through factories on the Black Sea. Europeans were at the court of Timur Khan, at Samarkand, in the early 15th century; and in 1559 Anthony Jenkinson, from Moscow, crossed the Oxus and reached Bokhara on the silk road (Fig. 64). At the end of the 16th century a Jesuit mission, travelling by sea to Macao, was established in Peking; and early in the next century adventurous journeys were made by Jesuits overland from India into China and Tibet. These confirmed the hitherto doubted identity of Marco Polo's 'Cathay' and the empire of 'China' reached by sea by the Portuguese and others.[9]

The western terminal ports of the sea routes across the Indian Ocean were also held by the Turks. Until the fourth decade of the 15th century China maintained a considerable maritime trade over these seaways; Chinese junks were to be seen in the harbours of the Persian Gulf and the Red Sea and on the east coast of Africa, and between 1405 and 1433 seven large Chinese armadas visited the coasts of the Indian Ocean from Java to Malindi in East Africa. As late as 1621 a Chinese collection of charts and sailing directions was published for the voyage from Nanking to East Africa.[10] But the principal carrying trade in the Indian Ocean was in the hands of Arabs. Marco Polo makes three references to 'charts and documents of experienced mariners who frequent that Indian Sea'; Fra Mauro's representation of East Africa and India appears to be drawn largely from Arab sailing directions; and in 1500, at Malindi, 'a Moor of Guzarat' showed Vasco da Gama 'a chart on which the whole Indian stretch of coast was mapped in the Moorish fashion, that is with meridians and parallels . . . but without other rhumb lines'.[11]

In the search for other sea routes to Cathay Marco Polo's Book remained the driving force. From Toscanelli's letter Columbus learnt of the wealth of Cathay and Cipangu, and of their longitudinal distance from Europe; all this came from Marco Polo.[12] Later, Columbus owned a copy of a Latin edition (1483–5) of Marco's Book, which, freely annotated in his hand, still exists.[13] His journals and letters abound in identifications of his discoveries with places recorded by Marco Polo, and in Cuba in 1493 he even sent an embassy in search of the Great Khan. The first Spanish version of Marco's Book, that by Rodrigo de Santaella, although not published until 1503 was—perhaps significantly—completed in August 1493. The belief that the discoveries of Polo, in the East, and Columbus, in the West, related to the same lands persisted long after Columbus, and in 1533 a German geographer[14] wrote: 'Behind the Sinae and the Seres . . . many countries were discovered by one Marco Polo a Venetian and others, and the sea coasts of these countries have now recently again been explored by Columbus and Amerigo

Vespucci in navigating the Indian Ocean.' Even cartographers who realized that Columbus had discovered a new continent superimposed it on Marco Polo's representation of East Asia (Fig. 7).

But it was the Portuguese who, opening a new sea-way into the Indian Ocean, were the veritable heirs of Marco Polo. It is certain that his work was known to them, and probable that it influenced their plans for discovery to the south and east

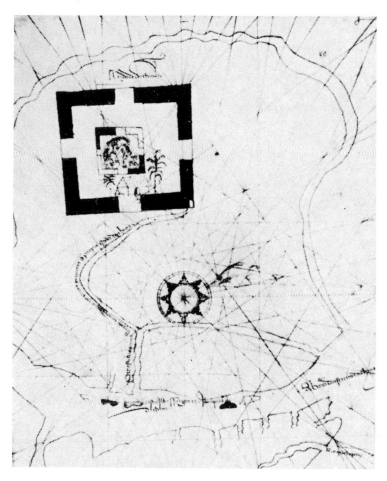

FIG. 12.—Chart of the mouth of the Canton River, drawn by Francisco Rodrigues about 1513

from the early 15th century.[15] About 1426 Prince Pedro (elder brother of Prince Henry 'the Navigator'), visiting Venice, was presented with a copy of Marco Polo's Book and a map said to be by Marco. About the same date Jafuda (or Jacme), Cresques, the son and assistant of Abraham who drew the Catalan Atlas, was summoned from Majorca to Portugal by Prince Henry. In 1502 a Portuguese translation of Marco Polo was printed with an address to those who were . . . 'going out to India'.

After the Portuguese expedition to the Spice Islands in 1511–12 their knowledge

Fig. 13.—Part of Linschoten's chart of South-east Asia, 1595.

of China grew rapidly.[16] Francisco Rodrigues, the cartographer who accompanied the expedition, drew charts of the China Sea probably copied from those of native pilots (Fig. 12). The first Portuguese ambassador to the Chinese court reached Peking in 1520. By 1557 they had obtained a base at Macao, for the China trade, and by 1571 at Nagasaki, for trade with Japan. The Spaniards in the Philippines made similar but unsuccessful attempts to establish themselves on the coast of China. Until the appearance of Dutch and English ships in these waters at the beginning of the 17th century, the cartography of the Far East was wholly derived from Portuguese and Spanish sources (Figs. 11, 13).

Remarks on the Illustrations

Chapter I

1   This 'Probable View of Marco Polo's own Geography' was published in Sir Henry Yule's edition of *The Book of Ser Marco Polo* (1871; 3rd edition, 1903).

The dominions of the Mongol khans are shown: the Khan of the Kipchak Tartars or Lord of the Ponent (west), the Ilkhan of Persia or Lord of the Levant (east), Chagatai ruling in 'Great Turkey' (Turkestan), and the Great Khan in Cathay and Manji (Manzi). The routes are those of Niccolo and Maffeo from Constantinople to Peking, 1255-66; of Niccolo, Maffeo and Marco from Venice to Peking, 1271-5; Marco's travels through China; and the return of the three Polos from Zayton to Venice, 1292-5.

2   The illustration is thought to represent Niccolo and Maffeo Polo, with the Mongol envoys, crossing the Tien Shan mountains on their way through Sinkiang to Peking. (South is at the top.) The legend above reads, in translation: 'This caravan has left the empire of Sarea to go to Cathay.' Sarai, on the Volga, was the capital of the Kipchak Tartars, from which the Polos had set out about 1262.

The Catalan Atlas, painted on eight panels of wood, is preserved in the Bibliothèque Nationale, Paris (MS Espagnol 30). The largest of the Catalan world maps, it has been called 'the most complete picture of geographical knowledge as it stood in the later Middle Ages'. It is one of the earliest maps to depict India as a peninsula.

3   This is the only map found in a manuscript of Marco Polo's Book (Royal Library, Stockholm; 14th century). It is a conventional diagram of the early Middle Ages, with east at the top and showing the northern and southern hemispheres of the old world as land masses surrounded and separated by the ocean. That on the left—the northern—represents the three known continents of Europe, Asia and Africa divided by the Mediterranean and the rivers Nile and Don.

4   This representation should be compared with Yule's reconstruction (Fig. 1). To the north is 'Catayo', with the Great Khan and his capital of 'Chanbalech';

to the south Manji (not named), with the great cities of Zayton and 'Cansay'. The vertical waterway is the Grand Canal built by Kublai 'from Manji to Cambaluc'; below are the 7448 islands, rich 'in all manner of spicery', placed by Marco in the 'Sea of Chin'.

5, 6   Fra Mauro's representation of the Far East is still derived from Marco Polo. His illuminator has conceived the cities and palaces of Cathay, as described by Marco, in the architectural styles of the Venetian Renaissance. (South is at the top of the map.) This is the earliest map in which 'Chipangu' or Japan is named. 'Sandu' is Marco Polo's 'Chandu', the 'city of peace' of Kublai, and Coleridge's Xanadu.

Fra Mauro's map is preserved in the Biblioteca Marciana, Venice. These details are reproduced from a 19th-century copy in the British Museum (Add. MS 11267).

7   This is one of the 'modern' maps added by Münster to his edition of Ptolemy, 1540. The Spanish discoveries in the New World are grafted on the Far Eastern geography of Ptolemy and Marco Polo. Ptolemy's 'Catigara' (Indo-China) has crossed the Pacific to Peru; and from Marco Polo come Cathay, the 7448 islands of the China Sea, and 'Zipangri'.

8   On Mercator's world chart of 1569, the promontory of the Southern Continent to the south of New Guinea ('Iaua major') bears names transferred from Marco Polo's geography of south-east Asia (cf. Fig. 1). The legend describing 'Beach' is taken from Polo's account of Locac (Indo-China), 'a wild region whither few travellers go'. Mercator's 'Lucach' and 'Beach' both derive from Locac by copyists' corruptions: Locac—Loeach—Boeach—Beach. 'Maletur' is Polo's Malaiur (Malaya); his Java Minor was Sumatra and is here displaced by a further misinterpretation.

9   This map by Ortelius was published in his atlas *Theatrum orbis terrarum*, 1570. By this date the Portuguese had reached south China and Japan, but they had not apprehended the identity of China with Marco Polo's Cathay. Ortelius, locating 'Xanton' (Shantung) in 40° N, has moved all Polo's place-names to the north of it, so that 'Mangi' is shown to the north of 'Cataio'.

10   In this map (as in Fig. 11) elements of Marco Polo's geography are still found alongside the new knowledge gained by the Portuguese and Spaniards. (South is at the top.) For Ramusio, see note 5 below.

11   Like Ramusio's map, that of Mendoza marks 'Zaiton' and the 'city of Quinsai, from Marco Polo the Venetian, called Civitas dei'.

The book by Juan González de Mendoza, *Historia de las cosas mas notables . . . del gran Reyno de la China,* was published at Rome in 1585 and translated into English in 1589. It remained the standard work on China for over a century. (See Chapter VIII.)

12   From a manuscript rutter of the East compiled by Rodrigues about 1513 (Chambre des Députés, Paris, MS 1248); published by A. Cortesão for the Hakluyt

Society in 1944. Rodrigues never visited the Canton river, and his chart was probably drawn from the sailing directions or charts of Chinese pilots whom he met at Malacca.

A note on the chart records that off the large island 'the junks from China anchor'. 'The City of China' with its walls represents Peking. The waterway leading to it, by which 'they carry the merchandise in small prows to the City of China itself', is probably the Grand Canal described by Marco Polo.

13   This chart, published in the *Itinerario* of Jan Huyghen van Linschoten (Amsterdam, 1595), is stated to be 'drawn from the most correct charts and rutters used to-day by the Portuguese pilots'. (East is at the top.) The Portuguese forms of names betray its origin. Here the Dutch cartographer is wholly free from the influence of Marco Polo and has taken his material from the voyages of the Portuguese and Spaniards or (for the interior) from Chinese information. The principal ports used by the Portuguese, Macao (here laid down on the wrong side of the Canton river) and Chincheo (Amoy), are marked. Japan is drawn in the conventional 'turtle-backed' form, and Korea appears as an island, as it does generally in the 16th century. (See also Chapters VII, VIII.)

Notes

Chapter I

<hr/>

[1] Whether Ptolemy himself prepared any maps is disputed. The earliest surviving manuscripts of his *Geographia* are of the 12th and 13th centuries A.D. The world map is stated to have been drawn by Agathodaimon of Alexandria, perhaps a contemporary of Ptolemy.

[2] Dr N. M. Penzer.

[3] *The Book of Ser Marco Polo*, ed. by Sir H. Yule, 3rd edition (1903), Introduction, vol. I, p. 129. [4] See Chapter VIII.

[5] G. B. Ramusio, like Marco Polo a native of Venice, prepared an Italian version of the Book, which was published in his travel collection, *Navigationi e Viaggi*, vol. II (1559), together with biographical notices of Marco. Jacopo Gastaldi, an associate of Ramusio who also worked in Venice, took Marco's place-names from Ramusio's text. (A. E. Nordenskiöld, in *Geogr. Journal*, 1899, pp. 396–406.)

[6] *Theatrum orbis terrarum*, Antwerp, 1570.

[7] Mercator's letter was printed in Hakluyt's *Principall Nauigations*, 1589. See below, Chapter V. [8] See Chapters IX–XI.

[9] Matteo Ricci, who established the Jesuit mission at Peking in 1601, asserted that 'Cathay was China'; and his hypothesis was proved by the journey of Bento de Goes from Agra to Suchow in 1604–7. Tomé Pires (see Chapter VIII), a century earlier, had written of 'Cambarra [Marco Polo's Cambaluc], which is called Peking'.

[10] The Chinese voyages in the Indian Ocean during the 15th century are described by J. V. Mills, 'Notes on early Chinese voyages', *Jnl. R. Asiatic Soc.*, 1951. Fra Mauro apparently knew of these voyages, no doubt from Arabic sources; his map shows Chinese naval junks off Aden and Sofala, in East Africa.

[11] The Portuguese commander here notices the difference from European charts, in which the sea areas were covered by a network of bearing lines radiating from centres arranged on the periphery of a circle (as in Figs. 4, 13).

[12] See Chapter III.

[13] Columbus' copy of Marco Polo, bearing his marginal notes, is preserved in the Bibliotheca Colombina, Seville.

[14] Johannes Schöner, *Opusculum geographicum*, 1533.

[15] See Chapter II. [16] See Chapter VIII.

II

THE PORTUGUESE SEA-WAY TO
THE INDIES

15th and 16th centuries

MARCO POLO'S TRAVELS, which at the end of the 13th century 'created Asia for the European mind', opened up the land routes between East and West. Over these passed missionaries carrying western Christianity into Asia, and caravans bearing the spices and textiles of Persia, India and China to European markets. When the Moslem Turks established themselves across these routes by the end of the 14th century, the Indian and Persian trade was canalized through the Genoese and Venetian 'factories', or agencies, on the Black Sea and in the Levant.

To break the monopoly of the Italian maritime states, the nations on the oceanic fringe of Europe looked to the sea routes. The means, as well as the motive, were at hand. By the 15th century, two vital advances in the design of ships had greatly improved their sailing qualities: the rudder hung on the stern-port had superseded the steering-oar, and the shape of bow and stern was differentiated. By 1440 the Portuguese expeditions were being fitted out with caravels: 'the best ships that sailed the seas' and able 'to go anywhere', as one commander claimed. Lateen-rigged and carvel-built on fine lines, they could sail close to the wind, although they became heavy to handle with a following wind; and their shallow draught made them apt for inshore navigation. These were the ships that were to discover America and the sea-way into the Indian Ocean.

The first stage on the ocean road to Cathay was the occupation of the Atlantic islands as advanced outposts. In the 14th century the Canaries were settled by Spain. The other groups fell to the Portuguese: Madeira and Porto Santo were colonized

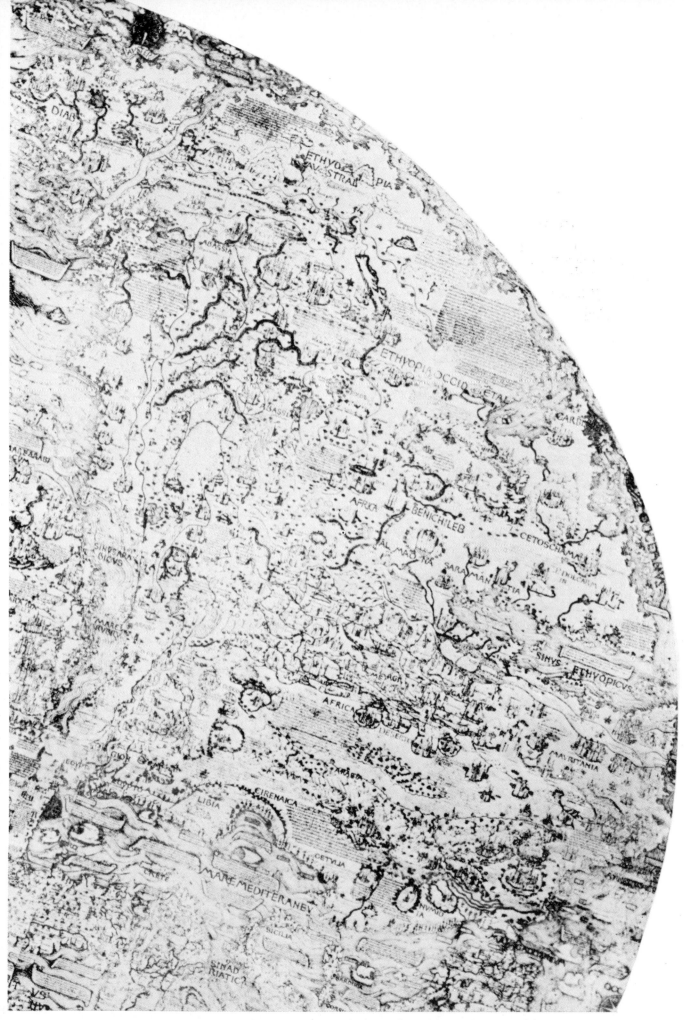

FIG. 14.—Africa, in the circular world map of Fra Mauro, 1459. (South is at the top.)

in 1418–19, the Azores from about 1440, and voyages were made into the Atlantic in search of the legendary islands which dotted the western edge of 15th-century charts. As late as 1487 a Portuguese expedition sailed with a royal charter to discover the Isle of the Seven Cities, or Antillia.

But it was by the east that the Portuguese were to find and develop a navigable route to India and Cathay. Whether this was deliberately conceived as the objective of the series of voyages along the African coast initiated by Prince Henry 'the Navigator' from 1418, is uncertain. By some mediaeval geographers the 'torrid zone' of the tropics was believed to be uninhabitable, with seas 'always kept boiling by the sun', and in Ptolemy's world map the Indian Ocean was closed on the south, in 15° S, by a continuous coastline connecting eastern Africa to the south-east peninsula of Asia; but other classical authorities could be quoted in support of the 'circumnavigability' of Africa.[1] Some maps of the 14th and 15th centuries[2] had shown a sea passage into the Indian Ocean round Africa, whose southward extension was underestimated by about half; and Fra Mauro (Fig. 14), thirty years before the Cape of Good Hope was rounded by Dias, drew Africa with a southern horn, derived no doubt from reports of Arab navigation along the east coast.

It is clear that Henry's plans developed in the light of reports from his captains as they pushed southward down the west coast of Africa. His overriding purposes— to pursue the crusade against Moslem powers, to extend Portuguese trade, and to add to geographical knowledge—did not necessarily call for an advance into the Indian Ocean. They found ample scope in the Negro kingdoms of Guinea, to whose markets the caravan trade in gold, ivory and slaves could be diverted from the Moorish merchants north of the Sahara. From here too the Christian kingdom of Prester John, identified with Ethiopia, might be reached overland.[3] In 1455 it was reported to lie six days' journey from the Gambia, and an Ethiopian mission visited Lisbon eight years before Henry's death in 1460. But the anxious scrutiny of the trend of the coastline by successive expeditions points to a growing belief in the possibility of a sea-way by the south and east; and there is evidence that long before his death Henry was thinking of Guinea as a stage on the way to India.

The initial phase in his plan however was the discovery of Guinea, and the first obstacle Cape Nun, lying in 28° N.[4] 'Because [wrote an early navigator] it was found that anyone who rounded it never returned, it was called "capo de non"—who passes never returns.' It was nevertheless passed by 1421, and in 1434 Gil Eannes, in an oared galley, rounded Cape Bojador, in 26° N. Nine years later the Gulf of Arguim, south of Cape Blanco, in 20° N had been reached; and in 1445 Dinis Dias passed the mouth of the River Senegal and Cape Verde. 'Thus was discovered at last

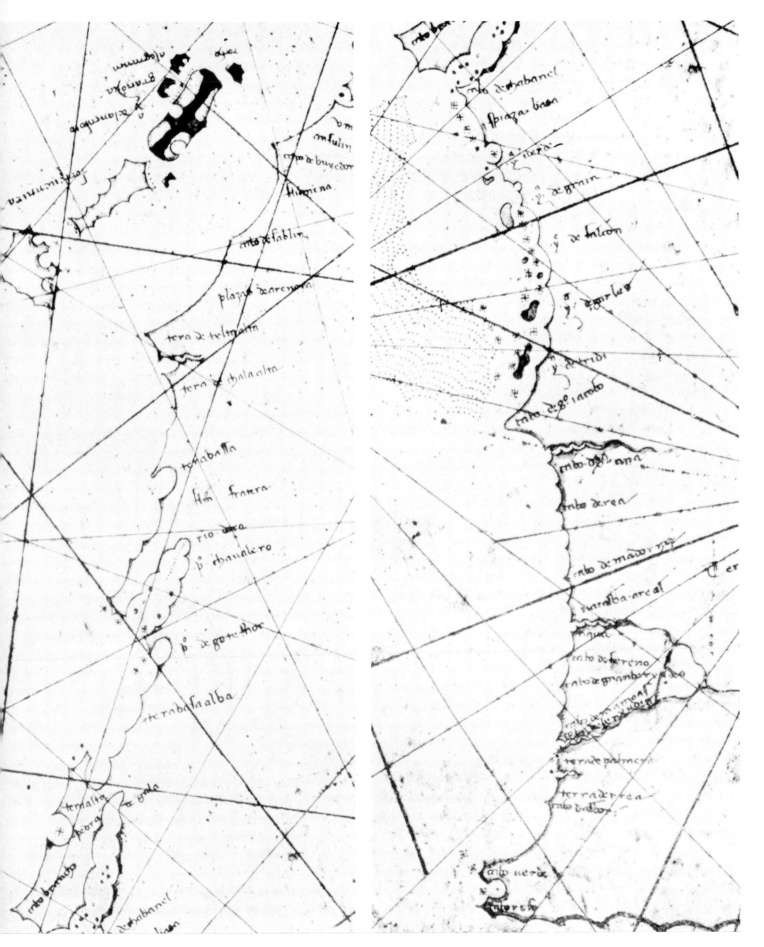

FIG. 15.—The west coast of Africa from the Canary Islands to Cape Verde, in a MS chart of Andrea Bianco, 1448.

the country of the first blacks', for the Portuguese had come to 'the end of the desert'. The coast, observes the contemporary chronicler, 'was found to run south with many headlands, which the Prince caused to be added to the navigating charts'. The extent of Portuguese discovery to this date is shown in the chart drawn at London in 1448 by the Venetian Andrea Bianco (Fig. 15).

In 1455 and 1456 Alvise Cadamosto made voyages to the Gambia and Rio Grande, sailing up the rivers and trading in the markets. By 1460 the Cape Verde Islands had been discovered, and two years later Pero da Sintra passed beyond Sierra Leone. These discoveries are laid down in the chart drawn in 1468 by Grazioso Benincasa of Ancona (Fig. 16). The tide of discovery now ran strongly, and successive voyages took the Portuguese eastward to the Gold Coast, where in 1481–2 the fort of São Jorge da Mina (Fig. 19, inset) was built, and to the head of the Gulf of Guinea, where to their discomfort they found the coast trending south; and they crossed the Equator to 2° S.

When Henry's nephew King John II came to the throne in 1481, the 'Indies' had become the objective for the African voyages. It was natural that Columbus should first (in 1484–5) have sought backing from Portugal, 'seeing that the King D. João frequently ordered the coast of Africa to be explored with the intention of going by that route to reach India'; nor was it less natural that his estimate of the distance to 'the Isle Cypangu by the Western Ocean' won little credit from the better-informed Portuguese cosmographers.[5] By now indeed John had made an encouraging advance southward along the African coast. In 1484 Diogo Cão returned from the two years' voyage in which he had reached the Congo and Cape Lobo (Cape Santa Maria) in 13° S. On discovering the Congo he 'set up beyond its mouth to the south-east a tall stone pillar with a threefold inscription, in Latin, Portuguese and Arabic, and it was accordingly called Rio do Padram'. This was the first of the stone columns or *padrões*, surmounted by crosses, to be erected by Portuguese captains, at King John's order, to mark their new discoveries. The two *padrões* set up by Cão on his voyage of 1482–4 are shown in the chart of Cristoforo Soligo (Fig. 17). Cão's second voyage (1485–7) took him as far south as Cape Cross, in 21° 50′ S (represented by the southernmost cross on Fig. 19), where he died.

From the results of Cão's expeditions, says an early writer, 'arose the hope and will to discover India', and King John now planned a double attempt, by land and sea, to reach the Indies and the empire of Prester John. Like the subjects of other mediaeval travellers' tales, the Priest-King's dominions in 'India' had formerly been located in Central Asia, but by the middle of the 15th century he was believed to reign in Ethiopia, accounted as part of 'hither India' but supposed to extend over a

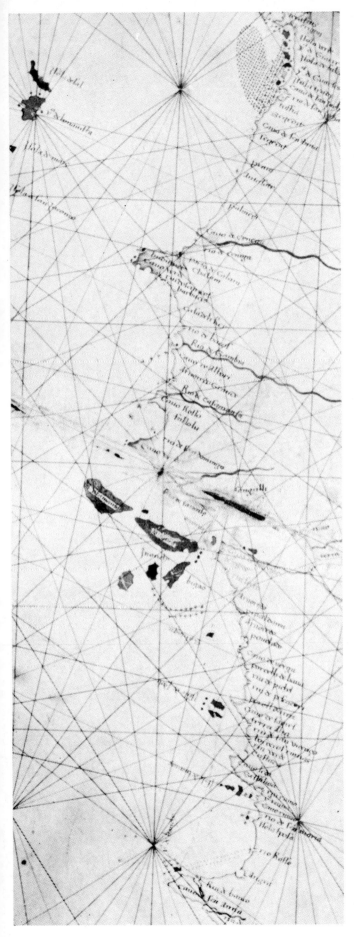

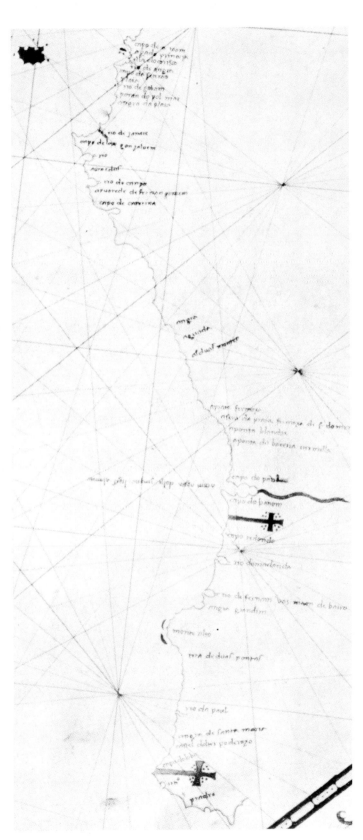

FIG. 16.—The west coast of Africa, in a MS chart by G. Benincasa, 1468.

FIG. 17.—Detail from a MS chart of 'Ginea Portugalexe', copied by C. Soligo, c. 1490, from a lost Portuguese original.

great area of the African continent.[6] Fra Mauro's map (Fig. 14) however confined 'Abassia' to eastern Africa, and Abyssinian monks had visited Portugal. Abandoning the attempt to communicate with Ethiopia overland from Guinea, John accordingly sent expeditions to seek the land route up the Nile and the sea-way round the southern tip of Africa.

Pero da Covilhão, setting out in May 1487, reached India in 1488 by way of Egypt and the Red Sea. The first Portuguese to visit India, he found spices on sale in the market of Calicut; and on his return to Cairo in 1490 he sent a letter to King John reporting 'that he had been in the cities of Cananor, Calicut and Goa . . . and to this they could navigate by their coasts and the seas of Guinea'. After further wanderings, in the course of which he visited Mecca and Medina, Covilhão arrived in Abyssinia, where he settled and was found by a Portuguese embassy in 1520.

Bartolomeu Dias, sailing in August 1487 with two caravels and a storeship, passed the southern point of Africa without seeing it and satisfied himself that the coast trended in a north-easterly direction. After setting up a column at a point just east of the Bushman's River and naming it Cabo do Padram,[7] he turned back at the Great Fish River, in 33° S. The southern cape, at which he erected another pillar on his return voyage, was named by King John Cabo de Boa Speranza because it

FIG. 18.—Africa, in a MS world map by Henricus Martellus, c. 1490.

gave 'great hope of the discovery of India'. The voyages of Cão and Dias are re-corded in the world map of Henricus Martellus (Fig. 18), drawn not long after the return of Dias in 1489. Following Ptolemy in its delineation of the Indian Ocean, this map abandons, in the light of the Portuguese voyages, Ptolemy's view that it was landlocked.

The sea-way to the East was now open to the Portuguese, but not until eight years later did John's successor King Manoel exploit it. The discovery of America had turned men's eyes westward. Portugal was not indifferent to western lands or islands, of which she may indeed already have had knowledge from unrecorded voyages. While the Portuguese probably never accepted Columbus's belief that he had reached the 'Indies', they succeeded in 1494 in moving the demarcation line between the Spanish and Portuguese spheres 270 leagues further west.[8] In 1498 an expedition was sent to discover 'the Western region' under Duarte Pacheco, who may have reached Brazil two years before Cabral. But Pacheco himself (writing in 1505) conceived this 'Western region' as 'a very large land-mass [continent]' extending from $70°$ N to $28\frac{1}{2}°$ S and effectively blocking the western route to Asia.

In 1497 Portugal had resumed her eastward advance. The instructions given to Vasco da Gama, based on Covilhão's report, ordered him to reach Calicut, the great spice emporium on the Malabar coast. After a three months' voyage in the Atlantic he rounded the Cape, and coasting East Africa he arrived at Calicut in May 1498. A second fleet under Pedro Alvares Cabral, who on Da Gama's advice set a course south-west, to avoid the calms of the Guinea coast, and touched at Brazil, sailed to India in 1500–1. The earlier voyages had exposed the weaknesses of the caravel in the open sea; and the commercial route to India, which was now open, called for ships of greater carrying capacity. Those which Dias designed for Vasco da Gama's fleet, heavier and bigger in beam, were the prototypes of the *nao* ('ship'), square-rigged on main- and foremasts with a lateen mizzen, the characteristic ocean-going vessel of the 16th century (Figs. 21, 24).

The world chart smuggled out of Lisbon and sent to Ferrara by Alberto Cantino in 1502 (Fig. 19) records the geographical results of the voyages of Da Gama, Cabral and their predecessors. This is the earliest surviving Portuguese map of the new discoveries in the east and west; and Pedro Reinel (Fig. 23) is the first Portuguese cartographer whose name is known from works still extant. That no earlier original Portuguese charts have come down to us is principally due to the official policy of secrecy by which the Portuguese authorities, notably under John II, sought to deny to foreigners both access to lands discovered for Portugal and information about them. Severe penalties were imposed to protect the Guinea trade

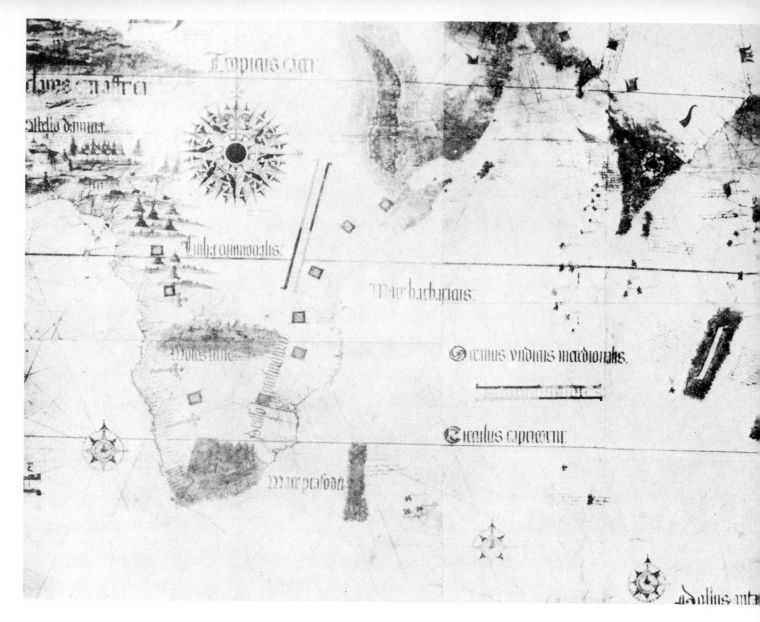

FIG. 19.—Africa, in the Cantino world chart, 1502. *Left:* The fort of S. Jorge da Mina, as shown on the Cantino chart.

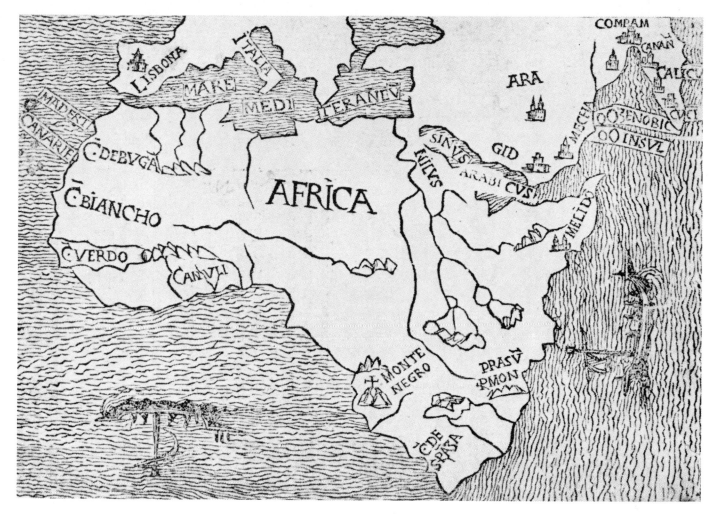

Fig. 20.—The first separate printed map of Africa, 1508.

from foreign intruders and to withhold charts from general circulation. The Casa da Mina e India, the office responsible for overseas territories, was charged with the production, revision and filing of charts; and pilots to whom they were issued were bound to surrender them on return from voyages. After Cabral's voyage an Italian agent in Lisbon wrote that 'it is impossible to get a chart of this voyage because the King has decreed the death penalty for anyone sending one abroad'. It is neverthe-less extraordinary that we have so few of the many charts drawn for Prince Henry and King John II, nor of those supplied to or brought back by their captains.[10]

The main cartographic record of the Portuguese discoveries before 1500 is to be found in maps which, from the use of Portuguese place-names or of information available only in Portugal, are presumed to be based on Portuguese originals or to be copies from them. Most of these maps are from the hands of Italian, and in particular Venetian, cartographers. The signature on Bianco's chart of 1448 (Fig. 15) calls him 'master of a galley', and he may have sailed in Portuguese ships. Fra

Mauro's world map (Fig. 14), in which Bianco and perhaps also Cadamosto collaborated, was completed for the King of Portugal at Venice in 1459, the year before Prince Henry's death, with the help of Portuguese charts; and a copy was sent to Lisbon. Benincasa's chart of 1468 (Fig. 16) has Portuguese names and reflects the recent discoveries of Cadamosto and Pero da Sintra. That of Soligo (Fig. 17), entitled 'Ginea Portugalexe', was plainly copied at Venice from a Portuguese chart drawn after Cão's first voyage.

FIG. 21.—Vasco da Gama's flagship, the *São Gabriel*: a 16th-century drawing.

These charts have some of the defects of compilations. The scale of the African coast as delineated by Bianco (1448) and Benincasa (1468) is not uniform, increasing as the coast runs south; and this suggests that they were 'carelessly assembled from sectional charts'.[11] The loss of their originals is the more to be regretted. The sea route to India presented problems in position-finding and navigation unfamiliar to European pilots. It embraced 75 degrees of latitude (from Lisbon to the Cape) and 110 of longitude (from Brazil to India). Charts which took no account of the convergence of the meridians could only mislead the seaman in laying his course;

and when he passed into the Indian Ocean his compass needle showed a westerly magnetic variation, instead of the easterly deflection of European waters. The solution eventually adopted by the Portuguese was empirical. Latitudes were carefully observed, by noonday observations of the sun's 'height'; after making sufficient 'southing' in the ocean to round the Cape, the pilot turned his ship's head to port and 'ran down the easting'. The use of the latitude to fix the ship's position is reflected in some of the earliest surviving Portuguese charts. The first to bear a meridian line graduated in degrees of latitude is a chart of the North Atlantic signed by Pedro Reinel and drawn about 1502.[12] Comparison of the outline of Africa as laid down on the map of Henricus Martellus (Fig. 18) and on the Cantino chart (Fig. 19) illustrates the striking development in cartographic representation which followed the Portuguese voyages. In the Cantino chart southern Africa has its correct orientation and approximately its true shape; although the width of the continent is underestimated, because of the difficulty of determining longitude by

FIG. 22.—MS chart of the Spice Islands by Francisco Rodrigues, c. 1513.

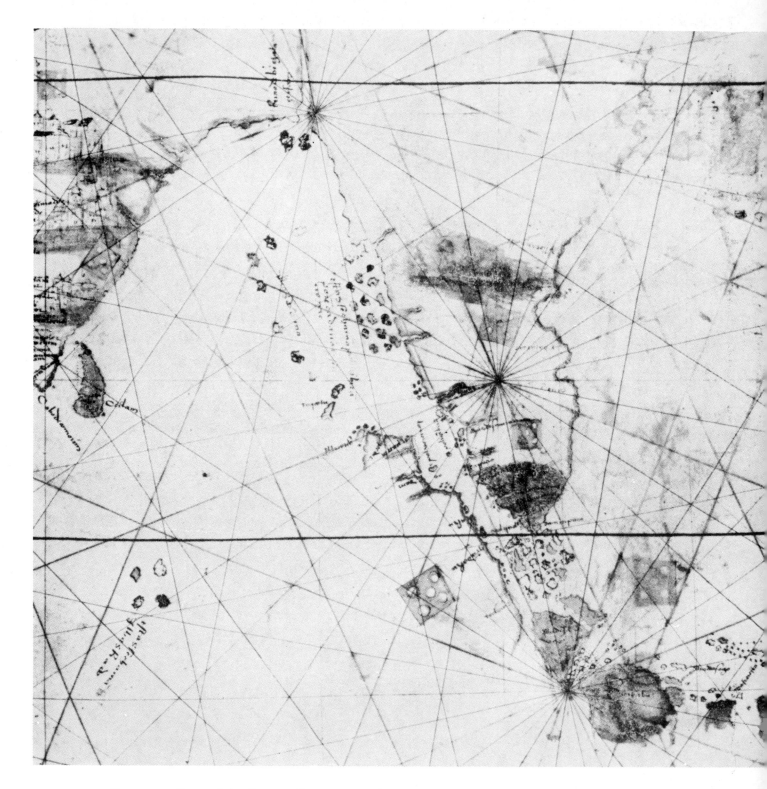

FIG. 23.—Part of the Indian Ocean, in a MS chart drawn *c.* 1518, probably by Pedro Reinel.

dead reckoning, the latitude of Cape Agulhas, the southern tip of Africa, is less than 3° in error (32° S, the correct figure being 34° 50').[13]

After the voyages of Da Gama and Cabral the foundations of the Portuguese empire in the East were quickly laid, and King Manoel assumed the style of 'Lord of the conquest, navigation and commerce of Ethiopia, Arabia, Persia and India'. As his title indicates, this was a commercial empire based on fortified posts and factories which commanded the trade routes of the Indian Ocean and protected them against the Moslems (Figs. 25–28). The capital of the empire was the colony of Goa, conquered by the second Viceroy Afonso de Albuquerque in 1510; and the principal trading centres and fortified bases were Ormuz and Malacca, captured by Albuquerque in 1508 and 1511 respectively. Ormuz commanded the Persian Gulf, and Malacca the Malay Peninsula and Archipelago. In 1511–12 an expedition under Antonio de Abreu and Francisco Serrão, accompanied by the chart-maker Francisco Rodrigues, reached Java and the Moluccas, or Spice Islands (Fig. 22); and Reinel's chart of about 1518 (Fig. 23) shows increasing Portuguese penetration into the Malay Archipelago.[14] In 1540–1, a fleet sailed up the Red Sea, hitherto closed to the Portuguese, as far as Suez; and this is recorded in the 'rutter' of João de Castro, illustrated by charts and views (Fig. 24). Macao, at the mouth of the Canton river, was founded about 1557 as a centre for the China trade.

Portugal's reach however had exceeded her grasp, and by the end of the 16th century her great empire was in decline. Her small military forces in the East were inadequate to defend it against disaffected tributary peoples and against piracy, and the blood of her settlers was diluted by intermarriage with natives. From 1580 to 1640 the Portuguese crown was united with that of Spain; and the first half of the 17th century saw the loss of Portugal's principal strongholds in the East to the English and Dutch.[15] Only Goa, Diu and Macao remained in Portuguese hands; but the empire which had once been ruled from Goa was gone.

FIG. 24.—Portuguese ships lying off Socotra in 1541. From the MS rutter from India to Suez, by João de Castro.

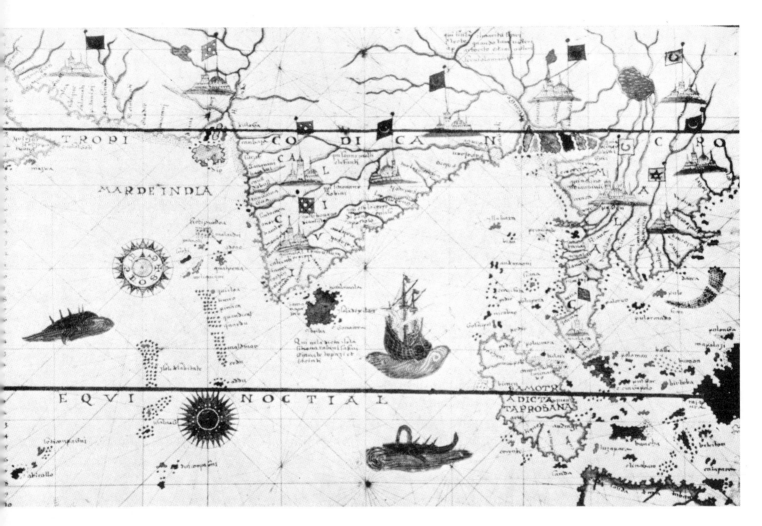

FIG. 25.—The Indian Ocean, in a MS chart by Joan Martines, 1578.

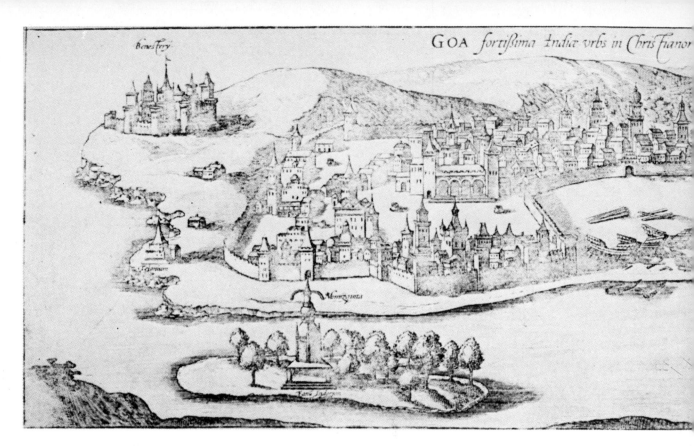

Beneffry

GOA *fortiſſima Indiæ vrbs in Chriſtianor*

FIGS. 26, 27.—Views of Goa and Calicut, from the

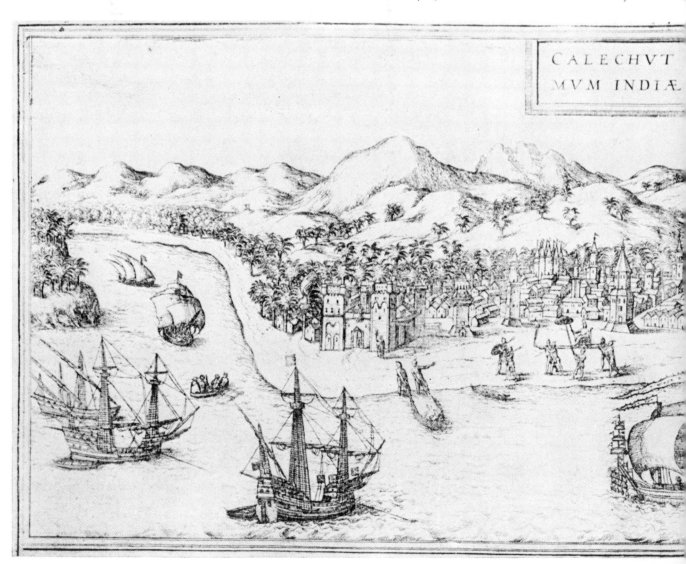

CALECHVT
MVM INDIÆ.

anno Salutis 1509 deuenit.

me of the city-atlas *Civitates orbis terrarum*, 1573.

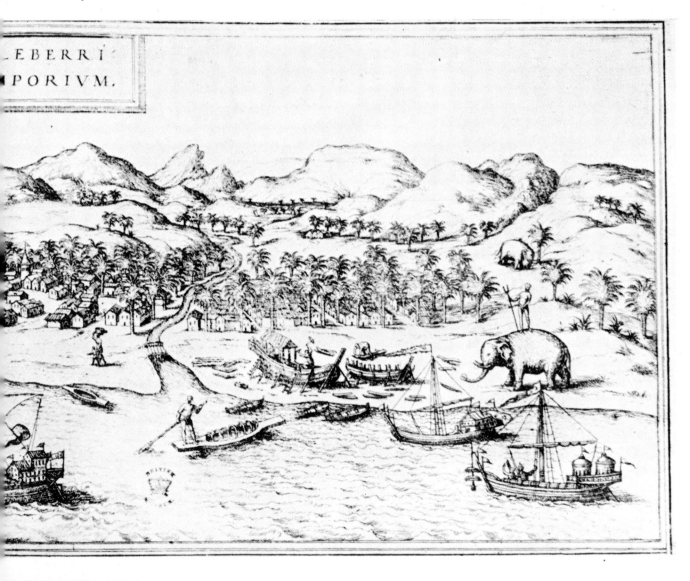

EBERRI
PORIVM.

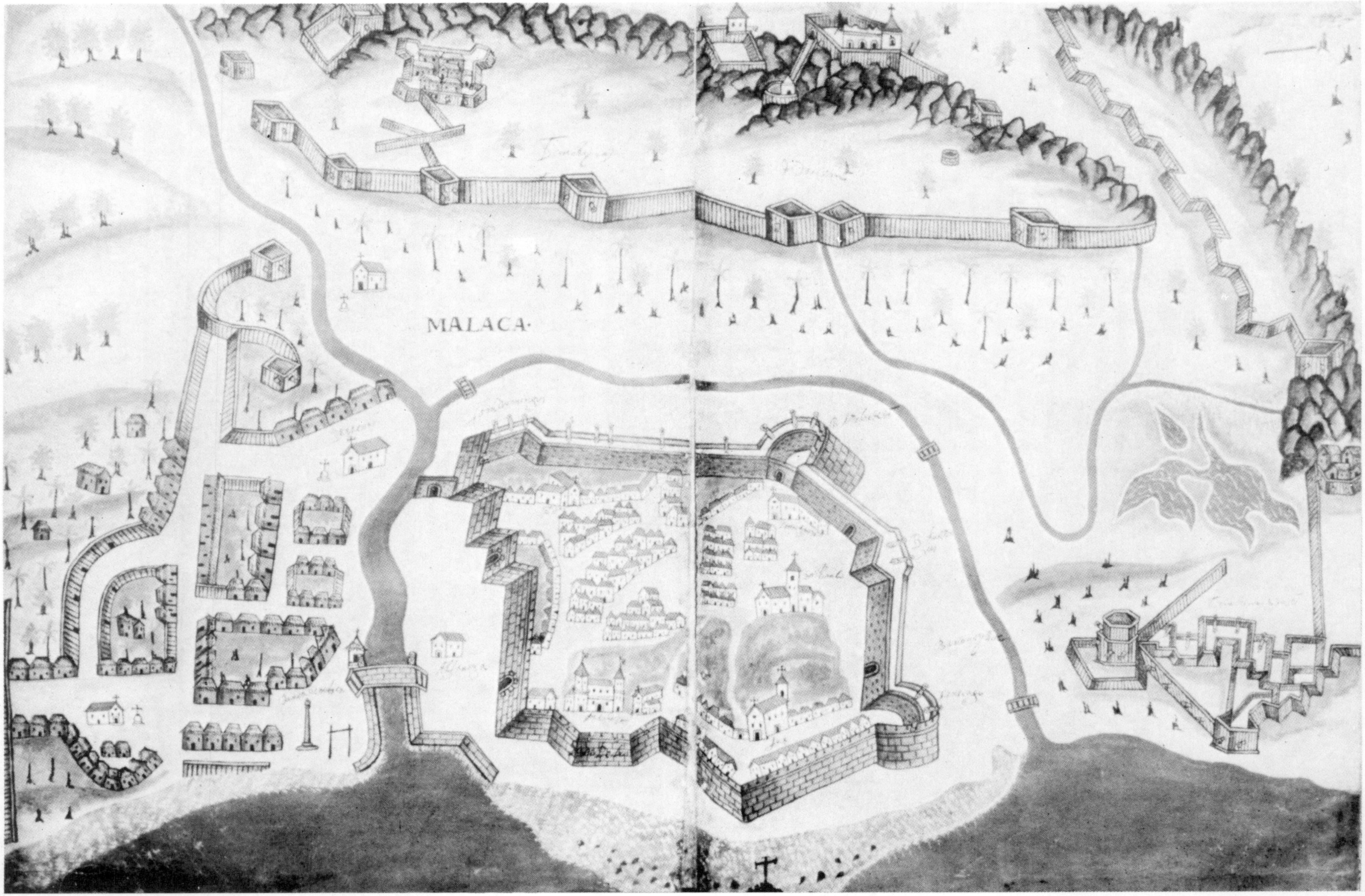

MALACA.

Fig. 28.—MS plan of Malacca by Pedro Berthelot, 1635.

Remarks on the Illustrations

Chapter II

◇-◇

14 The drawing of the west coast of Africa (on the right) is adapted to the circular shape of Fra Mauro's map completed in 1459. The 'Sinus Ethyopicus' is a feature taken over from mediaeval maps, and perhaps derived from rumours of the Gulf of Guinea. To the north of it (i.e. below it) Portuguese discoveries as far as Cape Verde and Cape Roxo are indicated—thus no further than in the Bianco chart of 1448 (Fig. 15). Prester John's Kingdom of 'Abassia' lies at the sources of the Nile, and 'Ethyopia' extends to the west and south coasts of the continent. In a legend Fra Mauro affirms his belief in an open sea-way (as shown on the map) between the 'Sea of India' and the surrounding ocean on the west. The large island of 'Diab' may represent Madagascar.

15 Andrea Bianco's chart of 1448 (in the Biblioteca Ambrosiana, Milan) is the earliest cartographic record of the Portuguese discoveries beyond Cape Bojador in 26° N. (The detail showing the African coast is here divided into two sections for convenience of reproduction.) The northern section (left) extends from Cape Bojador and the Canary Islands to Cape Blanco—'cabo brancho'—in 21° N; the southern (right) from Cape Blanco to the Senegal delta and Cape Verde (14° 40′ N), reached by the Portuguese in 1445.

16 The chart drawn at Venice in 1468 by Grazioso Benincasa of Ancona (British Museum, Add. MS 6390) has Portuguese names, like that of Bianco, and depicts the discoveries made by Cadamosto, on his two voyages of 1455–6, and by Pero da Sintra in 1462. At the top left are the Cape Verde Islands, opposite the shoals south of Arguim (also shown by Bianco, Fig. 15); further south are Cape Verde, the river Gambia (where Cadamosto turned back), the Bissagos Islands and Isles de Los, the Sierra Leone peninsula ('serralioa'; so named by Da Sintra 'because of the great noise of the thunder claps'), and Cape St Anne ('cauo sca Anna'). Da Sintra sailed 240 miles to the south-east before returning.

17 The MS chart of the West African coast, entitled 'Ginea Portugalexe' and

signed by Cristoforo Soligo, is found in an atlas drawn at Venice about 1490 and containing copies of 15th-century charts (British Museum, MS Egerton 73). Soligo's chart is evidently derived from a (now lost) Portuguese original. The lower part of the chart, here reproduced, shows the coastline from Cape Lopez ('capo de lopo gonzaluem'), in 0° 34′ S, to the farthest south reached by Diogo Cão on his first voyage (1482–4). A legend off the mouth of the Congo, called by the Portuguese Rio do Padram, reports fresh water five leagues to sea; and crosses indicate the stone pillars erected by Cão south of the river mouth and at Cape Santa Maria ('capo do lobo'), where he turned back. The scale of leagues is seen at the bottom right-hand.

18   The 'Insularium', or description of islands, written by Henricus Martellus Germanus at Florence about 1490 (British Museum, Add. MS 15760), contains a world map, the western half of which is here reproduced. In his representation of Asia Martellus follows Ptolemy; but Dias's voyage of 1487–9 was already known to the cartographer, and the land-connection between southern Africa and south-east Asia has disappeared. Africa is labelled 'the true modern form of Africa from the description of the Portuguese'; a legend refers to the point 'reached by the latest voyage of the Portuguese in 1489'; and place-names indicate the limit of Dias's exploration.

19   The 'Cantino' world map was obtained surreptitiously in Lisbon in October 1502 by Alberto Cantino, agent of Duke Ercole d'Este, of Ferrara; it is still preserved in the Biblioteca Estense, Modena. It thus testifies to Italian anxiety at Portuguese encroachment on Eastern trade by the new sea route.

The section of the map reproduced shows Africa and the Indian Ocean as known to the Portuguese after the voyages of Vasco da Gama (1497–9) and Cabral (1500–1) and later discoveries reported in Lisbon as recently as September 1502. At the extreme left is the fort of São Jorge da Mina on the Gold Coast (reproduced on a larger scale in the inset); crosses further south mark *padrões* set up by earlier expeditions. Portuguese flags on the east coast of Africa denote the ports touched at by Da Gama and Cabral. Comparison with the Ptolemaic outlines in the Henricus Martellus map (Fig. 18) shows a striking improvement in the delineation of Africa and India. South Africa no longer curves to the east; the peninsular form of India is now first suggested, with Ceylon reduced to true proportions and position. Madagascar, discovered in 1500, is shown for the first time. Two scales of degrees are given.

20   This woodcut map of Africa was printed on the title-page of the travel collection *Itinerariū Portugallēsiū e Lusitania in India* compiled by Montalboddo Fracanzano (Latin edition, 1508). This copy is in the second state, in which the name of the Red Sea has been corrected from 'Sinus Persicus' to 'Sinus Arabicus'.

21   Drawings of the ships in Vasco da Gama's fleet are found on the first page of the MS 'Livro das Armadas', of the early 16th century (Lisbon, Academia das

Ciências). The similarity between these designs and the ship-drawings in contemporary Portuguese charts, e.g. those of the Reinels, has suggested that the same illuminator was responsible for both. (A. Cortesão, *Cartografia e cartógrafos portugueses* (1935), I, 277.) The *São Gabriel* was barque-rigged, i.e. square-rigged on fore- and mainmasts, fore-and-aft on the mizzen.

22 The chart of the Spice Islands by Rodrigues, *c.* 1513, is from his MS description of the East (see Fig. 12). Rodrigues had in 1512 visited the islands in the expedition of Antonio de Abreu. The two large islands in outline on the right are Timor ('where the sandalwood grows') and Solor; those at the top Buru and Ceram (here joined to Amboina). To the right of Ceram are the Banda islands ('where the maces grow'). The legend above the compass rose states that four of the small islands drawn in profile 'are those of Maluco, where the clove grows'. The coastal profiles, unfamiliar in Portuguese cartography, suggest that Rodrigues may have had a native chart to copy.

23 This chart of the Indian Ocean, drawn about 1518, is attributed by Cortesão to Pedro Reinel, cosmographer to the King of Portugal (British Museum, Add. MS 9812). The configuration of the Bay of Bengal, which had by now been visited by the Portuguese, and of the Malay Peninsula, is remarkably accurate. The more southerly of the two Portuguese flags in the peninsula marks Malacca; others on Sumatra and farther east show Portuguese penetration of the Archipelago, which had by 1512 taken them to the Moluccas.

24 View of the port of Suk ('Xeque') on the north of the island of Socotra, by João de Castro; in his MS 'Roteiro em que se conten a viagem que fizeram os portuguezes . . . partindo da . . . Goa ate Soez' (British Museum, Cotton MS Tib. D. IX). This manuscript, taken from a Portuguese ship, formerly belonged to Sir Walter Raleigh. De Castro commanded a galiot in the Portuguese fleet which sailed from Goa to Suez in 1540–1. The ships on the left are *naos*, barque-rigged and broad of beam, with fore- and aft-castles.

25 The chart of the Indian Ocean, in a finely drawn atlas by Joan Martines of Messina dated 1578 (British Museum, MS Harl. 3450), shows the Portuguese empire in the East at its zenith, with the pivotal bases marked by Portuguese flags at Ormuz, Goa, Cananor (north of Calicut), and Malacca.

26, 27 The *Civitates orbis terrarum* (6 vols., Cologne, 1573–1618) was designed as an atlas of city-plans and views to accompany Ortelius' atlas *Theatrum orbis terrarum* (1570). The first volume, edited by Georg Braun and engraved by Frans Hogenberg, included these bird's-eye views of Portuguese commercial bases in India. Goa was colonized by the Portuguese and became their capital in the East, with the privileges of a city; Calicut was the principal trading centre of the Malabar coast.

28   Malacca, conquered by Albuquerque in 1511, was developed by the Portuguese as a base for their diplomacy and exploration in the Malay Peninsula and the Eastern Archipelago, and as a commercial centre for the control of the spice trade. In this plan of the fortified settlement and port, the numerous churches recall that here in 1545 St Francis Xavier founded the first Christian mission in Malaya. The plan, drawn by the pilot Pedro Berthelot in 1635 (six years before Malacca was taken by the Dutch), is one of the illustrations in his MS collection of charts of the Portuguese East (British Museum, MS Sloane 197; ff. 381–2).

Notes

Chapter II

[1] Notably Herodotus' report of the circumnavigation (from east to west) by Phoenician seamen under the Pharaoh Necho, *c.* 600 B.C.

[2] For instance, the world map in the Medici sea-atlas at Florence, 1351; but the African coast on this may be drawn by a later hand. That the Arabs knew the southern horn of Africa in the Middle Ages is suggested by a Chinese world map of 1402, showing the southern tip of the continent. (W. Fuchs, in *Imago Mundi*, X (1953), p. 50.)

[3] The location of Prester John's empire in Ethiopia dates from the early years of the 14th century. The first map to represent it thus is the chart drawn by Angellino Dulcert in Majorca, 1339.

[4] Cape Nun (or Non) was in fact so named by European seamen from its proximity to the Wadi Nun; it lies in the district of Ifni, Spanish Morocco.

[5] See Chapters III, VII.   [6] See above, note 3.

[7] The exact position is Kwaaihoek, or False Islet, three sea miles west of the Bushman's River. (Eric Axelson, *South-east Africa, 1488–1530* (1940), pp. 172 ff.) In 1938 Mr Axelson discovered fragments of the *padrão* at this point.

[8] See Chapters III, VII.   [9] See Chapter VII.

[10] It is probable that many old Portuguese charts perished in the great Lisbon earthquake of 1755.

[11] G. R. Crone, *Maps and their Makers* (1953), p. 53. Crone notes that in Benincasa's chart the scale of the most southerly section is 'nearly four times that of the northern'.

[12] The Reinel chart, preserved in the Staatsbibliothek, Munich, and sometimes known as 'Kunstmann I', is the earliest signed Portuguese chart now extant. It has in fact two graduated scales of latitude: one along the central meridian, the other (off the American coast) set at an angle, corresponding to the magnetic variation ($22\frac{1}{2}°$ W) in relation to the first. The second scale therefore also lies along a meridian, and it enabled the seaman to lay down on his chart, in their correct latitude, the positions which he had plotted on compass courses.

[13] A Portuguese manual of navigation written in 1505 gives the latitude of Cape Agulhas as 35° S. (Duarte Pacheco Pereira, *Esmeraldo de Situ Orbis*.)

[14] See Chapter VIII.   [15] See Chapter VII.

PART TWO

The Way of the West

III

CATHAY OR A NEW WORLD?

*The discovery of America, from
Columbus to Magellan*

❖❖

OF THE THREE PARTS into which the mediaeval world was divided, Asia was at once the largest and the most mysterious. It occupied the upper half of the circular diagrams in which Christian cosmographers depicted their world,[1] and in Asia contemporary fancy located the marvels which it drew from travellers' tales, from theological dogma, and from classical or Biblical legend. Within its bounds lay the empires of the Great Khan and of Prester John; here were lands rich in spices and gold, and a harvest of souls ripe for conversion; in the remotest east was placed the Earthly Paradise.

In the 15th century, when developments in the art of navigation increased the range of sea voyages, the Far East was still the magnet for adventurers. The search for a sea route to Cathay was the motive which inspired the two major enterprises of the great age of discovery—the opening of a sea-way into the Indian Ocean, and the discovery of America and the Pacific Ocean.

Neither of these conceptions was wholly new. That a ship could sail from the Atlantic into the Indian Ocean had been suspected as early as the 1st century A.D., and 15th-century mapmakers had indicated the passage by the southern part of Africa many years before it was rounded in 1488.[2] Columbus was not the first European to look west to Cathay, nor was he the first to search for land westward of the Azores. The westerly sea route to China was apparent to anyone who examined a globe in which, as in that of Martin Behaim (1492), the easternmost and westernmost known lands were separated only by about 120 degrees of sea. But to the interpretation of the geographical ideas and maps current in his day Columbus brought a fixity of purpose which, in the face of scientific orthodoxy, drove his project to its end, although not to that which he foresaw.

Columbus's objective has been the subject of voluminous, and largely idle, controversy. We need not doubt the arguments by which he recommended his plans to his patrons; King Ferdinand and Queen Isabella (he says) 'acting on the information that I had given to your Highnesses touching the lands of India, and respecting a Prince who is called *Grand Can* . . . resolved to send me, Cristobal Colon, to the said parts of India . . . and ordered . . . that I should go by the west, whither up to this day we do not know for certain that anyone has gone'. The maps which Columbus carried have not survived, but any seaman's chart drawn in Genoa

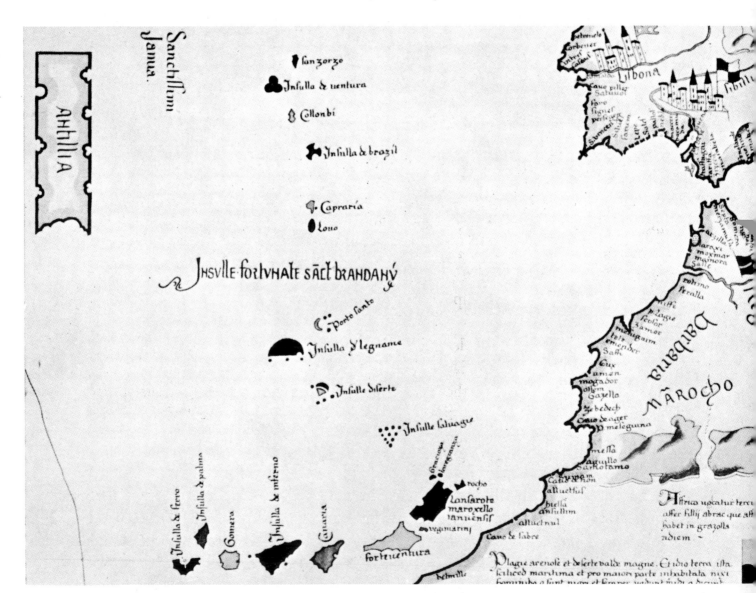

FIG. 29.—Atlantic islands, in the chart of Bartolomeo Pareto, 1455.

(Fig. 29) would have shown him supposed islands in the Atlantic to serve as stepping-stones to the Indies. The largest and most westerly of these was Antillia, or the Isle of the Seven Cities, and this may have been Columbus's first objective, for we learn from his log that he and his captains constantly expected to run down islands in mid-Atlantic. But his ultimate goal was Marco Polo's Cathay and (1500 miles off its coast) the 'island of Cipangu [Japan] . . . most fertile in gold, pearls and precious stones'.

Although Columbus owned a copy of Marco Polo's Book,[3] it was apparently from the Florentine physician Paolo Toscanelli that he had his original information on both the wealth and the location of these lands. The chart which Toscanelli forwarded with his letter to Columbus represented Cipangu as 3000 nautical miles west of the Canaries (less than one-third of the true distance), and in about the same latitude.[4] Columbus's problem was primarily that of sailing time, and it suited his purpose to shorten the projected voyage by making the largest credible estimate of the longitudinal extension of the old world. By using for this the highest figure (225°) to be got from classical geographers, adding 30° from Marco Polo, and adopting a shorter measure for the degree (45 nautical miles, against Ptolemy's 50 and the reality of 60), Columbus was able further to reduce Toscanelli's estimated distance by one-sixth. This placed Cipangu in the longitude of the western Antilles, and Cathay in that of the west coast of Mexico. In fact, when Columbus made his landfall at Watling Island in the Bahamas on 12 October 1492, he had passed the

FIG. 30.—Sketch of north-east Hispaniola drawn by Columbus, 1492–3.

Fig. 31.—Islands discovered by Columbus on his first voyage.
A woodcut in the printed edition of his letter, 1493.

point at which he had expected to find Japan by only 400 miles, or a week's sailing. On this voyage, to reassure the crew, 'it was always feigned to them that the distances were less, so that the voyage might not appear so long. Thus two reckonings were kept . . . the shorter being feigned, and the longer being the true one.'

Both Columbus's course, during his first Atlantic crossing of thirty-three days from the Canaries, and his identifications of the landfalls which he made in the course of his four voyages must be interpreted in the light of his purpose—the 'Enterprise of the Indies'. Four weeks out from the Canaries on the first voyage, he suspected that Cipangu had been missed and, deciding that 'it would be better to go at once to the continent and afterwards to the islands', he changed course south-south-west for the mainland of Cathay. In Cuba, which he at first took for Cipangu but later found 'to be so large . . . that I could not suppose it to be an island but the continental province of Cathay', he sent an embassy to seek out the Great Khan. On his second voyage (1493–4) he took sworn statements from his officers that Cuba was a peninsula—the south-east promontory of Asia, or 'Golden Chersonese', of Ptolemy. The discovery of the South American coast on his third voyage (1498) led him to suppose that this was the seat of the Earthly Paradise and (for the first time) that he had found 'a very great continent . . . until today unknown'. God had made him (so he wrote in 1500) 'the messenger of the new earth (*nuevo cielo y mundo*)' announced in the Apocalypse; 'and He showed me the spot where to find it'. On his last voyage (1502–4) Columbus coasted Central America,

FIG. 32.—A ship of the type of Columbus's *Santa Maria*. A woodcut in the printed edition of his letter, 1493.

assumed to be the kingdom of 'Catigara' (Indochina), from Honduras to Darien in search of a navigable passage to the west, perhaps into Ptolemy's 'Sinus Magnus' (Great Gulf); and he believed himself to be only nineteen days' journey from the Ganges.

Of the charts of his discoveries which Columbus drew, only one fragment in his hand is known (Fig. 30), although other representations may be derived from them (Figs. 31, 40). A contemporary sketch map (Fig. 33), based on information from

Bartholomew Columbus (who like his brother Christopher had been a chartmaker), suggests how Columbus reconciled his discoveries with the Asiatic geography of Ptolemy and Marco Polo. The name 'Mondo Novo' (New World) given in this map to the South American mainland reflects Columbus's belief that he had discovered a hitherto unknown land mass, of which he had written (as we have seen) in these very words.

This phrase had, as early as 1493, been used to describe the 'Indies' of Ptolemy and Marco Polo revealed by Columbus's first voyage;[5] but it did not then, nor much later, necessarily imply a new continent. By a historical irony however it was to rob Columbus of his laurels even before his death in 1506. A tract of 1503, entitled in its Latin editions *Mundus Novus*, contained a letter from the Florentine Amerigo Vespucci describing his voyage to South America in 1501–2 under the Portuguese flag.[6] Here Vespucci claimed to have 'found a continent' which (he asserted) 'it is proper to call a new world'; and Martin Waldseemüller, in a tract printed in 1507, saw 'no reason why we should not call this other part ... America after the sagacious discoverer Americus'. Geographers were becoming conscious that to the three parts (or continents) of the mediaeval world-map a fourth—a New World—had been added. Waldseemüller's large world map of 1507 is the earliest map to use the name of America, which he applied only to the southern part of the continent.[7]

Even in Columbus's own day neither the chroniclers of his voyages nor the

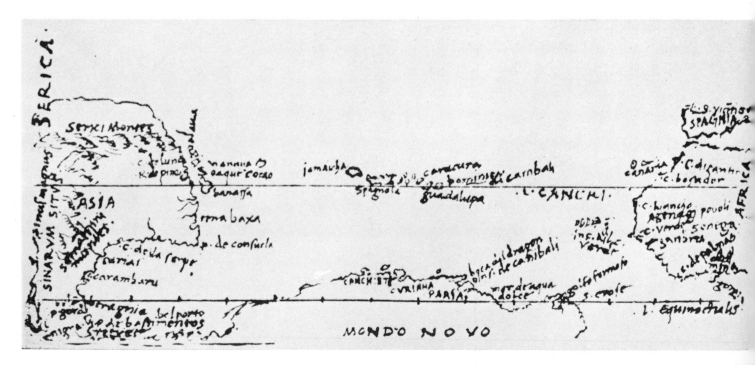

FIG. 33.—Sketch map by Alessandro Zorzi, showing the coasts of Central and South America: based on a map Bartholomew Columbus.

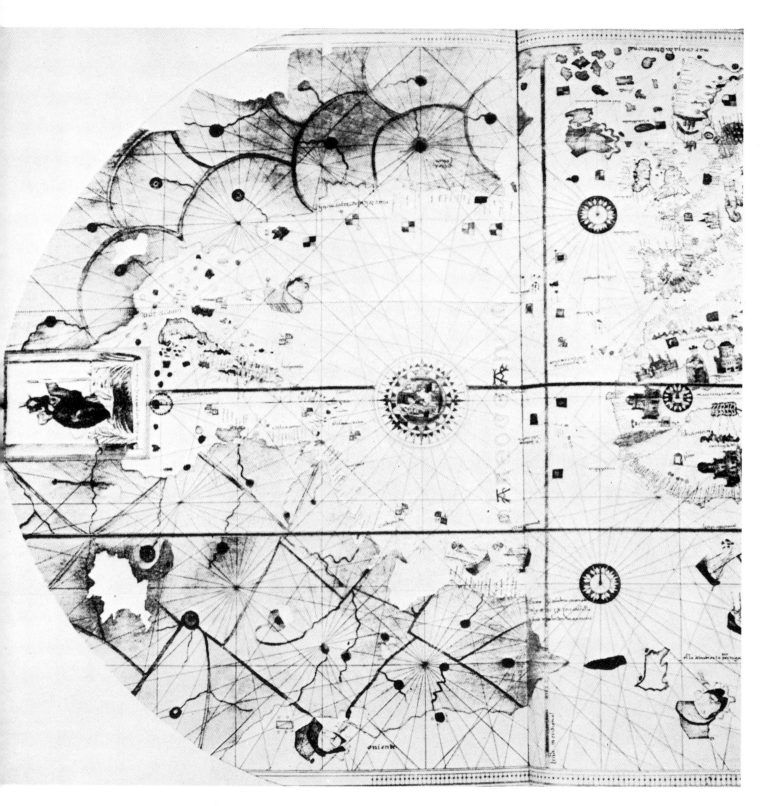

FIG. 34.—Western portion of the world map drawn by Juan de la Cosa, dated 1500.

FIG. 35.—Western portion of the Cantino world map, 1502.

Spanish and Portuguese mapmakers agreed in accepting his cosmographical views. Varying estimates of the longitudinal interval westerly from Europe to eastern Asia determined the interpretation of the new discoveries by geographers and cartographers. In 1494 Peter Martyr introduced the concept of a 'Western Hemisphere',[8] and in 1496 Columbus's friend Bernáldez told him that another 1200 leagues sailing westward would still not have brought him to Cathay. Contemporary maps (e.g. Figs. 34–40), ingeniously grafting the new discoveries on the old stock of Ptolemy and mediaeval lore, present widely divergent views on the relation between the new lands and the east coast of Asia. The world map drawn in 1500 (but perhaps not completed until 1508) by Juan de la Cosa, Columbus's pilot (Fig. 34), shows a continuous continental coastline from north to south, interrupted only (at the neck of the vellum) by a picture of St Christopher covering the area in which Columbus sought a strait in 1502–3. Here, as in the Portuguese 'Cantino' chart of 1502 (Fig. 35), it is not clear whether the lands in the west were regarded as joined to Asia or divided from it. The Portuguese were quicker than the Spaniards to appreciate that the westerly sea-way to Cathay was closed by a continent; nevertheless they were in 1502 still prepared to accept their discoveries in North America as a north-easterly extension of Asia.[9]

The map of 1506 by G. M. Contarini (Fig. 36), the earliest printed map to show the new discoveries, is drawn on a projection which makes the relationship plain. A wide sea passage divides the North American discoveries of the English and Portuguese (here drawn as a promontory of Asia) from the Spanish discoveries in South America. The cartographer appears to reject Columbus's assertion that on his first voyage he reached Cipangu (here laid down 15 degrees west of Cuba and in a lower latitude) and the coast of Cathay, 40 degrees further west. It is true that a legend, written between Cipangu and Cathay, reads: 'Christopher Columbus . . . sailing westward reached the Spanish islands . . . weighing anchor thence he sailed to the province called Ciamba [Cochin China]. Afterwards he betook himself to this place [Cipangu] which . . . has great store of gold.' This statement (which has been thought a later insertion on the copper plate) seems to reflect Columbus's claim to have arrived, in the course of his fourth voyage, on the coasts of south-east Asia. In this map we may see an early guess at the existence of the Pacific Ocean, perhaps from rumours picked up by the Portuguese in the East. Peter Martyr's map of Central America of 1511 (Fig. 37), however, shows an unbroken shore from Yucatan to Cape Nassau; and in the Stobnicza hemispheric map of 1512 (Fig. 38), based on a map published by Waldseemüller in 1507, an uninterrupted coastline is drawn from 50° N to 40° S. By this time the division of the world into two hemispheres was firmly established.

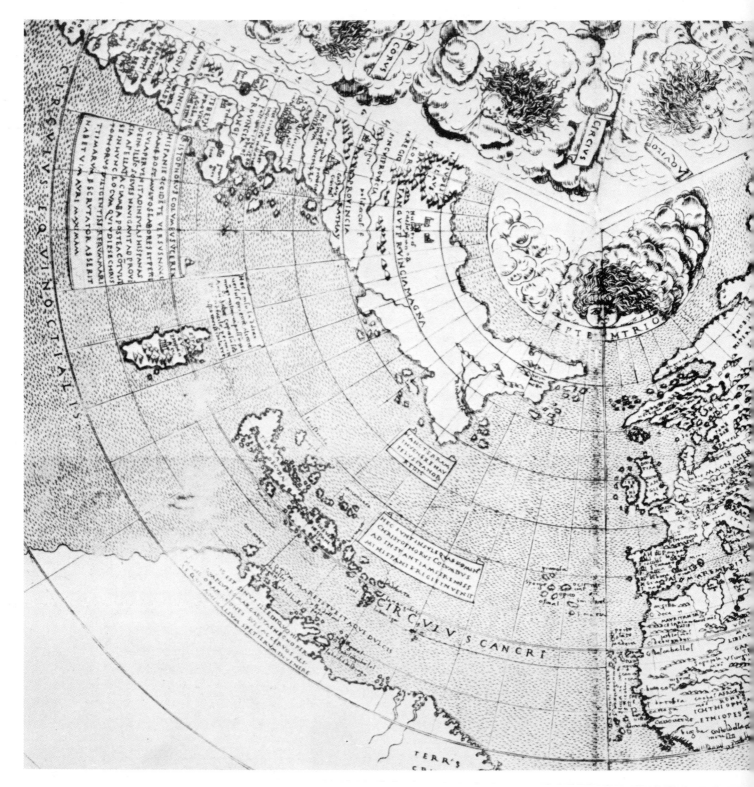

FIG. 36.—Part of the world map by G. M. Contarini, engraved in 1506 by F. Rosselli.

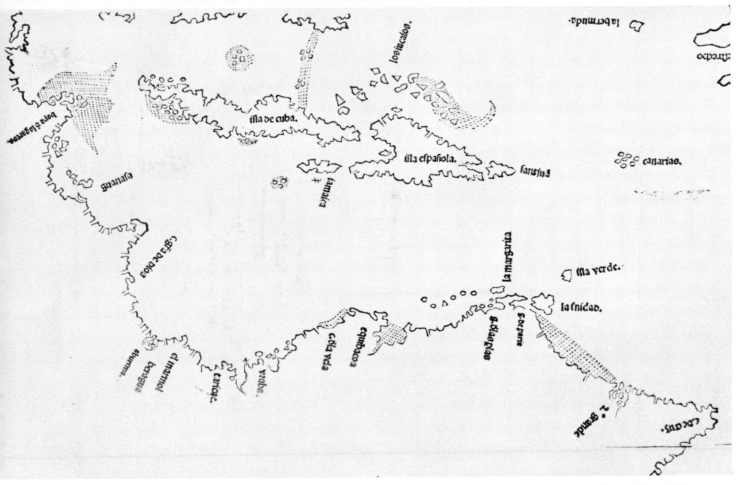

FIG. 37.—Map of the Caribbean, published in 1511 with Peter Martyr's first 'Decade of the New W

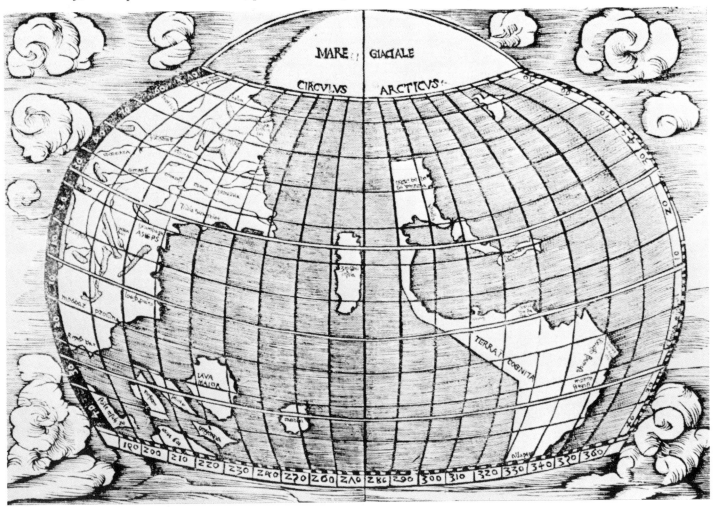

FIG. 38.—The Western Hemisphere, by Joannes de Stobnicza, 1512.

Meanwhile English and Portuguese navigators had made landfalls in North America, and Spanish expeditions had revealed the coast of South America as far as the River Plate. In 1497 John Cabot, sailing from Bristol and like Columbus seeking Cathay by the west, had reached Newfoundland or Nova Scotia, which he took to be the continent of Asia. The English flags on Juan de la Cosa's map (Fig. 34) indicate the coasts discovered by Cabot on this voyage and perhaps on his second, in 1498, of which there is no written record.[10] In 1500 and 1501 the Azorean Gaspar Corte Real made two voyages on which he rediscovered Greenland and coasted Labrador southward. These discoveries are drawn in the Cantino chart (Fig. 35) on the east, or Portuguese, side of the demarcation line between the Spanish and Portuguese spheres, determined by the Treaty of Tordesillas in 1494.[11] Pedro Alvares Cabral, leading the second Portuguese fleet to India in 1500, sailed south-west from the Cape Verde Islands, perhaps to make use of the trade winds and to avoid calms off the African coast, perhaps to discover lands in South America on the Portuguese side of the Tordesillas line.[12] This course in fact took him to Brazil, where he landed in 17° S before resuming his voyage to the Cape of Good Hope. In 1501–2 Vespucci, who had met Cabral near Cape Verde on his return from India (June 1501), continued the exploration of the South American coast, apparently reaching a latitude of 50° S.[13] A manuscript world chart of about 1508 (Fig. 39) presents an early interpretation of the American continent in the light of these discoveries.

In September 1513 Vasco Nuñez de Balboa, on a land exploration from Darien, climbed a peak 'from whiche he myght see the other sea soo longe looked for, and never seen before of any man commynge owte of owre worlde' (Fig. 121).[14] He was the first European to set eyes on the Pacific, called by the Spaniards 'Mar del Zur' (South Sea).[15] By 1520 the Gulf of Mexico from Yucatan to Florida had been uncovered by Cortes and other Conquistadors, but no strait was found (Fig. 41); and it was becoming plain that, if Cathay was to be attained on a westerly voyage, the great land mass of America which barred the way must be outflanked either by the north or by the south.

The search for a sea passage in the north will be described later.[16] To the south, a navigable route into the Pacific had been rumoured to exist several years before Magellan passed through his Strait (October–November 1502); and this route had been conjecturally drawn on maps and globes (e.g. Fig. 42) before his circumnavigation. The earliest authentic representation of the Magellan Strait is to be found in the sketches by Antonio Pigafetta who sailed in one of Magellan's two ships, the *Vitoria* (Fig. 43).

Magellan dispelled for ever the geographical illusions as to the length of the

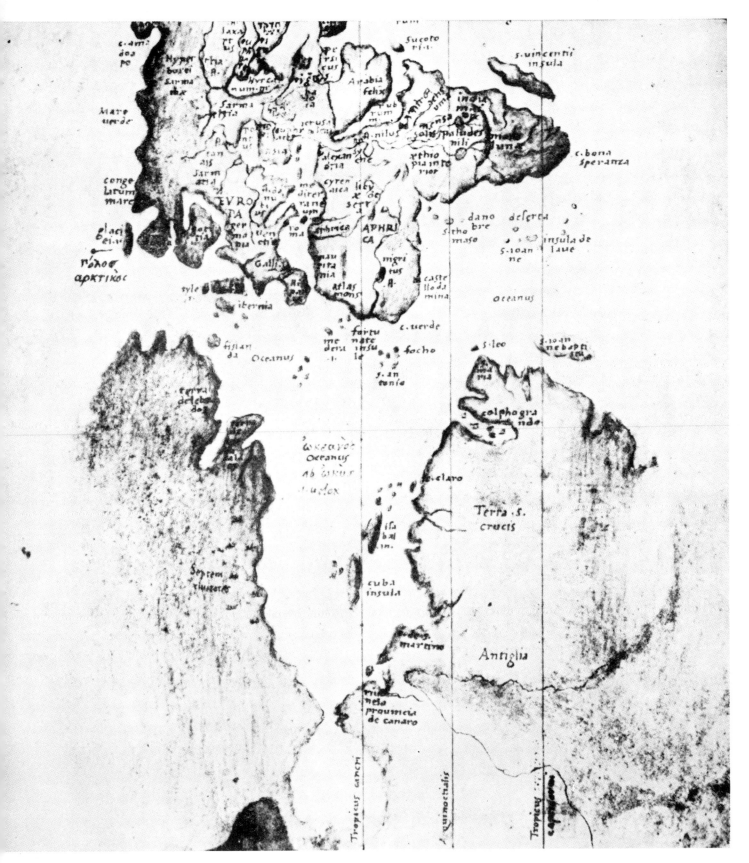

FIG. 39.—Part of a MS world map drawn about 1508.

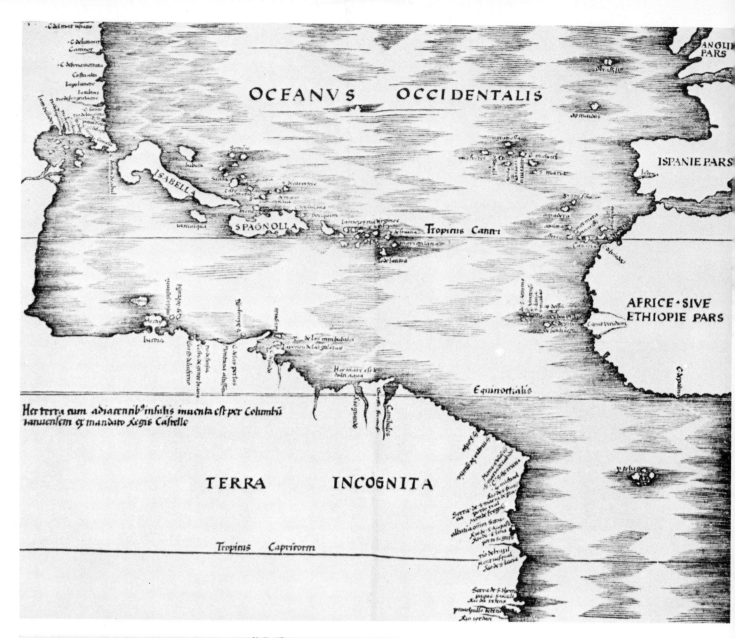

OCEANVS OCCIDENTALIS

ISABELLA

SPAGNOLLA

Tropicus Cancri

TERRA INCOGNITA

Tropicus Capricorni

ANGLI PARS

ISPANIE PARS

AFRICE·SIVE ETHIOPIE PARS

Equinoctialis

Hec terra cum adiacentib° infulis inuenta eft per Columbu ianuenfem ex mandato Xegis Caftelle

FIG. 40.—Map of the New World, in Ptolemy's *Geographia* (Strassburg 1513).

FIG. 41.—Map of the Gulf of Mexico, printed in 1524 with the second letter of Cortes from Mexico.

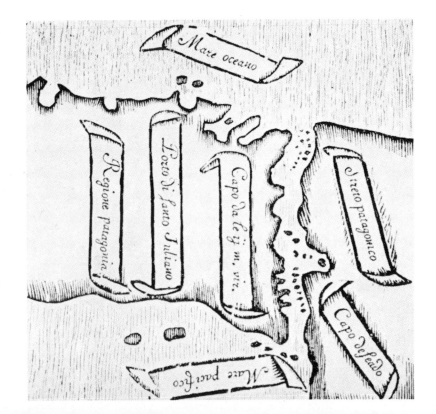

G. 42.—The Western Hemisphere in the globe of Johannes Schöner, 1515.

G. 43.—Sketch of Magellan Strait, in the MS journal of Antonio Pigafetta.

FIG. 44.—Map of the We

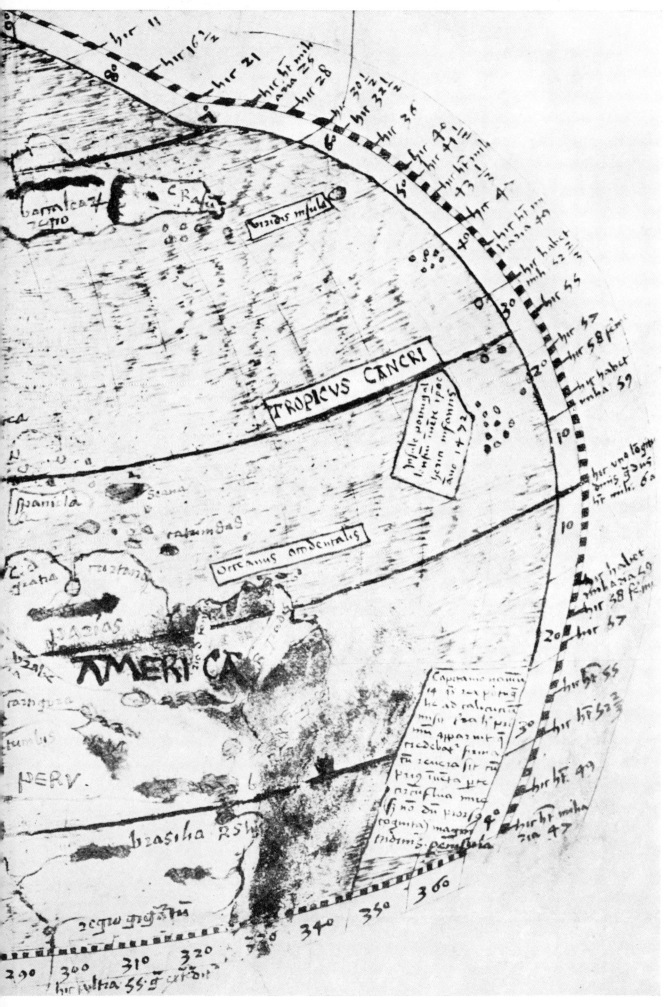

isphere, drawn about 1535.

westerly voyage to Asia, upon which earlier projects had been built. Columbus, at the Isthmus, thought himself 19 days from the Ganges; but 98 days were required by Magellan for the passage from the Strait to the Ladrones. His great voyage secured for Spain access to the Pacific by sea (Fig. 46), but it solved the geographical problem of the South Pacific only. A land connection between North America and north-east Asia could still be believed in (Figs. 44, 45), and this question was to remain unanswered until the age of Bering and Cook in the 18th century.[17]

The history of the name America on maps deserves a final note. After its introduction by Waldseemüller in 1507, he himself discarded it, probably because he came to ascribe the discovery of the New World to Columbus rather than Vespucci (Fig. 40); but other cartographers, following his lead, continued to apply it to South America (Figs. 42, 44, 45). The name was for the first time placed on both halves of the American continent by Mercator in his world map of 1538. This was in fact a recognition of the unity and continuity of the New World.

FIG. 45.—Hemispheric world map by Franciscus Monachus, published in 1529.

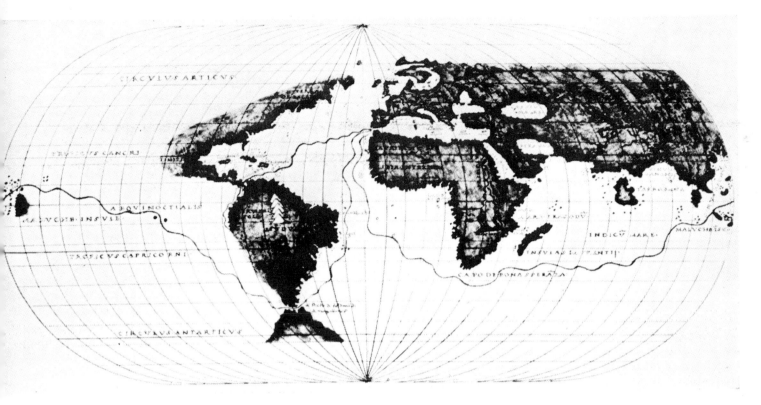

FIG. 46.—World map drawn by Battista Agnese in 1536, showing the track of the *Vitoria* round the world 1519–22.

Remarks on the Illustrations

Chapter III

◇◇

29   Islands of the Atlantic, in a portolan chart drawn at Genoa by Bartolomeo Pareto, 1455 (Biblioteca Nazionale, Rome). In the south are the Canaries; north of them the Madeira group ('Insulla de legname'); the general name 'Fortunate Islands of St Brendan', written above, refers to the Irish saint believed to have discovered islands out in the ocean in the sixth century. Due west from Portugal lie the Azores, with the legendary island of Brasil, and the large island of Antillia, first recorded on 15th-century charts; a Portuguese expedition sailed in search of it in 1487, and Columbus, advised by Toscanelli, expected to touch it on his first crossing of the Atlantic. (The reproduction is from a 19th-century copy.)

30   This sketch of north-east Hispaniola, drawn by Columbus as he coasted east in December 1492–January 1493, is preserved in the collection of the Duke of Alba. The features named are Cape S. Nicolas, the island of Tortuga, and the point of Monte Cristi. In Caracol Bay (just above the *s* of *española*), on Christmas Day, the *Santa Maria* struck a coral reef and could not be got off. From her timbers Columbus built at Navidad the first European settlement in the New World.

31   This illustration of Columbus's ship, the *Santa Maria*, in the Bahamas in 1492 is one of three woodcuts—the earliest representations of the New World—published in a Latin edition of his letter to the Treasurer of Aragon 'concerning the islands lately discovered in the Sea of India' (*De insulis nuper inuentis*, Basle, 1494). The islands of the Bahamas discovered and named by Columbus are grouped in conventional perspective: San Salvador or Guanahaní (Watling I.), his first landfall, Fernandina (Long I.), S. Maria de la Concepcion (Rum Cay), Isabella (Crooked I.), 'Hyspana' (Hispaniola).

32   'Oceanica classis', another woodcut in the Latin edition of Columbus's letter (1493), represents a three-masted ship of the type of the *Santa Maria*, with square rig on fore and main masts and an after-castle above a round stern. This

design, like the ship and fortress in Fig. 31, was copied from an illustration in Bernhard von Breydenbach's *Peregrinatio in Terram Sanctam* (Mainz, 1486).

33   This is one of three sketches, forming sections of a world map, found in the geographical notes compiled about 1522–5 by the Venetian Alessandro Zorzi (Florence, Biblioteca Nazionale, MS Magl. VIII, 81, fol. 6ov). This section is probably based in part on a map drawn by Columbus's brother Bartholomew, also an experienced cartographer. The longitudinal width of the Atlantic is grossly underestimated (cf. Figs. 34, 35); each division on the Equator represents 10°. The sketch connects the discoveries of Columbus's fourth voyage (1502–4), along the coast of Central America, with those parts of the West Indies and South America previously known, and relates them to Ptolemy's geography of Asia. The land-mass in the north-west, recalling that in the Cantino map (cf. Figs. 35, 40), bears Ptolemaic names—Serica, Serici Montes, Sinarum situs. The mainland of Honduras, along which Columbus in 1502 sought a passage into the Indian Ocean, is thus identified with Asia; in the south it tapers to an isthmus washed on the west by the 'Sinus magnus' which Ptolemy laid down in south-east Asia. The South American coast ('Mondo Novo') is drawn from the explorations of Columbus (1498) and Ojeda and La Cosa (1499); 'mar de aqua dolce' (sea of fresh water) marks the mouth of the Orinoco.

34   The world map dated 1500 and drawn by Juan de la Cosa, who sailed with Columbus in 1493–4 and made three later voyages to America, is preserved in the Museo Naval, Madrid. The Central and South American sections of the map are drawn on a larger scale, perhaps for emphasis. The coasts of South America are laid down from Spanish discoveries to 1499, and fall almost wholly on the western, or Spanish, side of the demarcation line. The large island 'discovered by the Portuguese', lying in the South Atlantic, seems to indicate knowledge of Cabral's landfall on Brazil in 1500. Although La Cosa was one of Columbus's officers who in 1494 certified that Cuba was a peninsula of the mainland, it is here drawn as an island; since it was first circumnavigated in 1508, it has been suggested that the chart may have been revised or completed then. The discoveries of John Cabot in north-east America are indicated by English flags and by the legends 'Cauo da Ynglaterra' (apparently Nova Scotia or Newfoundland) and 'Mar descubierta por Yngleses'. The extension of the land to the western edge of the map suggests a connection with Asia.

35   The Cantino map represents the geography of the New World from the Portuguese point of view. The demarcation line 'between Castille and Portugal', 370 leagues west of the Cape Verde Islands, is drawn, and the lands on the Portuguese (east) side of the line are more elaborately depicted than those on the Spanish side. The discoveries made for Portugal are displaced to the east to bring them within her sphere. In the north the Corte Real landfalls in Greenland and Labrador

(1500–1) are marked by Portuguese flags and by the legend (against Greenland) 'This land which was discovered by order of . . . Dom Manoel, King of Portugal, they think is the end of Asia'. To the north-west of the 'Antilles of the King of Castille' a coastline is laid down marked 'Parte de Assia' and bearing names from Columbus's first two voyages (cf. Figs. 33, 40). Brazil is decorated with drawings of the parrots reported by Cabral. At the bottom left-hand corner is the title of the map: 'Chart for the navigation of the islands lately discovered in the parts of India.'

36   The map by Contarini engraved at Florence by Francesco Rosselli in 1506, is the earliest printed map to show any part of the New World; one impression only, in the British Museum, has survived. The islands discovered by Columbus on his first two voyages are separated by nearly 20 degrees of longitude from 'Zimpangu', and by over 60 degrees from Marco Polo's Cathay. The legend (top left) relating to Columbus's voyage to 'Ciamba', i.e. his fourth voyage (1502–4), may be a later addition to the plate. The province of 'Tangut', another name from Marco Polo, extends east in a great promontory, the discovery of which is attributed in another legend to the Portuguese, that is, identified with the Corte Real discoveries. The South American coasts explored by the Spanish and Portuguese are represented as part of a continent extending to the south edge of the map.

37   This woodcut map, the earliest printed Spanish map of any part of America, was published in Peter Martyr's first *Decade of the New World*, Seville, 1511. Land-falls on Yucatan and Florida, otherwise unrecorded, are indicated; and Bermuda, recently discovered, is marked for the first time on a map.

38   Stobnicza's woodcut map, published at Cracow in 1512, is copied from an inset of Waldseemüller's large world map of 1507. The eastward extension of Asia corresponds to that given by Ptolemy; it has no land connection with America, and the existence of the Pacific Ocean is prefigured a year before Balboa set eyes on it. The lands of America are represented as a continuous continental coastline from 50° N to the south edge of the map.

39   This world map is found in a portolan atlas in the British Museum (MS Eg. 2803), attributed to the cartographer Vesconte Maggiolo of Genoa and to the year 1508. (East is at the top.) The Atlantic coast of South America has been extended southward, from Vespucci's voyage of 1501–2 to the Plate river; and its Pacific coastline is probably a later insertion. The names 'Antiglia' and 'Septem ciuitates' associate the New World with legendary Atlantic islands. North and South America are joined by an isthmus, and their westward extension is left obscure.

40   This woodcut map of the New World is one of the 'modern' maps added by Waldseemüller to the edition of Ptolemy printed at Strassburg in 1513. The editor states that it was prepared from information derived from 'the Admiral', who

is presumed to be Columbus. The delineation of the West Indies, however, follows that of the Cantino chart (Fig. 35) except that it connects the coast in the north-west to South America, thus incorporating the results of Columbus's last voyage. The inscription on South America gives Columbus (not, as earlier, Vespucci) the credit for discovering America.

41 Map of the Gulf of Mexico, printed in 1524 with the second letter of Hernan Cortes from Mexico (1520). Yucatan, discovered in 1517, was believed to be an island, as shown here. This is the earliest map to use the name Florida.

42 In Schöner's globe of 1515 the outline of America and its relation to Cipangu and Asia follow Stobnicza's map (Fig. 38), but Schöner makes two notable innovations. Straits into the Pacific are shown in 10° N and 45° S; the southern, no doubt a misrepresentation of the River Plate, divides America from a land mass which anticipates the 'Southern Continent' of later cartographers; and it was perhaps from this globe that Magellan learnt that 'he had to sail through a very well-concealed strait, having seen it in a chart in the King of Portugal's Treasury'. In the south, the land styled 'Brasilie Regio', which cannot be related to any known discovery, prefigures the southern continent of 16th-century maps (see Chapter IX).

43 Pigafetta's sketch of the Magellan Strait is drawn in his MS journal in the Biblioteca Ambrosiana, Milan, fol. 14v. The strait, here called 'Streto patagonico', was first to be known by Magellan's name some fifteen years later, in a map of 1534 (Fig. 53).

44 This MS map of the Western Hemisphere, drawn about 1535 and now in the British Museum (MS Sloane 117), illustrates the persistent attempts of contemporary geographers to reconcile the geography of the New World, as revealed by discovery, with that of Ptolemy's Asia. The outline of the American continent is recognizable. To the north-west, however, it reaches to the edge of the map, suggesting a connection with Asia; the Spice Islands are laid down some 10° west of the coast of Mexico; and on the North American mainland a later (but still early) hand has inserted names from Ptolemy and Marco Polo, in a darker ink—Ciamba, Thebet, India Superior, Zaiton (near Mexico!), Chatay, etc.

45 The woodcut hemispheres, published in the *De orbis situ* of Franciscus Monachus (Antwerp, 1529), are divided at the meridian delimiting the Spanish and Portuguese spheres. In the New World both Magellan Strait and the supposed Central American strait indicated by Schöner (Fig. 42) are marked; but North America is represented with a land connection with Asia. The name 'America' is applied only to South America. South of Magellan Strait, and across the whole map, extends a continent 'not yet discovered by our navigators'. This is the earliest representation of Terra Australis on a printed map, apart from Schöner's globe of 1515.

46   Between 1536 and 1564 Battista Agnese drew at Venice some sixty portolan atlases, each with an oval world map of this type. This map, in one of his earlier atlases, drawn in 1536 (British Museum, Add. MS 19927), shows the track of the *Vitoria* through 'El streto de ferdinādo de magallanes' to complete the first circumnavigation of the world, 1519–22. The Spanish trade route from Peru across the Isthmus of Panama to Europe is also marked.

Notes

Chapter III

[1] In such diagrams (the so-called T-O maps), the three known continents of Europe, Asia and Africa were divided by the rivers Don and Nile and by the Mediterranean. They were drawn with East at the top. Cf. the representation of the northern hemisphere in Fig. 2.

[2] See Chapter II.

[3] See Chapter I, note 13.

[4] About 1480 Columbus, then in Lisbon, wrote to Toscanelli, who forwarded to him copies of a letter and world chart which he had prepared for the King of Portugal in 1474. In these he supported Marco Polo, against the authority of Ptolemy, in extending Asia much further to the east; he reckoned from Lisbon westward to Quinsay 6500 miles, and from 'the island of Antilia, which is known to you [i.e. to the Portuguese],' to Cipangu 2500 miles. Toscanelli's letter survives in a transcript in a volume which belonged to Columbus; his chart is lost.

[5] Peter Martyr, in a letter from Barcelona dated 1 November 1943: 'that Columbus, discoverer of a new world (*novi orbis*)'.

[6] It has been doubted whether by *mundus novus* Vespucci implied a fourth continent; but the readers of the tract throughout Europe certainly took it in this sense.

[7] Waldseemüller's woodcut map, only one copy of which has been preserved, depicts North and South America as separate land masses; but an inset of the map shows an isthmus connection between them.

[8] Peter Martyr, in a letter dated 31 October 1494, referred to the 'antipodes in the western hemisphere' (*ab occidente hemisperii antipodum*).

[9] These were the discoveries of the Corte Real brothers in 1500-2 (see below).

[10] Some writers have supposed that Cabot made his first American landfall in 1494, or even earlier; but recently published documents suggest that in that year he was in Spain.

[11] See Chapters IV and VII.

[12] Cabral received instructions drawn up by Vasco da Gama, who advised a course south or south-west from the Cape Verde Islands and then east to the Cape. That discoveries of land in the west were expected on this course is also very probable.

[13] Vespucci's discoveries on this voyage, made under the Portuguese flag, are represented on contemporary Portuguese charts, e.g. the Cantino chart.

[14] Peter Martyr, *Decades of the New World* (1516), translated by Richard Eden in 1555.

[15] In distinction from the 'Mar del Norte', the North Atlantic. The isthmus of Panama lies roughly WNW–ESE.

[16] In Chapters V and VI.

[17] See Chapters VIII and XI.

IV

THE NEW WORLD IN THE SIXTEENTH CENTURY

*The search for a western passage and the
charting of the American coasts*

◇◆◇

BEFORE BALBOA SET EYES on 'the greate mayne sea heretofore unknowen' in
1513, before Magellan's crossing of the Pacific in 1520–1, mapmakers had given the
'new world' of America a continuous Atlantic seaboard from 50° N to 40° S.[1]
Whether this fourth continent had any land connection with eastern Asia across the
north of the Pacific was a question which received no answer for over two centuries.[2]
Yet Cathay and the Spice Islands remained the objective for westward exploration
throughout the 16th century, and the search for a sea-way through the American
continent continued until its existence was finally discredited in the 18th century.[3]
Parallel with the quest for a western passage grew the concept of settlement and
empire, nourished on the one hand by realities—the fabulous conquests of Spain in
Mexico and Peru, the rich fur trade of Canada—and on the other by travellers' tales
and beckoning myths—kingdoms of gold, the Fountain of Everlasting Youth, the
Seven Cities of Cibola, El Dorado.[4] In the pursuit of these, the map of America was
gradually pieced together.

That Columbus in 1492 had discovered a westerly route to 'the Indies' was at
first generally accepted.[5] At his interview with King John II of Portugal on his
return, the king did not conceal his chagrin, exclaiming, 'Why did I let slip an
enterprise of so great importance?' The interests of Portugal, long committed to the
quest for an easterly sea-way to the Indies, were indeed deeply involved, and a
diplomatic settlement with the new colonial power of Spain was needed to safeguard

her own expansion and overseas discoveries. This was reached in the 'capitulation' or treaty of Tordesillas, concluded between Spain and Portugal in 1494, which drew a *raya*, or line of demarcation, in the Atlantic 370 leagues west of the Cape Verde Islands.

The new world, with the exception of Brazil, lay on the Spanish side of the Tordesillas demarcation line, and Spanish cartography of the 'Indies' was from the first carefully organized. In the Casa de la Contratación (or 'Board of Trade') of Seville, the governing body of Spain's territories overseas, the Pilot Major was responsible for the instruction of pilots and for the examination of sea-charts. On his appointment in 1508 the first Pilot Major, Amerigo Vespucci, was ordered to draw up a royal *padrón general* (master chart) 'of all the lands and islands of the Indies', and to ensure that no pilot used any chart not drawn from the *padrón*. As a kind of 'inventory' of the lands discovered, settled, or claimed by Spain, the *padrón general* was kept up-to-date by continuous addition and correction from the charts brought back by pilots and explorers. Although its revision was a fruitful source of discord among the cosmographers of Seville, it supplied a systematic record of known coasts and new discoveries such as no other nation disposed of; and to the bureaucratic administration of the Casa de la Contratación is due the survival of many Spanish charts of the 16th and 17th centuries, although few were printed (Figs. 47, 53). By contrast, the maps of early French and English explorers suffered heavy mortality. The pages of Richard Hakluyt abound in references to maps now lost—the 'Sea card' of John Cabot, Sebastian Cabot's world map ('the copye whereof was sette out by Mr Clemente Adams and is in many merchantes houses in London'), Jacques Cartier's maps, 'an olde excellent map which [Master John Verarzanus] gave to Henrie the eight, and is yet in the custodie of master Locke', a globe 'in the Queenes privie gallery at Westminster wch also semeth to be of Verarsanus making', and many others.[6]

Of the two voyages for Cathay set forth by John Cabot from Bristol in 1497 and 1498, we have neither his journals nor his maps. The geographical ideas which prompted his enterprise, and in the light of which he identified his North American landfalls, are illustrated by the Contarini map which, to the north of the oceanic islands discovered by Columbus, depicts a great promontory extending from north-east Asia into the Atlantic (Fig. 36).[7] Cabot's tracks, as indicated by the evidence of early maps and by the conflicting recollections of his son Sebastian, have been variously interpreted. His 'Prima vista', or first landfall, may be Cape Breton (as in the map of 1544 ascribed to Sebastian Cabot; Fig. 47) or Cape Bonavista in Newfoundland; Hakluyt and some later writers suppose him to have coasted

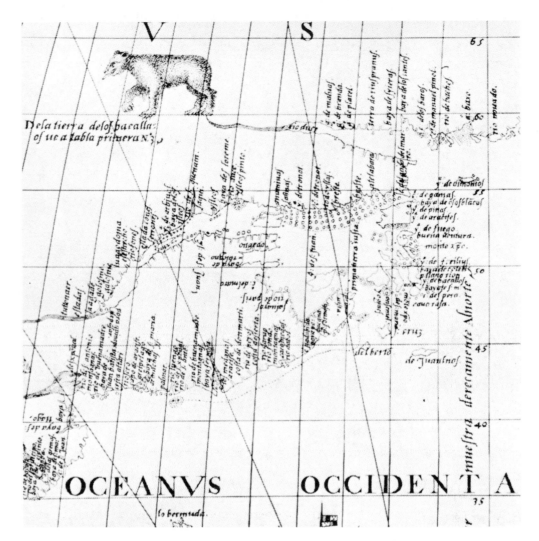

Fig. 47.—Part of the world map of Sebastian Cabot, 1544.

as far south as Florida. Cabot was followed by the brothers Corte Real who, in three expeditions under the Portuguese flag in 1500–2, rediscovered Greenland, navigated the east coast of Newfoundland, and perhaps penetrated into the Gulf of St Lawrence (Figs. 35, 47, 49). The entrance of Hudson's Strait may have been found by the Portuguese and was probably reached by Sebastian Cabot on a voyage of 1509.[8] By this date it was plain that the continental lands revealed by his father's voyages bore no resemblance to Marco Polo's Cathay, and Cabot's venture was undertaken in the belief 'that a passage might bee founde to Cathay by the north seas, and that spices might bee brought from thense soner by that way, then by the vyage the Portugales vse by the sea of Sur'. After being turned back by ice and mutiny in $67\frac{1}{2}°$ N, Cabot sailed south-west from Labrador to 38°, the latitude of Virginia (Fig. 47).

The charting of the Atlantic seaboard of North America was completed by

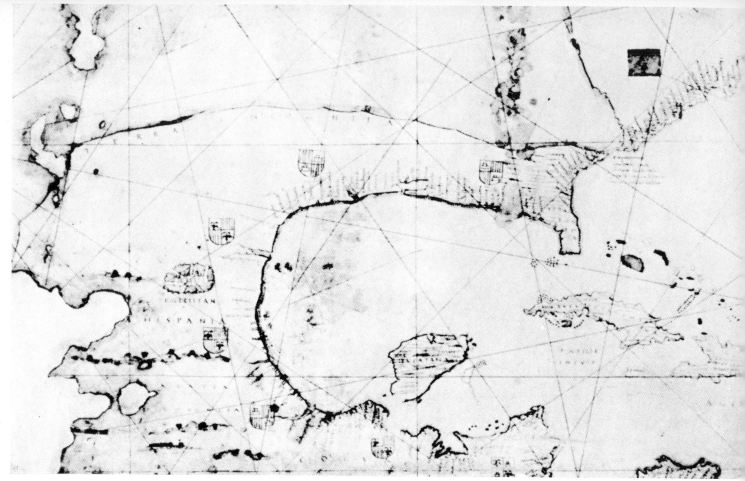

FIG. 48.—The New World, in Verrazano's map, 1529.

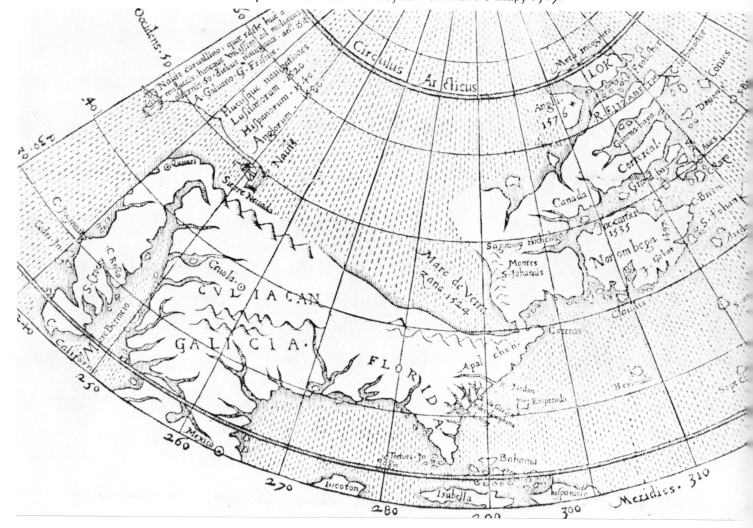

FIG. 49. Part of Michael Lok's map, published by Hakluyt in 1582.

coasting voyages made under the Spanish and French flags in search of a western sea-lead. The Spaniards, naturally apprehensive of such a discovery to the north of their Caribbean colonies, despatched Estevão Gomes in 1524 with orders 'to examine all the coast from Florida to Baccalaos [Labrador], whether any passage can be found leading to the kingdom of the Great Khan'. Gomes, a Portuguese pilot who had deserted from Magellan's expedition before it reached the Pacific, had a personal interest in discovering a more direct passage than that by the strait named after his rival; and the voyage in which he examined 'every bay, creek, river, and inlet, whether it extended over to the other side [of the land]', can be traced in the charts of the royal cosmographers in the Casa de la Contratación (Fig. 50). Meanwhile in 1523 the King of France, whose ships had captured the Mexican

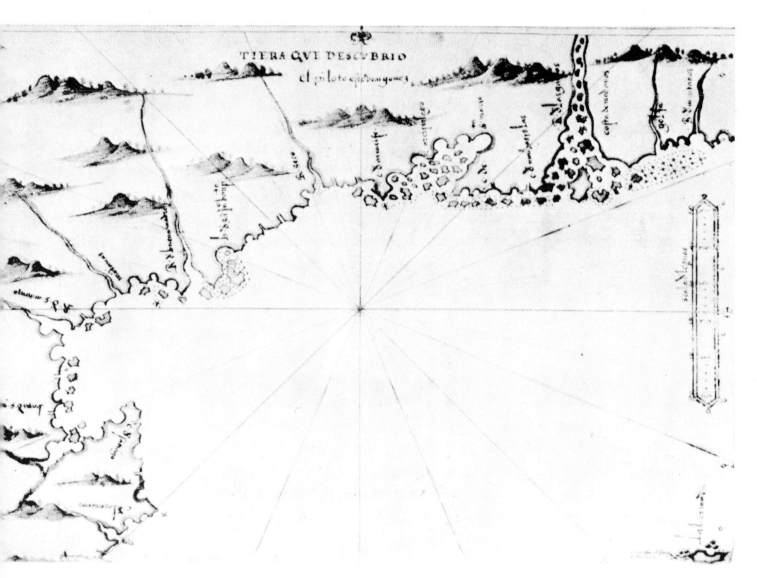

Fig. 50.—Chart by Alonso de Santa Cruz, c. 1545, showing the coasts of New England explored by Gomes.

treasure sent home by Cortes, despatched Giovanni da Verrazano, a Florentine exile living at Dieppe, 'on the discovery of Cathay'. On his second voyage, in 1524, Verrazano navigated and charted the American coast from 34° N, near Cape Fear, to Nova Scotia and Newfoundland, naming the mainland New France. The voyages by which Verrazano 'established the cartography of the north-east coast of America between Florida and Cape Breton, including the Hudson River', are recorded on a world chart by his brother Girolamo (Fig. 48). Here, and on other maps of the 'Verrazanian' type, we see, to the south of Norumbega (the New England region) a conspicuous 'little necke of lande in 40 degrees of latitude' dividing the Atlantic from the Sea (or Gulf) of Verrazano, which (could it be doubted?) 'bathed the limits of India, China, and Cathay'. This neck of sand (*arena*) was in fact the Hatteras sandspit, and what Verrazano saw across it in 1524 was no ocean but the waters of Pamlico Sound; yet over half a century later his 'colossal error', perpetuated by the cartographers, was to sustain the projects of Hakluyt and Raleigh for English exploration and settlement in this region (Fig. 49).[9]

By 1529, as Girolamo da Verrazano's map shows, the Atlantic coastline of North America had been traced in detail from Florida to Nova Scotia and Cape Breton, and its principal indentations between Chesapeake Bay and the Bay of Fundy placed on the charts. This coast was, it is true, shown as trending ENE–WNW (instead of NNE–SSW). The 16th-century chart was laid down from compass bearings and drawn for the use of pilots sailing on compass courses; its meridians therefore indicated magnetic and not true north. The westerly magnetic variation, which prevailed along the American shores of the Atlantic and for which seamen familiar with the easterly variation of European waters were unprepared, resulted in the incorrect orientation given to the North American coast by early cartographers (Figs. 47–9, 53). This explains too why the American landfalls of pilots 'running down the latitude' on a westerly course were commonly plotted too far north.

North of Cape Breton a deep sound represented the Gulf of St Lawrence, and Newfoundland was connected to Labrador, for the Strait of Belle-Isle had not yet been navigated from east to west; on many later maps Newfoundland was drawn as an archipelago (Figs. 47, 49, 51). In this region there remained hope of a passage, and here the French resumed the initiative which they had taken with Verrazano's expeditions. In 1534 Jacques Cartier, a sea-captain of St Malo, 'made his first discouerie', as an Elizabethan propagandist wrote, 'of those partes of America, which lie . . . as it were on the backside of Newfoundland. In which voyage his principall intention was to seeke out the passage, which hee presumed might have beene found out into the East Indian Sea, otherwise called the passage to Cathaya'. On this voyage Cartier sailed through the Strait of Belle-Isle, along the west coast of New-

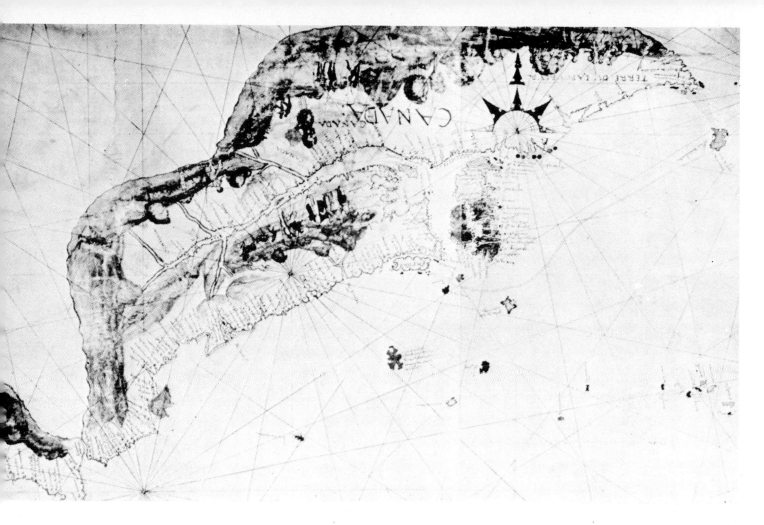

FIG. 51.—Canada and the St Lawrence ~~ri~~ver, in a world map drawn about 1544, ~~pe~~rhaps by Pierre Desceliers.

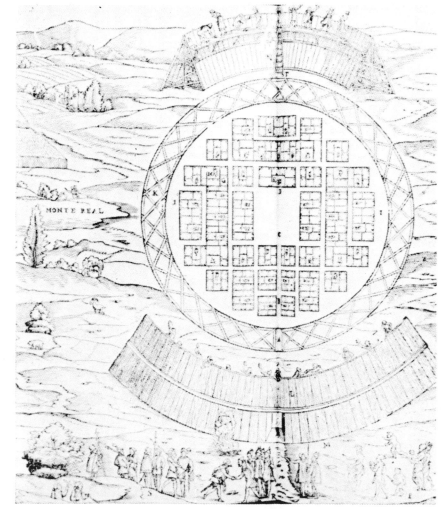

~~FI~~G. 52.—Jacques Cartier before the Indian town of Hochelaga, 1535.

foundland, and into the mouth of the St Lawrence. The Indians whom he brought back to France told of three Indian 'kingdoms', those of Canada or Stadacona, Saguenay, and Hochelaga, and described the St Lawrence as 'the great river of Hochelaga and the route towards Canada'. Encouraged by this report to hope for a strait or river communicating with eastern Asia or for wealthy native kingdoms like Mexico, Cartier in 1535 sailed up the St Lawrence past the Saguenay river to

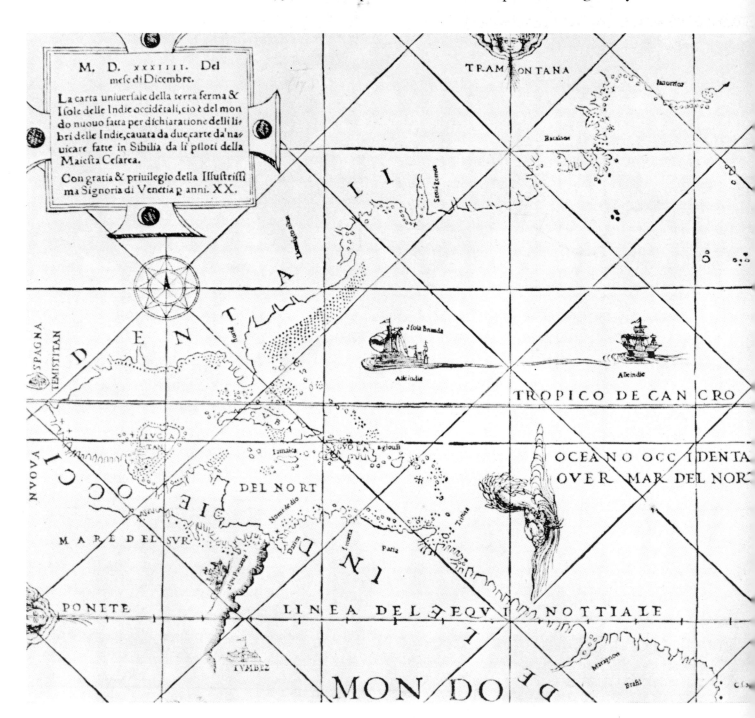

FIG. 53.—'Map of the mainland and islands of the West Indies', engraved at Venice in 1534.

the Indian settlement of Stadacona (Quebec) and went on by boat to Hochelaga (Montreal; Fig. 52). A third expedition, under Roberval and Cartier, was sent out in 1542 to colonize 'the lands of Canada and Hochelaga, forming the limit of Asia by way of the west', but did not extend Cartier's earlier discoveries. On this voyage Jean Alphonse, Roberval's pilot, compiled sailing directions (printed by Hakluyt) and rough charts for the 'River of Canada'. Cartier's own maps have not been preserved, but his discoveries were promptly laid down in contemporary charts by Dieppe hydrographers (Fig. 51).[10]

The conquests of Mexico (1519–21) and of Peru (1531–33) provided the Spaniards with bases for the exploration of Central America and the continental lands to the north and south. Before the fall of Mexico the outline of the Gulf of Mexico had been taking shape on the maps (Fig. 53). Florida had been discovered in 1513 and Yucatan in 1518–19, both peninsulas being first charted as islands; and in 1519 the whole northern shore of the Gulf, from Florida to the Rio Panuco, was coasted by Alonso de Pineda in search of a western strait. Soon after the conquest, Spanish overland expeditions from Mexico had reached the Pacific in the west and Panama to the south-east; and in 1533 a fleet sent out by Cortes discovered California. Although the Gulf of California was navigated to its head in 1540 and contemporary charts correctly delineated the peninsula (Fig. 54), California became the victim of a curious retrogression in cartography. Described on an English map of 1625 as 'sometymes supposed to be a part of ye western continent, but scince by a Spanish Charte . . . it is found to be a goodly Islande', it continued to be laid down as an island throughout the 17th century.[11] The territory to the north of the Gulf of Mexico was explored by two grandiose Spanish expeditions from Florida, impressive alike for their tenacity and for the magnitude of their failure. Of the first, which set out in 1528, only four survivors led by Cabeza de Vaca lived to bring to the Spaniards in Mexico, in 1536, their tale of the 'Seven Cities of Cibola'.[12] Three years later Hernando de Soto led an expedition into the Mississippi valley; the survivors, after traversing 'over 350,000 square miles of unexplored North America', at length reached Tampico, on the Gulf, in 1543. These journeys, with others from the Pacific coast, placed on the maps the fringe of the vast interior of the North American continent (Fig. 55).

From Peru, Spanish expeditions by land thrust south into Chile in 1535, north into Colombia in 1539, and east into the Amazon basin. The course of the Amazon, from its headwaters to its mouth, was followed by Francisco de Orellana in 1540–1, and that of the Orinoco by Lope de Aguirre in 1561 (Fig. 57). To Guiana, adventurers were drawn by the tale of El Dorado, the gilded king of the legendary

E.M.—G

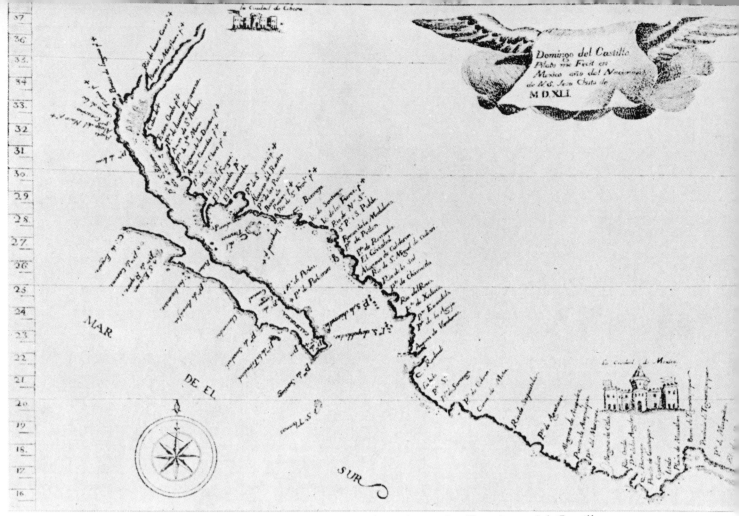

FIG. 54.—The Gulf of California, in a chart drawn by Domingo del Castillo, 1541.

FIG. 55.—The north coast of the Gulf of Mexico, in a chart drawn by Santa Cruz, c. 1541

FIG. 56.—South America, from a map by Diego Gutiérrez, engraved in 1562.

city of Manoa, first reported to the Spaniards about 1530.[13] In the second half of the 16th century numerous expeditions, culminating in that of Antonio de Berrio in 1590-1, sought El Dorado in the highlands of Guiana; and thither in 1595 Sir Walter Raleigh led an expedition to win 'a better Indies for her Majestie then the King of Spaine hath any'.[14] After sailing up the Orinoco to the mouth of the Caroni river, Raleigh returned with eloquent accounts of gold, of monsters, and of 'that mighty, rich and beautiful Empier of Guiana, and of that great and golden Citie, which the Spaniards call El Dorado, and the naturals Manoa'. In 1596 Laurence Keymis, sent out again by Raleigh, brought back news of 'a Sea of salt water, named Parime', lying 'farre within' on the route to Manoa. These and other features of the

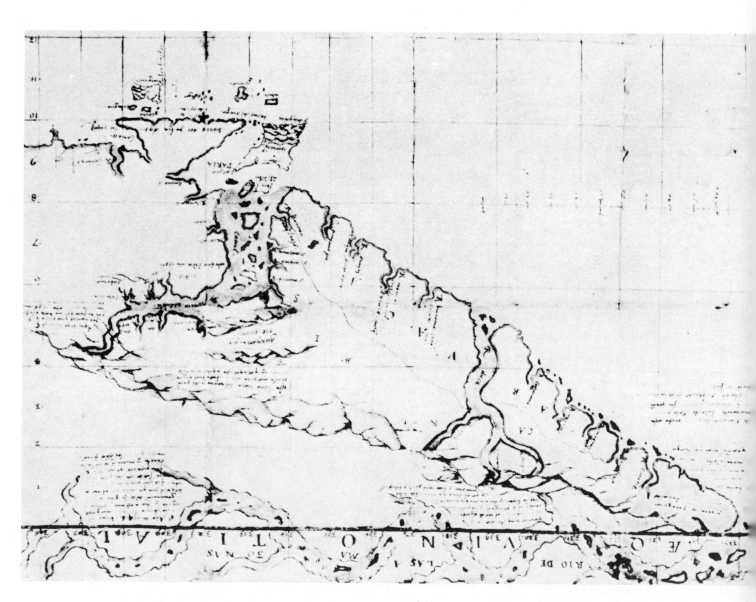

FIG. 57.—A Spanish map of the rivers Orinoco and Amazon, drawn about 1560

FIG. 58.—Map of Guiana, engraved by T. de Bry in 1599.

real or conjectural geography of Guiana were laid down 'in a large Chart or Map, which [Raleigh wrote in 1595] I haue not yet finished' and which has been identified with a manuscript map in the British Museum;[15] other maps were engraved from material furnished by seamen who had been on Raleigh's voyages (Fig. 58).

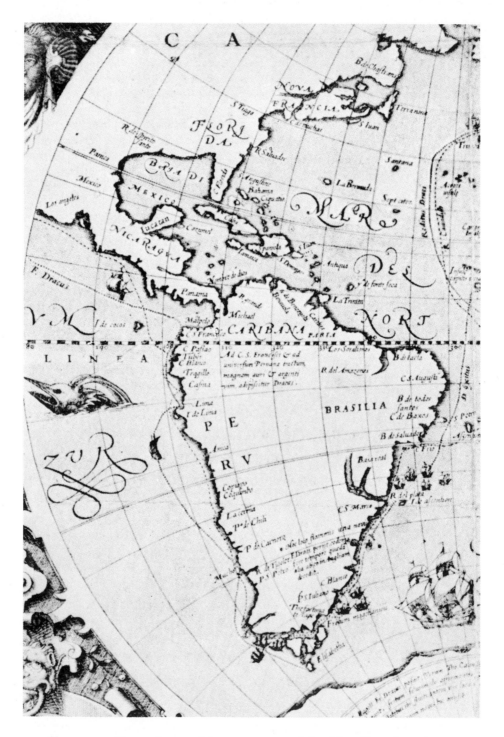

FIG. 59.—Part of a world map engraved by Hondius about 1590.
Showing the tracks of Drake and Cavendish.

The third great river estuary, that of the River Plate discovered by Vespucci in 1502, visited by Magellan in 1519, and explored by Sebastian Cabot in 1526–9, was settled between 1537 and 1580. Inland the city of Potosí, in Bolivia, said to be the largest city of the New World in the 16th century, sprang up near its silver mines discovered in 1545. By the middle of the century Spanish seamen had navigated almost the entire coasts of South America (Fig. 56). A ship from Spain made her way in 1539–41 through the Magellan Strait and north along the Chilean coast to Callao in Peru, but not until 1553 was the voyage made in the reverse direction. In October 1578, on his voyage of circumnavigation, Drake noted an error in the Spanish charting of this coast: 'We ran, supposing the coast of Chili to lie as the generall Maps haue described it, namely North-west, which we found to lie and trend to the Northeast and Eastwards, whereby it appeareth that this part of Chili hath not bene truely hitherto discouered, or at the least not truely reported for the space of 12 degrees at the least' (Fig. 59).

During the 16th century European enterprise in the exploration and colonization of the Americas had been seaborne. The bases in which Spanish, French and English adventurers had established themselves lay for the most part along the coasts or on river estuaries, and they were supplied by oceanic lines of communication.[16] In cartography the characteristic form was the sea chart. To the next two centuries fell the task of extending the landward frontiers of knowledge by exploration, mapping, trade and plantation. In South America the leading pioneers were Jesuit missionaries. In North America, French settlers in the St Lawrence basin, English colonists of the Atlantic seaboard and fur-traders in the North-West, and the Spaniards of New Mexico were to open up the continent from ocean to ocean.[17]

Remarks on the Illustrations

Chapter IV

◇◇

47   Sebastian Cabot is known to have drawn maps during his residence in Spain, where he was Pilot Major in the Casa de la Contratación 1518–47. These are lost, and the only surviving map attributed to him is the engraved world map dated 1544 of which the unique example is preserved in the Bibliothèque Nationale, Paris (see note 6). This is no doubt derived from the Spanish *padrón general*; and one of the printed legends issued with Cabot's map states that it was compiled in part from the maps 'made by his father [John Cabot] and him'. Another legend gives the date of John Cabot's North American landfall as 1494, a date which has suggested an earlier voyage than 1497. This landfall was probably at Cape Breton, marked on the map as 'Prima tierra vista'. The coasts shown in the detail here reproduced are those of Labrador, Newfoundland (represented as a cluster of islands), and Nova Scotia. (The reproduction is from a 19th-century copy.)

48   The chart drawn by Girolamo da Verrazano in 1529 (preserved in the Vatican Library) shows the Atlantic coastline of America from Florida to Cape Breton, explored by his brother in 1524. Opposite the supposed isthmus in 40° N, recorded by Giovanni, is the legend: 'From this eastern sea you may behold the western sea and there are six miles of land between them.' The cartographer has introduced the name Norumbega (here, in the form 'Noranbega', applied to a river), by which the New England region was known in the 16th century.

49   Michael Lok's map, drawn from 'Verrazano's plat' in his possession, was published by Hakluyt in his *Diuers voyages* (1582) to support English claims in North America and to illustrate western access routes to the Pacific. The isthmus and 'Sea of Verrazana 1524' are shown, with (to the north) the discoveries of 'J. Gabot 1497', 'De Cartier 1535', 'Corte real', and 'Angli 1576', i.e. Frobisher's expedition (see Chapter V, and Fig. 75).

50   This chart by Alonso de Santa Cruz, *cosmografo mayor*, is included in his

manuscript 'Islario General' of about 1545 (Biblioteca Nacional, Madrid). It depicts the coast of New England which Estevão Gomes explored in 1524–5, from Cape Cod (or perhaps a point further south) to the Penobscot river in Maine, with the names given by him.

51   This is one of a group of manuscript world maps and atlases drawn by hydrographers of Dieppe between about 1540 and 1566; four of these were made by Pierre Desceliers, of Arques near Dieppe. They give the earliest cartographic representations of the discoveries of Jacques Cartier (a native of Brittany) in the St Lawrence basin in 1534, 1535–6, and 1541–2. The map from which the reproduction is taken, sometimes known as the 'Harleian' or 'Dauphin' mappemonde, is preserved in the British Museum (Add. MS 5413); it is unsigned and undated, but was probably drawn by Desceliers about 1544. The detail reproduced shows the St Lawrence river to the most westerly point reached by Cartier (in 1535), marked by the name of his native town St Malo; this lies beyond the junction of the Ottawa and St Lawrence rivers ('Ochelaga', on the site of Montreal). To the west lies the ocean which Cartier sought. The conjectural strait linking it to the Atlantic further south may be compared with Verrazano's 'isthmus' (Fig. 48). The Indian name 'Canada' (three times repeated) is given to the region north of the St Lawrence.

52   This woodcut plan of the 'city' of Hochelaga in New France was published with the narrative of Cartier's second voyage in Ramusio's *Nauigationi e viaggi*, vol. III (Venice, 1556). In front of the stockades of their town below 'Monte Real', Huron Indians are shown greeting the Frenchmen.

53   This is a woodcut map, 'taken from nautical charts made in Seville by the pilots of His Imperial Majesty', and published in the *Summario de la generale historia de l'Indie occidentali* (Venice, 1534), perhaps edited by Ramusio. The Caribbean islands are accurately drawn, but Yucatan still appears as an island (cf. Fig. 48); 'Temistitan' (Mexico) and 'Tumbez' (in Peru) represent the latest conquests of Spain. The Atlantic coastline of North America is marked 'Steuā Gomes'. Ships indicate the sea routes between Spain and the Indies and from Peru to Panama. In the southern part of the map (not reproduced here), the name 'Stretto de magallanes' appears for the first time on a map.

54   Domingo del Castillo, who drew this chart at Mexico in 1541, was a pilot in the second of the two Spanish fleets which navigated the Gulf of California in 1539–40 and 1540–2. The original chart, formerly in the Cortes archives in Mexico, is not now known; the reproduction is from a copy of it engraved in 1770, and there may have been corruption of the original, e.g. in the premature use of the name California for the peninsula. The tracks of the Spanish expeditions are indicated by coastal names.

55   The map by Santa Cruz (in the Archivo General de Indias, Seville) shows

numerous Indian settlements inland, reported by survivors of De Soto's expedition on their return to Mexico in 1543. The route followed by his men is not precisely known, but they seem to have ranged as far north as Georgia and west into Texas before returning down the Mississippi and along the western shore of the Gulf to the Spanish town of Panuco.

56   The map of America by Diego Gutiérrez, cosmographer in the Casa de la Contratación, was engraved by Hieronymus Cock at Antwerp in 1562. This shows the extent of Spanish exploration along the coasts and river-valleys, and inland from Peru and from settlements on the north coast and in the River Plate basin. The Amazon, revealed by Orellana in 1540-1, is in the serpentine form common to all early maps; and the Plate estuary is grossly exaggerated. The names on the (wrongly oriented) Pacific littoral record Spanish penetration from Peru southward into Chile in the decade 1540-50. The legend 'Gigantum regio', and vignette above it, show the early growth of the belief in Patagonian giants. Tierra del Fuego is represented as a continental land.

57   This map (in the Archivo Histórico Nacional, Madrid) records the exploration of the Orinoco and Amazon rivers to about 1555. (The map is drawn with south at the top, and is reversed in the reproduction so that it is oriented to the north.) The Amazon is drawn with a serpentine course (cf. Fig. 56); the estuary of the Orinoco is delineated, but its headwaters were unknown until Lope de Aguirre, from Peru, descended the river from source to mouth in 1561.

58   The map of 'the powerful and gold-bearing Kingdom of Guiana', published in Theodore de Bry's *America*, Part VIII (Cologne, 1599), is copied from a slightly earlier map by Jodocus Hondius, although its title asserts that it is 'drawn by a sailor who accompanied Walter Raleigh on his voyage [of 1595]'. To the south of the Orinoco lies the salt lake 'called by the cannibals Parime', reported to Keymis in 1596; and on its north shore stands 'Manoa or Dorado, the greatest city in the world'. These features suggest that the author of the map (or Hondius, who had lived in London and maintained his English connections) may have seen a map drawn by or for Raleigh. The geography of the interior is derived from the accounts of Raleigh and Keymis. At the foot are pictures of an Amazon and a man of the Ewaipanoma, a tribe reputed to have their heads on their chests. A legend relates that Amazons live with men only in April—a story that goes back to Marco Polo.

59   South America, from a world map engraved by Hondius in London about 1590, with the tracks of the circumnavigations of Drake (1577-80) and Cavendish (1586-8). Drake's correction to the charting of the Chilean coast (cf. Fig. 56) will be noted. Tierra del Fuego is depicted as a group of islands, with Elizabeth Island as the southernmost, separated by a channel from Terra Australis (see Chapter IX and Fig. 124).

Notes

Chapter IV

<hr>

¹ For Balboa, see Chapter III; for Magellan, see Chapters III, VII, IX.

² See Chapter II; and Fig. 14.

³ See Chapters VI and XII.

⁴ The Spaniards in the Bahamas had, before 1511, picked up from Indians a tale of a 'fountain of youth' in a land to the north called Bimini; this played its part in the discovery of Florida. Cibola was a Zuñi *pueblo* where (as Indians of the Colorado reported in 1536) there were 'seven very large cities'; it became the objective of Spanish expeditions from Mexico to the north. The legend of El Dorado, the gilded king of the city of 'Manoa' on 'Lake Parima', was told to the Spaniards about 1530; they supposed his kingdom to lie in the Orinoco basin.   ⁵ See Chapter III.

⁶ For the maps of Sebastian Cabot and Verrazano, see above, Figs. 47–9, and below, note 9. Sebastian Cabot's map, engraved by Clement Adams in 1549, was still in the Royal Library a hundred years after Hakluyt wrote in 1582, and probably perished in the burning of the Palace of Whitehall at the end of the 17th century. The only surviving example of Cabot's map (Fig. 47) was probably engraved in the Netherlands.

⁷ Cabot's discoveries are also represented on the map of Juan de La Cosa (Fig. 34), and may therefore have been known to Columbus.

⁸ Cabot was at this date still in the English service.

⁹ As Hakluyt noted, maps by Verrazano reached England; and his interpretation of North American geography long influenced English and French enterprise (cf. Figs. 49, 51, 62, and Chapters VI and XII).

¹⁰ See 'Remarks', Fig. 51. The principal chartmakers of Dieppe at this period were Pierre Desceliers, Nicolas Desliens, Nicolas Vallard, and Jean Rotz.

¹¹ See Chapter XII. The map quoted is that by Henry Briggs (Fig. 175).

¹² See above, note 4.   ¹³ See note 4.

¹⁴ For Raleigh's earlier colonial venture in North America, see Chapter XII.

¹⁵ B.M., Add. MS 17940.

¹⁶ Spain's trade routes by sea in the 16th century are shown in Figs. 46, 110.

¹⁷ See Chapter XII.

PART THREE

The Way of the North

V

THE NORTH-EAST PASSAGE

13th to 16th centuries

THE STRONGEST MAGNET for exploration in the 16th century was still the reputed wealth of Cathay and the Spice Islands: 'the most richest londes and ilondes in the worlde, for all the gold, spices, aromatikes and pretiose stones . . . from thens thei come', as Roger Barlow wrote to King Henry VIII in 1541.[1] When the English and Dutch entered the field of discovery, the southern sea-routes to the Far East were already claimed by Spain and Portugal. By the easterly route round the Cape of Good Hope the Portuguese had developed a seaborne traffic with India and eastern Asia. Spanish ships had passed the Magellan Strait and crossed the Pacific, and the main Spanish trade route was established across the Isthmus of Panama. The continuity of the American coast from the St Lawrence to the Magellan Strait had been disclosed by repeated searches for an easier channel into the South Sea. The younger seafaring nations who aspired to a share in Eastern trade had to seek a route into the Pacific by a portage or strait across North America, or by navigable passages to the north of the two contingents which barred the way to the Far East. Even in the Virginia colony of 1607, the first permanent English settlement in the New World, the prospect of 'a certaintie of the South Sea' had not been abandoned;[2] but it was to the search for northern passages that the main effort of English and Dutch seamen was directed. 'There is one way to discouer, which is into the North,' wrote Robert Thorne in 1527, 'for out of Spaine they have discouered all the Indies and Seas Occidentall, and out of Portingall all the Indies and Seas Orientall.'[3]

Thorne and his friend Roger Barlow, English merchants trading in Seville, both prepared projects urging on King Henry VIII 'this waie of the northe' and 'the commodity and vtilitie of this Nauigation'. Thorne's letter was addressed to the

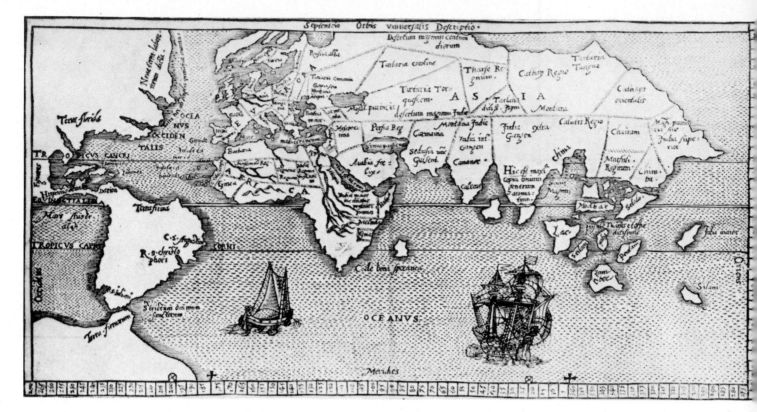

FIG. 60.—Robert Thorne's world map, 1527; printed by Hakluyt in 1582.

King in 1527, and his 'book and card of the viage to Cataia' came into the hands of Dr John Dee fifty years later. The letter was first printed by Richard Hakluyt in 1582 as propaganda for the North-West Passage, with a somewhat edited woodcut reproduction of Thorne's 'little Mappe or Carde of the world' (Fig. 60).

The geographical conditions for the 'waie of the northe' were a navigable passage to the north of Asia or America and the existence of a strait dividing the two continents. Thorne boldly asserted his opinion that 'there is no land vnhabitable, or Sea innauigable', and was himself willing 'to attempt, if our Seas Northward be nauigable to the Pole, or no'. Armchair geographers of the 16th century held conflicting views, derived from theoretical reasoning, from the authority of ancient writers, or from their interpretations of explorers' reports, about the relationship between the supposed Polar lands and the continents of Asia and America.[4] By the second half of the century (Figs. 61–3) it was generally agreed that no land bridge connected north-east Asia with north-west America and that the Polar lands were divided by sea from both continents; and debate turned on the question whether the north-east or the north-west offered the easier or more 'commodious' passage.

It is not surprising that Polar geography was the subject of active speculation, for in the 16th century (as today) national interests hung upon the answer. To those Englishmen who, like Thorne, studied geography from a globe it was plain that 'sayling Northward and passing the Pole . . . it should be a much shorter way [to the Spice Islands], than either the Spaniards or the Portingals haue'. Maps drawn on a polar projection (e.g. Fig. 62) drove this point home. Countries in high latitudes would also offer a better market for woollen cloth, the staple English export, than

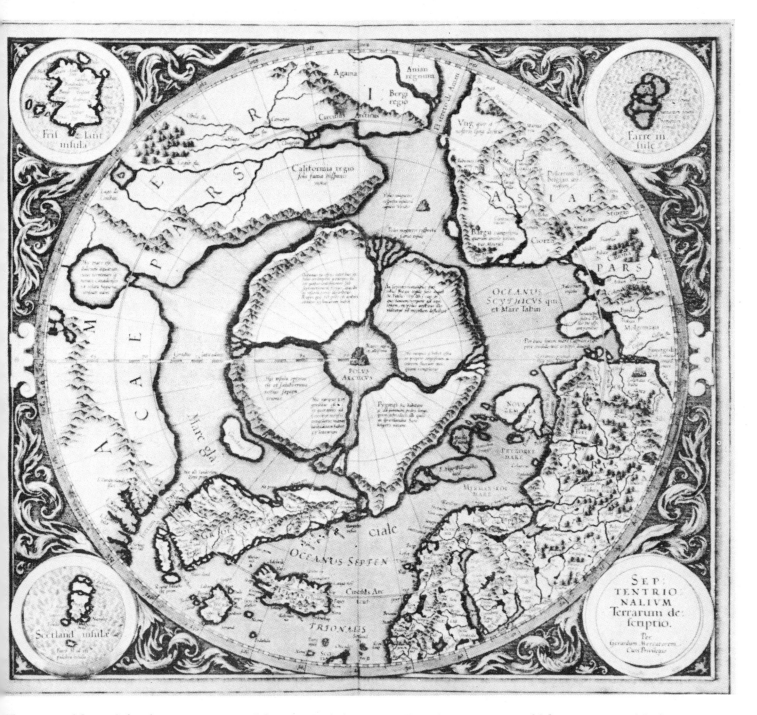

FIG. 61.—Map of the Arctic region, in Mercator's Atlas, 1595. Based on an inset of Mercator's world chart, 1569.

tropical lands. Both these arguments were urged by Thorne, and they were echoed 150 years later (as we shall see) by a later English adventurer for the North-East Passage.

Thorne had offered his countrymen three northern routes which he believed to be navigable: 'toward the Orient', 'towards the Occident', and 'right toward the

FIG. 62.—'Sir Humfray Gylbert Knight his charte', probably drawn by John Dee about 1582.

in 1556–7 Stephen Borough and his brother William (then sixteen years old) had in the pinnace *Spendthrift* boldly penetrated to Vaygach Island ('Waygats'), south of Novaya Zemlya, and through the Kara Sea before being turned back by ice (Fig. 65). Further enterprise in this direction was checked by the expectation of richer profits from the Russian trade and by increasing interest in the north-west route.

That belief in a sea-passage to the north of Asia was still lively is shown by William Borough's 'entire sayling plat that we use for those parts' (Fig. 65) and

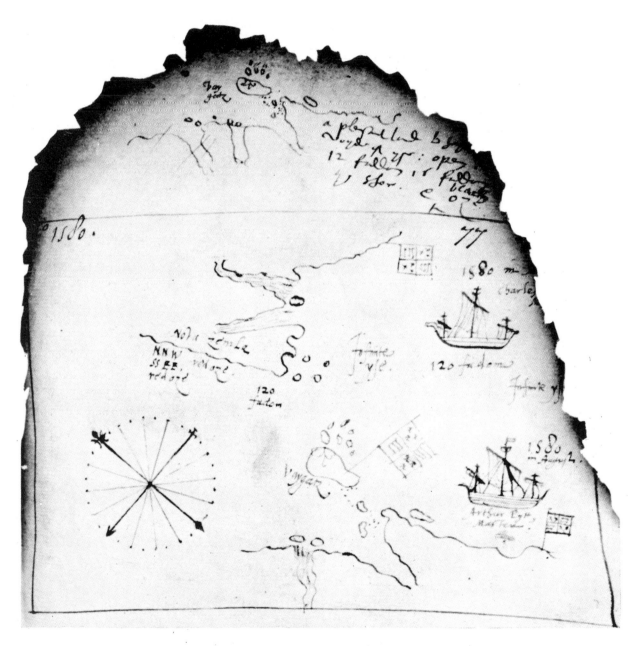

FIG. 66.—Sketch by Hugh Smyth, showing the ships of Pet and Jackman icebound in the Kara Sea in 1580.

FIG. 67.—Map of the North Polar regions eng

98 from the charts of Willem Barents.

by George Best's world map of 1578 (Fig. 63); and as late as 1580 Mercator could assert to Richard Hakluyt that 'the voyage to Cathaio by the East is doubtlesse verie easie and short' (Fig. 61).[7] These hopes were sustained by Dee's zealous advocacy and by Borough's 'continuall practise in the voyages made yeerely' to Russia by sea. Borough and Dee drew up the instructions for William Pet and Charles Jackman, masters of the two ships sent out by the Muscovy Company in 1580 to search for the passage. A sailing time of thirty-six days was allowed to 'the Promontory Tabin', whence the land was forecast to run south and east. The ships passed through the Kara Strait, north of Vaygach, or perhaps through the Yugor Strait (also known as Pet's Strait), south of the island, into the Kara Sea, where they were beset by 'infinite yse', and on the return Jackman's ship was lost without trace. To the manuscript journal of the voyage brought back by Pet is attached a chart (Fig. 66), showing the ships in the Kara Sea. Drawn by one of Pet's company, as we learn from a note in Dee's handwriting ('Hugh Smyth did inform me by mouth and made a little draught with his own hand of this place and there aboutes anno 1582'), this sketch graphically suggests both the fortitude of the Elizabethan seamen and their inevitable failure to pierce the shallow and ice-packed coastal waters to which they clung.[8]

The running was now taken up by the Dutch, whose interest in opening a northern passage to the Far East was no less than that of the English. Two expeditions were sent out in 1594. An Amsterdam ship, commanded by Willem Barents, sought the passage to the north of Novaya Zemlya and navigated its west coast as far as 77° N. The merchants of Zeeland, advised by Hakluyt, preferred the channel south of Novaya Zemlya followed by the English voyagers, and their ships passed through the Yugor Strait into the Kara Sea. In 1595 a combined expedition, with Barents as chief pilot, failed to penetrate the ice in Yugor Strait. Two ships sailed from Amsterdam in the following year, again with Barents as chief pilot. Their course is marked on Barents' map of the three voyages (Fig. 67) and on Gerrit de Veer's map (Fig. 68), both engraved in 1598; and a contemporary English chart (Fig. 69) also records their discoveries. Sailing on a more westerly course, they discovered Bear Island ('T'veere Eylandt'), and Spitsbergen ('Het nieuwe land'). After the ships had separated, Barents coasted Novaya Zemlya and rounded its north-east cape to a bay where his ship was frozen in. Here the crew constructed a hut for their winter quarters ('Het behouden Huys' in Fig. 68). They were the first party of Europeans to survive an Arctic winter. On the return voyage in open boats to the Kola Peninsula in the following summer Barents died of scurvy. His hut, built of fir-wood planks, was found by a Norwegian ship in 1871. Among the relics left by Barents' crew in 1597 and recovered in 1875 was a Dutch translation

Fig. 68.—Part of a chart by Gerrit de Veer, 1598, illustrating Barents' voyage of 1596–7.

Fig. 69.—An English chart of the Arctic, drawn about 1610.

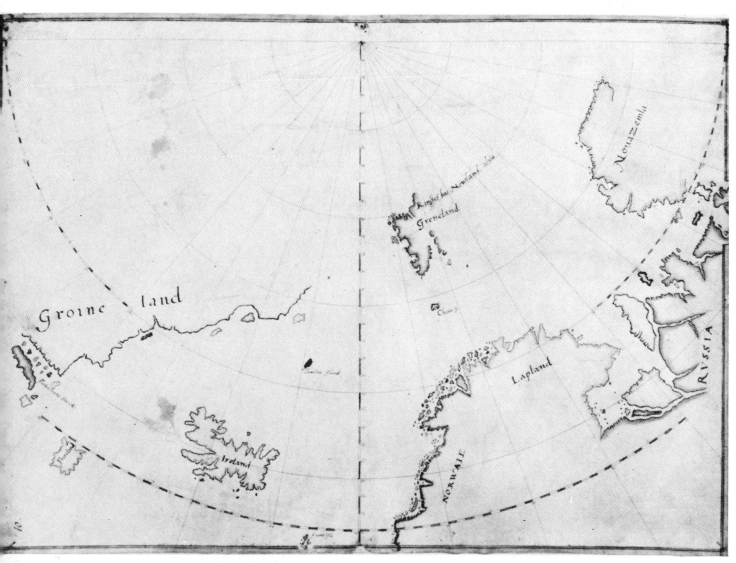

of the journal of the voyage made by Pet and Jackman in 1580, no doubt furnished by Hakluyt.

Henry Hudson, leading Dutch expeditions in 1605–7, found no way through the ice to the east and west of Spitsbergen, and further search for the North-East Passage was discouraged for half a century, although the Dutch whalers who frequented the northern seas brought back reports of open sea to the north and east of Novaya Zemlya.[9] In 1675 speculation on the north-east route was revived by rumours which reached England from Holland. Joseph Moxon, whose map (Fig. 70) shows the supposed geography of the passage, told a curious story in a paper to the Royal Society.[10] Twenty-two years earlier, he recalled, he had met, in an Amsterdam beer-house, a seaman from the Greenland whaling fleet, who reported that the Dutch ships 'had sailed two degrees beyond the pole', without meeting land or ice. 'I asked him', wrote Moxon, 'what weather they had there? He told me fine warm weather, such as was at Amsterdam in the summer time.' By such 'Arguments and

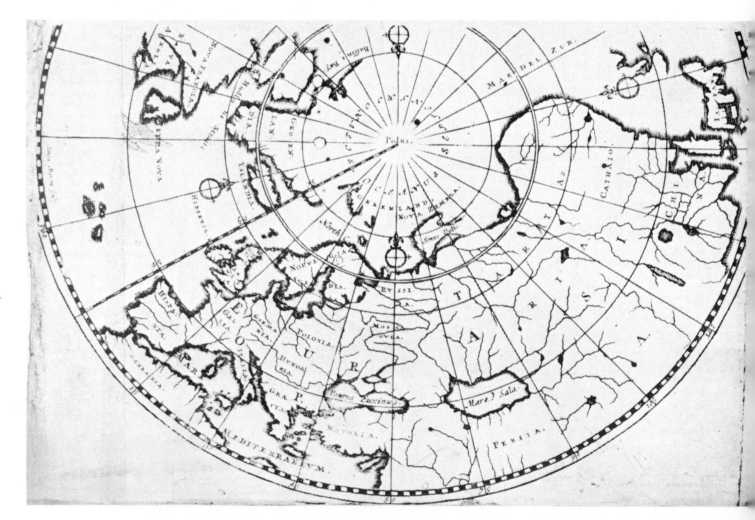

FIG. 70.—Joseph Moxon's map of the North-East Passage, published in 1674.

Reasons', flimsy as they must seem to us, Captain John Wood was persuaded of the 'Possibility of a Passage to ye Northward of Nova Zembla to China and Japan'. He defined the advantages of the discovery in terms similar to Thorne's: the north-east offered the shortest route, involving a mere six weeks' voyage to Japan, and a market in Tartary for English cloth, 'wch now is a great Drugg'. Wood's project was supported by King Charles II and the Duke of York, for whom he 'drew a Polar Draught', and in May 1676 he sailed with two ships, the frigate *Speedwell* and the pink *Prosperous*. His voyage was a fiasco, the *Speedwell* being wrecked on the west coast of Novaya Zemlya. Wood drew the ungenerous conclusion that his predecessors in discovery had misled him and that Novaya Zemlya and Spitsbergen 'are the same Continent'.[11]

Meanwhile the eastern end of the passage had been discovered. Russian expeditions by land had explored the northern coastline of Siberia, and in 1647–8 the Cossack

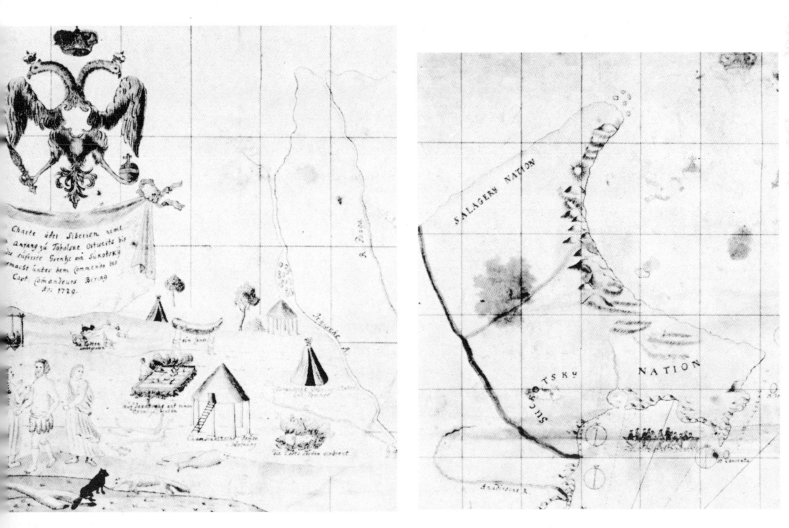

Figs. 71, 72.—Details from a MS map of Siberia drawn for Bering in 1729 and illustrating his first expedition.

Deshnev sailed round the north-east point of Asia.[12] The great Russian expeditions sent out under Vitus Bering (1725–9 and 1734–43) were designed to investigate the strait supposed to lie between Asia and America. Its existence was not proved beyond doubt, but Bering himself was convinced (Figs. 71, 72, 119), and from 1754 the strait has borne his name. In 1778 Cook navigated it to 70° N in search of a passage from the Pacific to the Atlantic by the north of Asia or of America.[13]

The last English venture for the passage reverted to Thorne's alternative route directly across the Polar region. In 1773, on the proposal of the Royal Society, the Admiralty despatched two ships, the *Racehorse* and the *Carcass*, selected for their

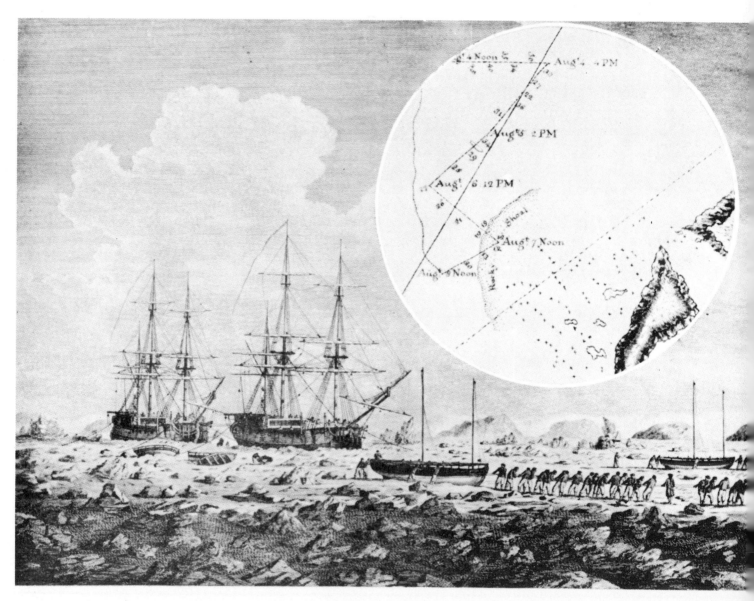

FIG. 73.—Captain Phipps's ships locked in the ice north of Spitsbergen, 7 August 1773. *Inset:* Part of a sketch chart drawn by Phillip d'Auvergne, midshipman in the *Racehorse*, August 1773.

strength of construction, 'for the purpose of trying how far navigation might be practicable towards the north pole'.[14] The expedition was commanded by Captain C. J. Phipps, and Horatio Nelson served as a midshipman in the *Carcass*. Phipps was unlucky in meeting unfavourable ice conditions. North of Spitsbergen he was checked by ice in 81° 37′ N, and on working to the east he found only a 'wall of ice, extending for more than twenty degrees between the latitudes of eighty and eighty-one' (Fig. 73).[15]

Of the three northern passages proposed by Thorne, that by the north-east was, at the beginning of the 19th century, considered to be the most discouraging; yet it was the first to be navigated throughout in a single vessel.[16]

Remarks on the Illustrations

Chapter V

❖◇❖

60 'The forme of a Mappe sent in 1527 from Siuill in Spayne by maister Robert Thorne marchaunt' was engraved and printed by Hakluyt in his *Diuers Voyages touching the Discouerie of America*, 1582. Thorne's letters to King Henry VIII and to the English ambassador in Spain, also printed by Hakluyt, contained an apology for the 'imperfection' of his 'little Mappe or Carde of the worlde', emphasized the length of the Spanish and Portuguese routes to the Far East, and urged that the route 'sayling Northwarde' would be shorter 'by more than 2000 leagues'. A legend on the map, off the north-east coast of America, asserts the English claim by discovery.

61 Mercator's concept of the Northern Regions admits the possibility of navigable passages from the Atlantic to the Pacific not only by the north of Asia and America, but also across the Pole. The North Pole ('a very high and black rock') lies in a sea connected by four channels, separated by large islands, with the 'indrawing sea' to the South. This view of the geography of the North was derived by Mercator (as he explained in a letter to Dee in 1577) from older records, now lost—the narrative of one Jacob Cnoyen and a work entitled 'Inventio Fortunatae', the author of which may have visited Greenland and America. Mercator shows an open sea passage north of Asia, rounding Cape Tabin (in 80° N), beyond which two magnetic poles are marked, and issuing in the Strait of Anian, which divides Asia and America. The insets depict the Shetlands, the Faroes, and the mythical island of 'Frisland', thought to lie south-west of Iceland.

62 The map, also on a Polar projection, drawn by John Dee for Gilbert about 1582 and now in the Free Public Library, Philadelphia, reproduces Mercator's version of the geography of the North Pole. Like Mercator's map, it reflects contemporary belief in an open passage to the north of Asia. It was however chiefly designed to illustrate western routes into the South Sea. In addition to the channel thought to have been found by Frobisher in 1576 (cf. Chapter VI, and Figs. 63, 75,

76), it indicates a navigable strait from the St Lawrence emerging into the Pacific by the Gulf of California. Further south (in 40° N) is drawn the supposed isthmus dividing the Atlantic from the 'Sea of Verazano, 1524' (see Chapters IV and VI, and Figs. 48, 49, 76).

63   This oval world map was published in *A true discourse of the late voyages of discouerie . . . under the conduct of Martin Frobisher generall*, by George Best, 1578. Like Dee's chart (Fig. 62), it shows an open north-east passage, but it emphasizes the short route offered by 'Frobisshers Straightes' and the Strait of Anian to the Moluccas. The 'strait' that Frobisher discovered in 1576 was in fact an inlet on the west coast of Davis Strait (see Chapter VI, Fig. 75). This woodcut map may be from a drawing by James Beare, who is reported to have 'drawne out the cards of the coast' on Frobisher's expeditions.

64   Anthony Jenkinson, who in 1557 went to Moscow as an agent of the Muscovy Company, travelled in 1558-9 down to the Volga to the Caspian Sea and east to Bokhara. His map of 'Russia, Moscovy and Tartary' is stated in its title to have been 'edita Londini Anno 1562', but the earliest version of it known is that published by Ortelius in his *Theatrum* in 1570. The map records Jenkinson's first journey (of 1558-9), from which he brought back an unfavourable report of the prospects of trade with the country round the Caspian.

65   William Borough's 'sayling plat' with notes on navigation, drawn about 1568, depicts the Muscovy Company's annual route by North Cape and 'Ward hows' (Vardö) to 'St Nicholas' (Archangel) and the channel to the south of Novaya Zemlya by which he entered the Kara Sea in 1557. The chart (British Museum, Royal MS 18. D. III, fol. 124) is bound in a collection of maps put together by Lord Burghley.

66   The sketch by Hugh Smyth (British Museum, Cotton MS Otho E. viii, fol. 73) is bound with the journal of Pet's voyage which was given to Dr Dee, and has his marginal notes. As a seaman's chart, it gives soundings and information on the sea-bottom; English flags are drawn on Novaya Zemlya, Vaygach, and the mainland.

67   The Polar chart engraved by Baptista van Deutecum in 1598, and published in Linschoten's *Itinerarium* (Latin edition, The Hague, 1599), marks the track of the Dutch ships in 1596, resulting in the discovery of Spitsbergen ('Het nieuwe Land'), and that of Barents' ship to winter quarters on Novaya Zemlya, in 76° N (see Fig. 68). Open sea is shown to the Pole; Mercator's Arctic islands have disappeared, although his magnetic pole, east of Cape Tabin, remains. The sketches of whales and walrus suggest commercial possibilities. In the north-west, 'Martin Forbischers straytes' are wrongly drawn as a passage to the south of Greenland

(cf. Fig. 75). The north-east passage issues southward to the Pacific by the Strait of Anian.

68   Gerrit de Veer, who sailed with Barents on his second and third voyages to the Arctic, described them in his *Waerachtige beschrijvinghe van drie seylagen* (Amsterdam, 1598). The detail reproduced from his map shows Barents' ship fast in the ice, the hut ('Het behouden Huys') built for wintering in the ice in 1596–7, and the return by open boat, on which Barents died of scurvy.

69   This English chart drawn about 1610 (British Museum, Cotton MS Aug. I. i. 10) reproduces the Arctic geography of the Barents chart (Fig. 67). The discoveries made by Captain James Hall for the King of Denmark on the west coast of Greenland in 1605–7 (see Chapter VI) are erroneously located in Spitsbergen, here named 'Kinges his Newland alias Greneland'.

70   Moxon's Polar map was published in his tract *A brief discourse of a passage by the North-Pole to Japan, China, &c.* (London, 1674). Open sea lies between Novaya Zemlya and the Pole, although the passage to the south is now represented as a gulf ('Sinus Dul[c]is'). In the north-west also a channel leads through Hudson's Straits and Baffin's Bay.

71, 72   The map drawn by order of Captain Vitus Bering in 1729 is now in King George III's Topographical Collection in the British Museum (K. Top. CXIV. 43). It extends 'from Tobolsk eastward to the farthest border of Sukotskÿ [Siberia]', and illustrates his first expedition (1725–9), under instructions drawn up by Peter the Great to determine whether an open strait existed between Asia and America; Bering took three years to cross Siberia to the Sea of Okhotsk and thence to the north-east coast of the Kamchatka peninsula. Here he built a ship and sailed north to $67°$ $18'$ N, without seeing the American coast or showing that a sea passage linked the Pacific and Arctic Oceans. Although satisfied that the strait existed, he undertook his second expedition in 1733 to demonstrate it.

The vignette (Fig. 71) illustrates the habits of the Siberian tribes observed by Bering. The detail of his sea voyage (Fig. 72) shows a line of soundings to above $67°$ N, where Bering decided that 'our task had been carried out and that the land did not extend farther north'. His observations of magnetic variation are also marked. (See Chapter VIII, and Fig. 119.)

73   The view of Captain Phipps's ships icebound north of Spitsbergen was engraved from a drawing by the marine artist James Cleveley, who accompanied the expedition. These ships were naval 'bombs', roomy and strongly built.

The inset is from a 'Plan of the Bay in which the *Racehorse* and *Carcass* were inclosed by the ice from July 31 to August 10, 1773. Latitude . . . $80°$ $37'$. Drawn by Phillip D'Auvergne, Midshipman on board the Racehorse'. The ships' track, August 4–8, is marked.

Notes

Chapter V

[1] In *A Brief Summe of Geographie*, translated from a Spanish work of 1519 by Martín de Enciso (ed. E. G. R. Taylor for the Hakluyt Society, 1931).

[2] See Chapter XII.

[3] For Thorne's letters, see 'Remarks', Fig. 60. The writings of Barlow and Thorne were circulated in manuscript during the 16th century.

[4] For various interpretations of this relationship, compare Figs. 36, 49, 60-3, 67, 197.

[5] 'Anian' was first recorded by Marco Polo as a kingdom of northern Asia (cf. Fig. 74). Most 16th-century maps located it in north-west America (cf. Fig. 61); and the 'Strait of Anian', dividing America from Asia, was first named in a pamphlet of 1562 by the Venetian cartographer Jacopo Gastaldi. The form and extent given to it by mapmakers is seen in Figs. 10, 61, 63. (See also Chapters VI and XII.)

[6] In Professor E. G. R. Taylor's phrase.

[7] Mercator's letter was printed by Hakluyt in his *Principall Nauigations* (1589).

[8] For the expedition of Pet and Jackman, as for all English voyages of discovery in the 16th century, small merchant ships were employed. Thus, in voyages for the North-west Passage (Chapter VI), Frobisher in 1576 had two pinnaces of under 30 tons, and Davis in 1585 two ships of 50 tons burden.

[9] The Dutch whaling ships, of an average burden of 300 tons, were 'very strong built, and doubled at the Bow, to resist the Shocks of the Ice'.

[10] Printed by Moxon in *A brief discourse of a passage by the North-Pole to Japan, China, &c.* (London, 1674).

[11] Wood's proposals, the journal of his voyage, and his conclusion were printed in *An account of several late voyages and discoveries to the south and north* (London, 1694).

[12] Whether Deshnev thus anticipated Bering and Cook in the discovery of the strait separating Asia from America is disputed. His voyage, from the Kolyma river on the Arctic coast round East Cape to the Anadyr river north of Kamchatka, was either unknown to, or not accepted as authentic by, Peter the Great in preparing Bering's instructions.

[13] See Chapters XI and XIV.

[14] Phipps's ships were bomb ketches; see Chapter XIV.

[15] A. E. Nordenskiöld's *Vega*, in 1878-9; see Chapter XIV.

E.M.—I

VI

THE NORTH-WEST PASSAGE

16th to 18th centuries

⬦━━⬦

WITH THE ESTABLISHMENT of the Russia trade from about 1560 and the failure of Pet and Jackman in 1580,[1] English enterprise towards the north-east had spent itself, and the Elizabethan adventurers looked west, by 'the backe side of the new found land', for the short route to Cathay.

Contemporary maps (Figs. 62, 76) reflect the belief in sea or land passages, lying south of the Arctic Circle, by which the American continent might be crossed or out-flanked. In about 40° N a narrow isthmus divides the Atlantic from the gulf, or 'Sea of Verrazano', which Giovanni da Verrazano thought he had seen on his voyage along the American seaboard in 1524.[2] On 'Sir Humfray Gylbert knight his charte' (Fig. 62), the St Lawrence is drawn as a strait traversing the continent to the Gulf of California. Further north, a navigable sea passage is shown just above the 60th parallel. Other fabulous or semi-fabulous passages, developed from travellers' tales, fed willing belief and conspired to cheat the hopes of explorers. The 'Strait of Anian', conceived in the 16th century as the sea passage between Asia and America, came to be sought as a waterway from the Pacific to the northern shores of the American continent.[3] Michael Lok, examining an old Greek pilot at Venice in 1596, learnt that he had four years earlier, on a voyage for the Strait of Anian, discovered a sound in 47° or 48° N, by which he sailed from the South Sea into the Atlantic and back; and for 200 years navigators searched for the Strait of Juan de Fuca.[4]

From such speculative geography sprang the Tudor and Stuart enterprises. Some were aimed at the establishment of a North American colony as a stepping-stone on the western passage. This motive lay behind the ventures of Gilbert in 1583 and of Raleigh in 1585–7 and even the colony planted in 1607 at Jamestown, where

Captain John Smith commented satirically on Captain Newport's 'five peeced Barge, not to beare us to that South sea, till we had borne her over the mountaines'.[5] Other projects were directed to the search for a sea-route to the north of the continent. Gilbert had himself, as early as 1565 or 1566, taken the lead in urging 'how that the passage by the Northwest, is more commodious for our traffick, then the other by the East', and he and Anthony Jenkinson debated the advantages of the two routes before the Queen and Council.

Gilbert's *Discourse of a discouerie for a new passage to Cataia*, with his map (Fig. 74), was printed in 1576 and served as propaganda for the voyages made by Captain Martin Frobisher in 1576–8 for the newly founded Company of Cathay. The 'supposed straight' into the South Sea discovered by Frobisher at his first attempt was a bay, and his search for the passage was diverted into a hunt for gold-bearing ore; but on his third voyage he sailed 200 miles into Hudson Strait—'The Mistaken Straightes' in James Beare's chart (Fig. 75). Frobisher's voyages disappointed their promoters and, as Michael Lok wrote in 1579 with the bitterness of a ruined man, 'now the passage to Cathay is by him left vnto vs as vncertain as at the beginning'. Yet the Asiatic appearance of the captive Eskimos or 'strange men of Cataye' whom he brought to England, 'much like [suggested Lok] to the Tartar nation', encouraged belief in access to Cathay by the north-west.[6]

Lok himself had lost faith in Frobisher but not in the Passage. Richard Hakluyt, reprinting Thorne's papers and Verrazano's narrative in his *Diuers voyages touching the discouerie of America* (1582), pointed to the possibility of a land passage, laid down on the map (Fig. 76) which Lok drew for Hakluyt from 'an olde excellent mappe which [Verrazano] gaue to Henrie the eight, and is yet in the custodie of master Locke'. As a base for discovery and command of the passage, Hakluyt advocated a western colony; but he did not fail to notice the 'great probabilitie, of a passage by the North-west part of America'.

Fortified by this propaganda, a syndicate headed by William Sanderson promoted a new search for the North-West Passage. John Davis's first voyage, in 1585, took him into Davis Strait to a latitude of nearly 67° N and, writing to Sir Francis Walsingham on his return, he affirmed that 'the northwest passage is a matter nothyne doubtfull but at any tyme almost to be passed, the sea nauigable, voyd of yse, the ayre tollerable, and the waters very depe'. On his third voyage, in 1587, Davis penetrated his Strait to a point on the Greenland coast in 72° 12′ N, 'naming the same Hope Sanderson', crossing the Strait and returning by Cumberland Gulf and the 'furious overfall' of Hudson Strait, 'a very great gulfe, the water whirling and roaring as it were the meetings of tydes'. From Hope Sanderson, Davis had seen 'no ice towards the north, but a great sea', and the day after he

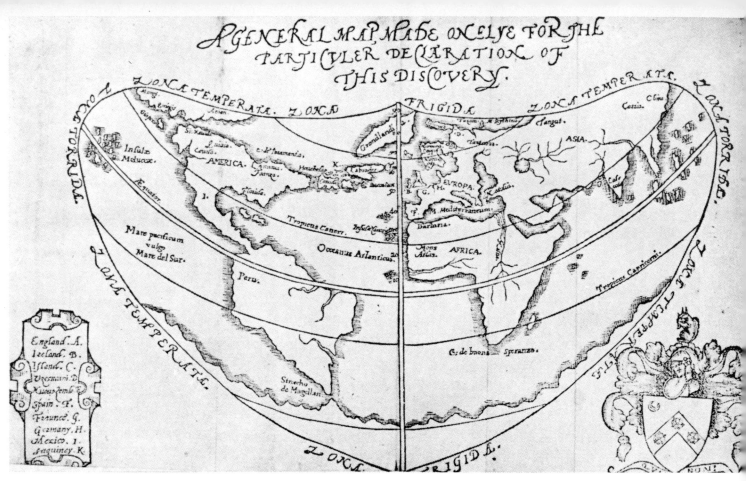

FIG. 74.—Sir Humphrey Gilbert's world map, published in 1576.

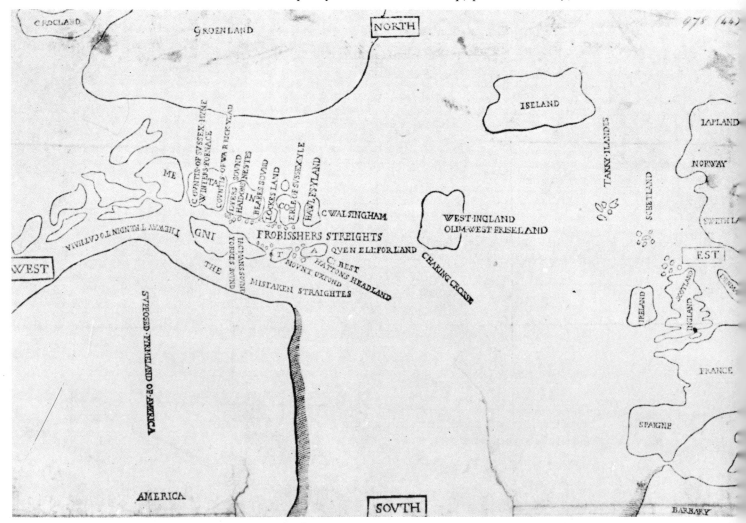

FIG. 75.—Chart illustrating Frobisher's voyages to the north-east in 1576–8, perhaps by James Beare.

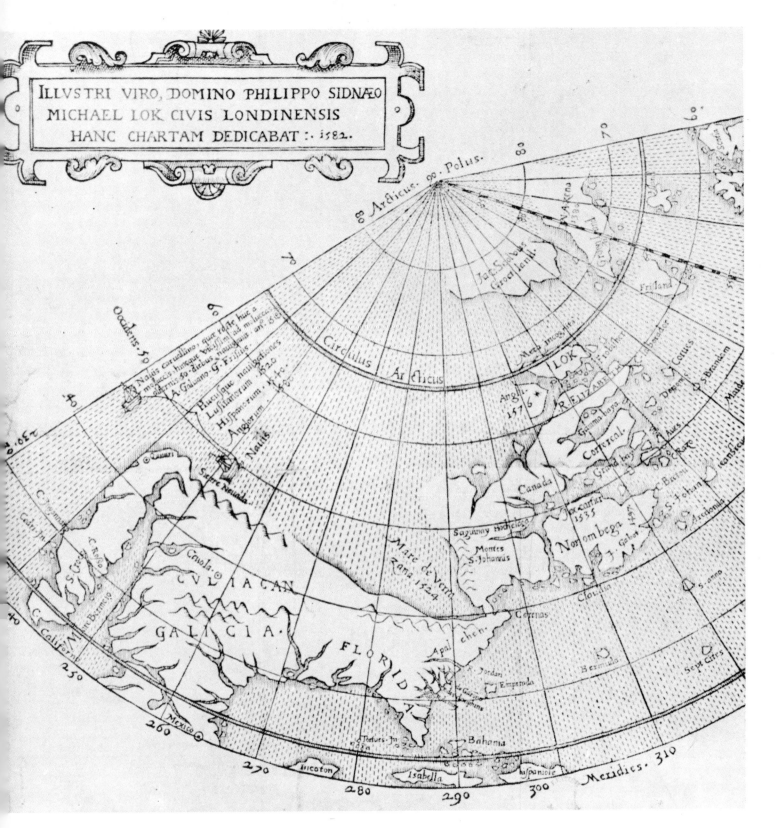

FIG. 76.—Part of Michael Lok's world map, published by Hakluyt in 1582.

FIG. 77.—The North-West Passage on the terrestrial globe of Emery Molyneux, 1592.

landed at Dartmouth he wrote to Sanderson, 'I haue bene in 73 degrees, finding the sea all open. . . . The passage is most probable, the execution easie.' Sanguine as this assertion may seem, Davis had in fact discovered the eastern entrance by which the North-West Passage was eventually to be navigated.[7]

The charts which were doubtless drawn by so careful an observer have not survived; but 'how far I proceeded [Davis wrote in 1595] & in what fourme this discouery lyeth, doth appeare vpon the Globe which M. Sanderson to his very great charge hath published'. This was the 'very large and most exact terrestriall Globe . . . composed by M. Emerie Mollineux of Lambeth', announced by Hakluyt in 1589 and completed by Molyneux at Sanderson's expense in 1592. In the preparation of the first English terrestrial globe Davis certainly had a hand. He tells us that he was 'the only meane with master Sanderson to imploy master Mulineux therein'; his discoveries are drawn with authority and precision (Fig. 77); and a legend on the globe has been plausibly interpreted as a record that Molyneux had sailed with Davis.[8]

Of the four possible channels proposed by Davis in 1587 for further examination, those by Hudson Strait and by Davis Strait were to be the scene of the attempts made in the next half-century. The voyage made by Captain George Waymouth in 1602 apparently took him into Hudson Strait; 'hee neither discovered nor named any thing more than Davis . . .' commented Luke Foxe in 1635, 'yet these two, Davis and he, did (I conceive) light Hudson into his Straights'. Dutch expeditions led by Henry Hudson in 1607–8 had vainly sought a northern passage through the ice to the east and west of Spitzbergen; and his third voyage, prompted by 'letters and maps which Captain Smith had sent him from Virginia, informing him of a sea leading into the Western Ocean' to the north of the English colony, had brought him as far south as the Hudson River in search of a passage.[9] In 1610 Hudson was engaged by a London syndicate to follow up the strait entered by Waymouth, whose log-books he had seen at Amsterdam the year before. Passing through the strait, he sailed south 'into a spacious sea . . . confidently proud that he had won the passage', and wintered in James Bay. Hudson, marooned by mutineers in an open boat, did not return, but —as the map of Hessel Gerritsz (Fig. 78) shows—the survivors' reports were acclaimed as proof that the passage into the South Sea had been opened, and Captain Thomas Button was sent out in 1612 to exploit the supposed discovery. Before his return in the following year, Gerritsz was writing 'we do not think that we shall hear anything about them before they return . . . from East India or China and Japan', and the Company of the Merchants of London Discoverers of the North-West Passage had been incorporated.

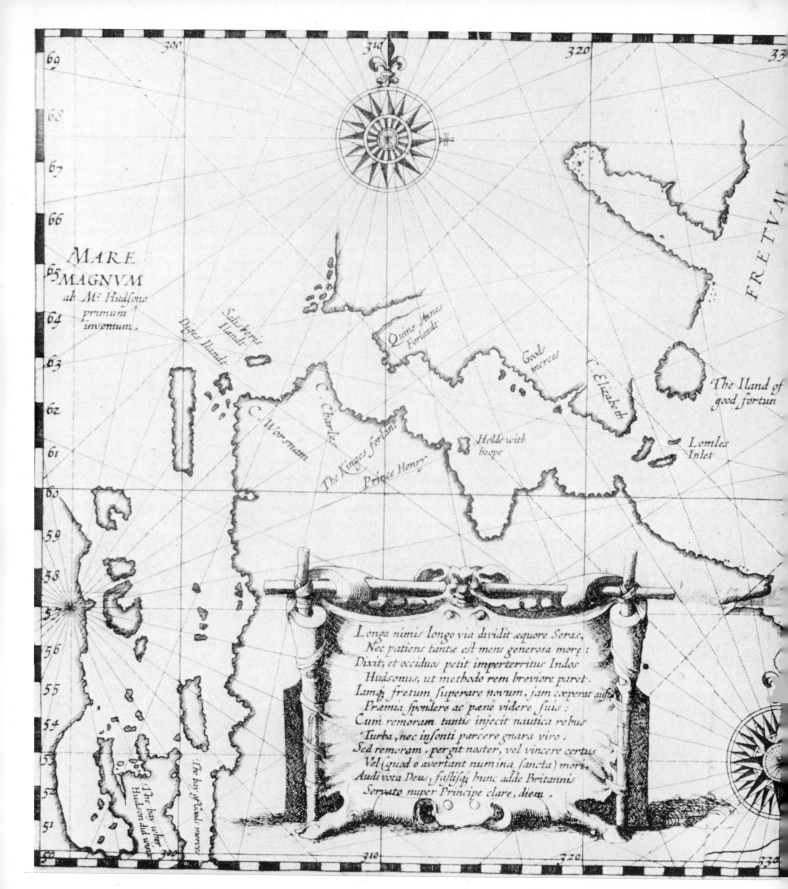

MARE
MAGNVM
ab Mr Hudsono
primum
inventum.

FRETVM

Salisberis Iland:

Digtes Iland:

Quine Annes
Forlandt

Gods
mercies

C. Elizabeth

The Iland of
good fortun

C. Charles

C. Worsnam

Lomles
Inlet

The Kinges forland

Holde with
hoope

Prince Henry

Longa nimis longo via dividit aquore Seras,
Nec patiens tante est mens generosa mora:
Dixit, et occiduos petit imperterritus Indos
Hudsonus, ut methodo rem breviore paret.
Lamq, fretum superare novum, jam cœperat aufit
Præmia spondere ac pænè videre suis:
Cum remoram tantis injecit nautica rebus
Turba, nec insonti parcere gnara viro.
Sed remoram pergit noster, vel vincere certus
Vel (quod o avertant numina sancta) mori.
Audi vota Deus, fastisq; hunc adde Britannis
Servato nuper Principe clare, diem.

The bay where
Hudson did winter

The bay of Gods mercies

Fig. 78.—Chart of Hudson's discoveries

Bredrans R.
Conigam R.
C. S.t Seffin
Romborts R.
enemarchshaven

nes C.

HONI SOIT QVI MAL Y PENSE

DIEV EST MON DROIT

GROENLANDIA

Meridianus per insulas Corni et Flovm traysfens,
& pro omnium primo usurpari potest.

The Catts chance

Desolation

Hals cape

Whyties cape

C. Goodhope

C. Record

C. Farewel

Quine Elizabets forlandt

rys land

Bus

The grand bay

C. Grat

I. S. Lucia

Bacalao

Ilha de Bacalhao

11, by Hessel Gerritsz, 1612.

Undeterred by Button's revelation of the western shore of Hudson's 'spacious sea', extending from the Nelson River in the south to 'Sir Thomas Roe's Welcome' in the north, the North-West Company dispatched a series of expeditions in search of a western outlet from Hudson Strait or the Bay. A considered opinion on the prospects of success in this quarter was given by William Baffin after his voyage with Robert Bylot in 1615 (depicted in Baffin's map, Fig. 79): 'doubtless theare is a passage. But within this strayte whom is called Hudsons Straytes, I am very doubtfull, supposing the contrarye . . . We haue not been in any tyde then that from

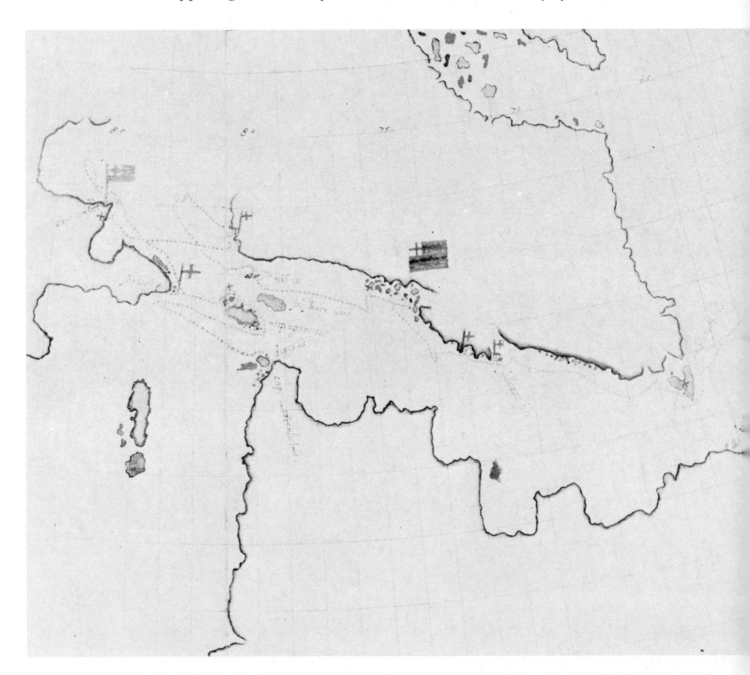

Fɪɢ. 79.—Map by William Baffin in the MS log of his voyage into Hudson Strait, 1615.

FIG. 80. — Chart of the west coast of Greenland by James Hall, 1605.

FIG. 81.—Hudson Bay, in a map by Henry Briggs, published by Purchas in 1625.

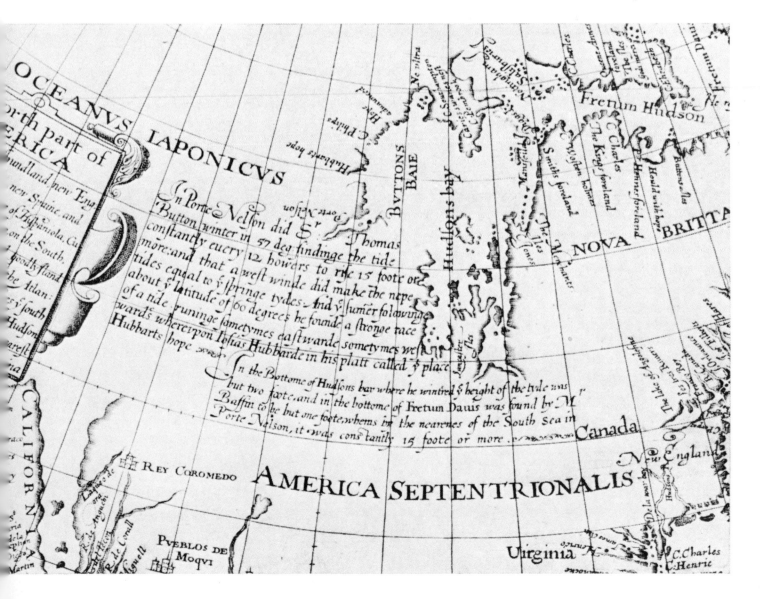

Resolutyon Iland, and the greatest indraft of that commeth from Dauis Strayts, and my judgment is . . . the mayne [passage] will be upp Fretum Dauis.'

On this northerly route, three Danish expeditions in 1605–7, with the Yorkshire-man James Hall as chief pilot, and an English expedition in 1612 under Hall and Baffin had already explored the west coast of Greenland. Hall's narrative of 1605 is illustrated 'with representations of Land-sights curiously delineated', perhaps by Josiah Hubbard of Hull (Fig. 80), whose 'plat' of Hudson Bay is also mentioned on Briggs's map (Fig. 81). In 1616 Bylot and Baffin were sent out by the Company with instructions to 'keepe . . . up Fretum Davis untill you come toward the height of eightie degrees . . . then West and Southerly . . . to the latitude of sixtie degrees: then direct your course to fall in with the Land of Yedzo about that height'.[10] This expedition reached nearly 78° N in 'Baffin's Bay' and recorded the openings from it to north and west (Smith, Jones and Lancaster Sounds), thus pointing to the true North-West Passage.[11] Foxe's map (Fig. 82) perhaps reproduces the outline of Baffin's lost chart of this voyage. Baffin, a level-headed man, reported to his em-ployers that 'there is no passage, nor hope of passage in the north of Dauis Streigths, wee hauing coasted . . . the Circumference thereof, and finde it to be no other then a great Bay'; but as a 'probabilitie or hope of profit' he recommended the 'killing of Whales' and 'of Sea-Morse [walrus]'. Here we see the motive of a quick commercial return displacing the remoter prospects of a northerly trade route to the Far East.

Ten years later, as Henry Briggs's map (Fig. 81) indicates, the North-West Company could still believe in a communication by water between Hudson Bay and the Pacific. In 1631 two expeditions sailed for the Bay, under Captains Luke Foxe of Hull and Thomas James of Bristol. Both captains searched the western shore of the Bay. Foxe's course, drawn on his 'Polar Map or Card . . . rough-hewen, like Shipwright's timber' (Fig. 82), led him to the entrance of Foxe Channel in the north. James, after meeting Foxe, who waggishly told him 'you are out of the way to Japon, for this is not it', in the south of the Bay, wintered like Hudson in James Bay. In his 'Platt of Sailing for the discoverye of a Passage into the South Sea' (Fig. 83), this bay, hitherto called after Hudson, first bears its modern name, although Hudson Bay is still called 'Button's Bay'. The supposed western outlet from Hudson Bay disappeared from 17th-century charts, and no serious attempt on it was made for over a century after Foxe and James.

In the north-west, as earlier in the north-east, enterprise was now diverted from discovery to trade. After the manner of 'proud and privileged' corporations, the Hudson's Bay Company, formed in 1670, preferred the immediate profits of the

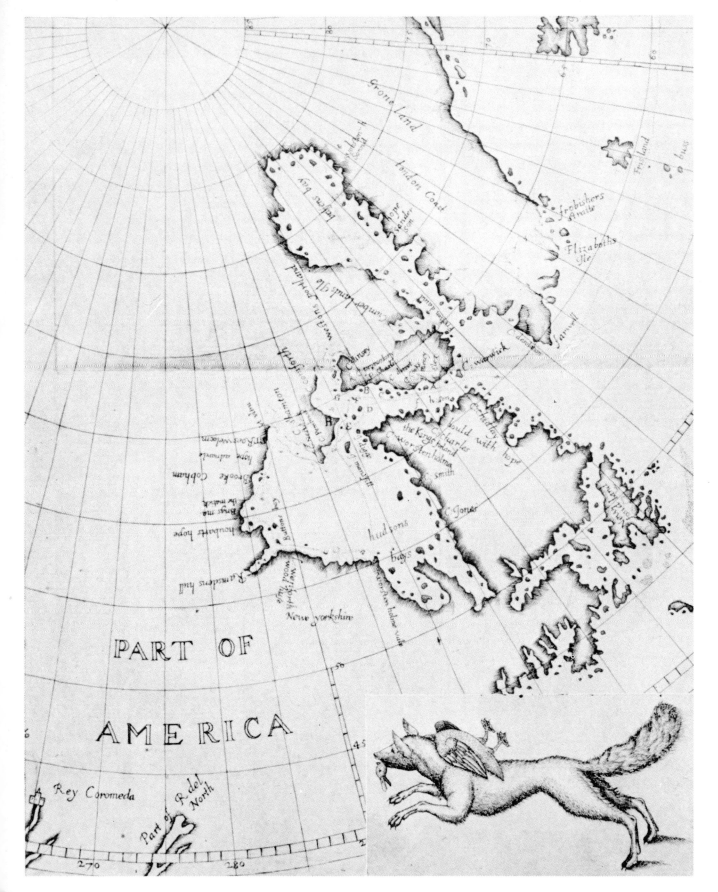

FIG. 82.—Part of Captain Luke Foxe's map, published in 1635; showing his track into Hudson Bay in 1631. *Inset:* Foxe's emblem.

fur-trade to speculative ventures further afield. Publicists of the 18th century however, with characteristic ingenuity, revived, and adapted to the known geography of Hudson Bay, the old tales of navigable western passages to the Pacific in temperate latitudes. The Strait of Juan de Fuca still haunted the minds and maps of geographers; and a Gulliverian piece of geography, launched in a London periodical of 1708, engendered belief in a channel supposed to have been found by a Spanish Admiral de Fonte in 1640.[12] In this apocryphal narrative, De Fonte tells how, on a voyage from Chile, he discovered a passage in 53° N—the 'Rio de los Reyes'—and sailed north-east by rivers and lakes until he met a Boston ship (presumably from Hudson Bay); one of De Fonte's captains followed another waterway to 79° N, and a sailor from his ship made his way to the head of Baffin Bay, which

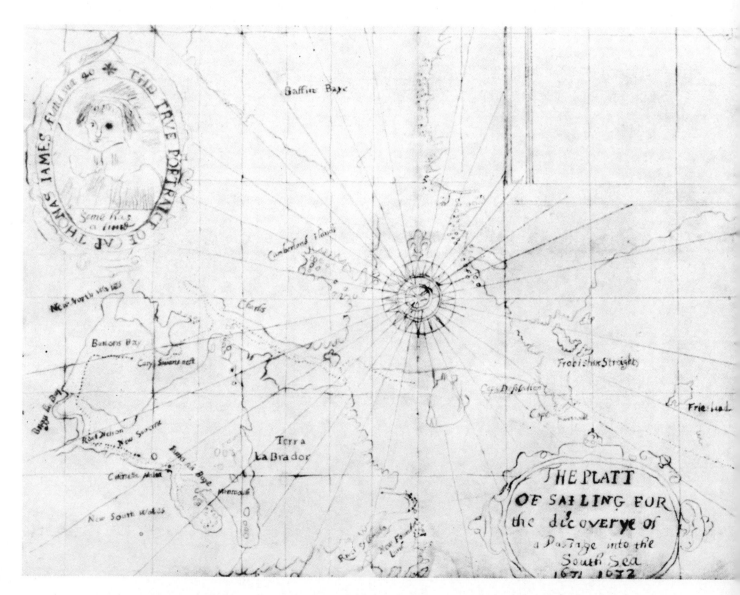

FIG. 83.—MS map by Captain Thomas James, with his tracks in 1631–2.

apparently ended in a freshwater lake. Expeditions between 1741 and 1747 failed to dispel these illusions, and in 1745 a reward of £20,000 was offered by the British government for the discovery of a western outlet from the Bay to the Pacific. As late as 1768 the anonymous author of a speculative work on the 'Great Probability of a North West Passage, deduced from observations on the Letter of Admiral de Fonte', could conclude that 'the proper passage is up the Streight of *de Fuca*, therefore that is the proper Streight of *Anian*' (Fig. 84), but could indicate only one possible entrance for the strait on Hudson Bay.[13]

All these fictitious passages were finally deleted from the map by the land journeys made from Canada by Samuel Hearne, down the Coppermine River in 1770–1, and by Alexander Mackenzie, down the Mackenzie River in 1789 (Fig. 85). The supposed western outlets of the 'invisible, because imaginary' straits were disproved by the surveys of the north-west coast of America by Captain Cook (1778) and Captain George Vancouver (1791–5). These investigations, as Vancouver wrote, 'set aside every opinion of a North-west Passage . . . existing between the Pacific and the interior of the American continent'. The instructions for Cook's last voyage had revived earlier projects, from the time of Drake, for discovering the western

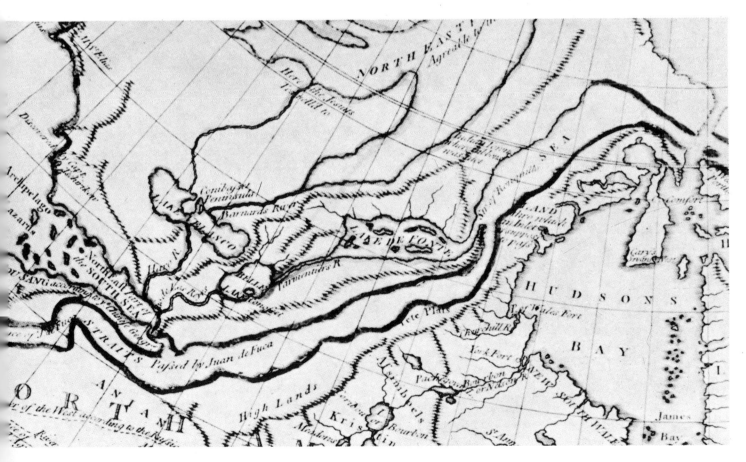

FIG. 84.—Map of the supposed passages from Foxe Channel to the Pacific, published by Thomas Jefferys in 1768.

entrance of the Passage off the north-west point of America. After examining rivers and inlets 'pointing towards Hudson's or Baffin's Bays', he was to proceed 'to the northward . . . in further search of a north-east or north-west passage, from the Pacific Ocean to the Atlantic Ocean, or the North Sea'. Having passed through Bering Strait in 1778, he reached Icy Cape (Fig. 85) before returning south to winter.[14]

The supposed passages through the North American continent, from Hudson Bay to the Pacific, had thus been discredited by 1800, and the ventures of the 19th century (to be described later[15]) were directed to the search for a westerly sea lead, starting from the point at which Davis and Baffin had left the problem.

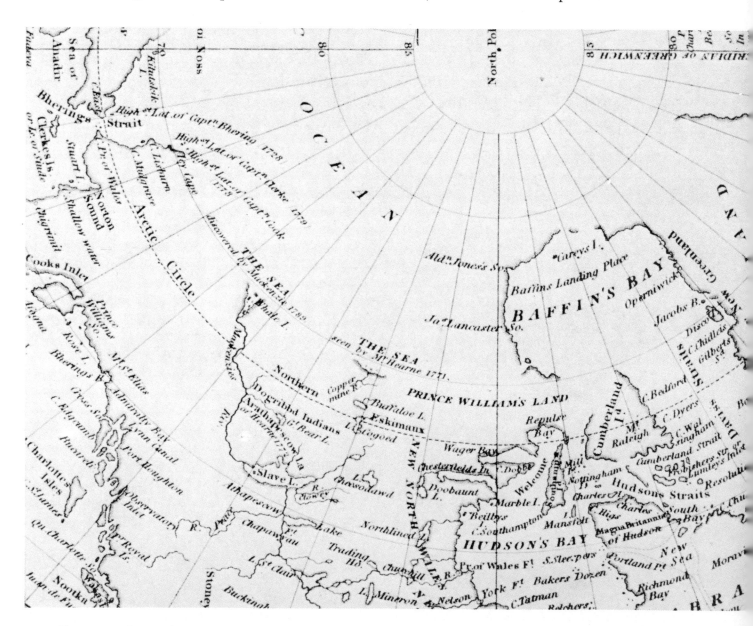

FIG. 85.—Arctic America, in a map published in 1818, illustrating the journeys of Hearne and Mackenzie.

Remarks on the Illustrations

Chapter VI

◇◇ ⟩◇◇◇

74   In *A discourse of a discouerie for a new passage to Cataia* (1576), with which this woodcut map was published, Gilbert employed arguments to demonstrate that a passage into the Pacific by the north-west was 'more commodious' than that by the north-east, which had hitherto received more attention. His map illustrates these arguments, emphasizing the shortness of the north-west route to the Moluccas (by comparison with those by Magellan Strait and the Cape of Good Hope), and showing it in temperate latitudes whereas the passage by the north-east lies within the Arctic Circle.

75   Frobisher's three voyages in 1576–8 were the first of the Elizabethan expeditions in search of the North-West Passage. This crude woodcut map, published in 1578 with Best's *True discourse* (see Fig. 63), shows the two channels which he supposed to open on 'the way trendin to Cathaia' and the names which he gave to the coasts discovered by him. These are all located between Greenland and the mainland of America—an error which was to mislead later cartographers (cf. Figs. 77, 78, 82, 83). 'Frobisshers Streights', discovered in 1576, were in fact an inlet (now Frobisher Bay) in Baffin Land, which is drawn as an archipelago named 'Meta Incognita' (the Unknown Bourne). 'The Mistaken Straightes' are the entrance to Hudson Strait, which Frobisher discovered by chance on his third voyage (1578) while searching for his own strait. This map is perhaps by James Beare, after whom 'Beares Sound' is named on it.

76   Michael Lok's map published in 1582 (see Fig. 49) exhibits the supposed routes into the Pacific by the north-west. Frobisher's supposed channels, south of the Arctic Circle, lead into an ocean greatly exaggerated in width; the St Lawrence, discovered by Cartier, rises in mountains bordering the 'Sea of Verrazano'; and in 40° N the Verrazanian isthmus is drawn (see Chapter IV, and Figs. 48, 49).

77   The globes drawn by Emery Molyneux and engraved by Hondius in 1592 are the earliest English globes. On the terrestrial globe, the coasts of 'Fretum Davis'

(Davis Strait) are laid down from information supplied by Davis, with whom Molyneux may have sailed (H. M. Wallis, 'The first English globe', *Geogr. Journal*, vol. CXVII (1951), p. 279). The names in the strait, to Davis's farthest north at 'Hope Sanderson', are those given by him in 1587. In the south-west of the strait, 'A furious ouerfall' indicates the opening of Hudson Strait, which Frobisher likened to 'the waterfall of London Bridge'. Frobisher's 'straytes', with the names which he gave to coastal features in 1576, are erroneously located in the south of Greenland (cf. Fig. 75); but Frobisher's Cape Walsingham is omitted, as Davis gave this name to a foreland on the west shore of his own strait. The mythical islands of Frisland and Grocland (doublets of Iceland and Greenland) still retain their place on the map.

78   The chart of Hudson's discoveries in 1610-11, engraved by Hessel Gerritsz, was published in *Descriptio ac delineatio geographica detectionis freti* (Amsterdam, 1612). On the return from his second voyage in 1608, Hudson had 'resolved to make triall of that place called Lumleys Inlet, and the furious overfall by Captain Davis'. This was the object of his last voyage. Entering Hudson Strait, he explored (wrote Gerritsz) 'all the shores laid down in his chart to 63°', giving them the English names in Gerritsz' chart. 'C. Worsnam' is an error for Cape Wolstenholme. Hudson's reconciliation of his discoveries with those of earlier explorers is indicated by the names 'C. Elizabeth' (given by Frobisher) and 'Lomles Inlet' (given by Davis). After wintering in 54° (James Bay), he sailed north into 'a wide sea' (Hudson Bay) with strong tides, which inspired in him 'no small hope of a passage'. As on the Molyneux globe, Frobisher's discoveries, e.g. 'Quine Elizabets forlandt', are wrongly plotted by Gerritsz in south-east Greenland. This persistent error goes back to the printed maps of Frobisher's voyages (cf. Fig. 75).

79   Baffin's route chart of his voyage in 1615 (British Museum, Add. MS 12206, fol. 6), in his log, marks by a 'red prickle line' his track into Hudson Strait and the mouth of Foxe Channel, and by crosses the places where he landed 'to make tryall of the tyde'. The apparent absence of tides convinced him that Hudson Strait gave no passage to the west. Some of Hudson's names (cf. Fig. 78) are repeated, e.g. 'Cape Wostenholme', 'Diggs ile'; the others were given by Baffin.

80   This chart, with soundings, of the west Greenland fjords north of Queen Anne's Cape, in 66° N, accompanies Captain James Hall's manuscript report to the King of Denmark on his expedition of 1605 (British Museum, Royal MS. 17. A. XLVIII).

81   The map by the mathematician Henry Briggs, published in *Purchas His Pilgrimes* in 1625, indicates several openings out of Hudson Bay to the west. The names on the north and west shores of the bay are those given by Button in 1611. The height of the tides in Port Nelson, where Button wintered in 1611-12, is quoted as evidence of 'the nearenes of the South Sea'. Hudson and James Bays bear their original names of 'Buttons Baie' and 'Hudsons bay' respectively.

82 Part of Foxe's 'Polar Map or Card', showing his course in 1631, from his book *North-West Fox* (1635), with (inset) his emblem. After traversing Hudson Bay he extended Baffin's exploration (cf. Fig. 79) until checked by ice at 'Foxe's Farthest' in 66° 47' N. He concluded that if a passage existed it must lie by way of 'Sir T. Roes Welcom' in 65° N; and the inlet named 'Ne vltra' (go no further) on Briggs's map (Fig. 81) is accordingly renamed 'Vt vltra' (go further) by Foxe on his map.

83 'The Platt for sailing for the discovery of a Passage into the South Sea' drawn by James (British Museum, Add. MS 5415, G. 1) marks his track in 1631-2 along the western and southern shores of Hudson Bay to winter quarters in 'James his Baye', here first so named. It also illustrates his conclusion that it was 'most probable that there is no passage'. An inset displays a portrait of James at the age of 40.

84 The map by Thomas Jefferys was published in an anonymous work entitled *The Great Probability of a North West Passage, deduced from observations on the Letter of Admiral de Fonte* (London, 1768). It is based on a map of 1752 by the French geographer J. N. Delisle, in which a variety of hypothetical geography was credulously combined. The Strait of Juan de Fuca and the waterways followed by De Fonte (by the Rio de los Reyes and Lake De Fonte) converge in a gulf opening into Foxe Channel. Further north, Barnards River, by which Bernardo was supposed to have sailed, leads to the 'Indian Town where Gibbons [from Boston] was met'.

85 This map of 1818 shows how all possibility of a passage by water through the continent south of the Arctic Ocean was removed by the explorers of the second half of the 18th century. The north-west coasts of America had been continuously traversed by Cook (1778) and Vancouver (1791–5), from Vancouver Island to Alaska; Cook had passed through Bering Strait to Icy Cape in 70° 44' N. Two land journeys had eliminated the conjectural channels westward from Hudson Bay; Hearne in 1770–1 travelled from Fort Prince of Wales and down the Coppermine River to its mouth, and Mackenzie in 1789, starting from Fort Chepewyan, went down the Mackenzie River to Whale Island on the sea. (The mouth of the Coppermine River is laid down nearly four degrees too far north, for, although Hearne had a good quadrant, he was unskilled in its use and recorded only one observation for latitude.) 'Baffin's Bay' was still drawn with an almost continuous shoreline, and the sounds leading out of it to the west were not explored before the voyages of Parry in 1819–20.

Notes

Chapter VI

<hr />

[1] See Chapter V.

[2] See Chapter IV.

[3] See Chapter V, note 5, and Chapter XII.

[4] See Chapters IV and XI.

[5] See Chapter XII.

[6] The ore brought back by Frobisher from his first and second voyages failed to yield gold; and Lok, Frobisher's principal backer, became bankrupt. John White (see Chapter XII) made drawings of the Eskimos brought to London by Frobisher.

[7] See Chapter XIV.

[8] Helen M. Wallis, 'The first English globe', *Geogr. Journal*, vol. CXVII (1951), p. 279. This would account for 'Molyneux's great care in the delineation of Davis's discoveries, for which evidently he had the help of Davis himself or his charts'.

[9] Smith seems to have sent a manuscript map of Virginia to Hudson in 1608; see Chapter XII, and 'Remarks' on Figs. 168, 169.

[10] 'Yedzo' (i.e. Yezo or Hokkaido, the northernmost Japanese island) is here used for Japan; see Chapter VIII.

[11] See Chapter XIV.

[12] De Fonte's supposed narrative was printed in *The Monthly Miscellany, or Memoirs for the Curious*, London, 1708. It was credulously accepted by the leading French geographers (J. N. Delisle and Buache), although John Green in 1753 expressed surprise that they should be 'so far imposed on by it as to take it for genuine, notwithstanding it carries so many glaring Marks of Forgery on the Face of it'.

[13] Alexander Dalrymple, with characteristic stubbornness, attempted as late as 1790 to reconcile the De Fonte fable with the discoveries of Hearne (see Chapter XII).

[14] For Hearne and Mackenzie, see Chapter XII; and for Cook, Chapter XI.

[15] See Chapter XIV.

PART FOUR

The Spice Islands and Cathay

VII

EUROPEAN RIVALRY FOR THE SPICE ISLANDS

16th and 17th centuries

THE TREATY OF TORDESILLAS, which in 1494 defined the rights of overseas expansion by Spain and Portugal, had drawn the *raya*, or demarcation line, 370 leagues west of the Cape Verde Islands.[1] This was the best settlement that Portugal was able to make; but her eagerness to establish the dividing line as far west as possible, in order to secure a foothold in the new world which she perhaps already suspected to exist, was to place in jeopardy her rights of discovery in the Far East. Her expansion eastwards across the Indian Ocean to the Malay Peninsula and Archipelago, in the early years of the new century, focused attention on the antipodal continuation of the *raya*, 180 degrees of longitude distant from the Atlantic line.[2] Magellan himself had perhaps been with Serrão to the Moluccas in 1512, and these islands, the source and centre of the spice trade, were the objective of his voyage under the Spanish flag begun in 1519. He intended (as a Portuguese agent in Seville wrote) to sail across the Pacific 'West and WNW direct to Maluco, which land of Maluco I have seen laid down in the globe and chart which Fernando de Reynell made here ... and his father [Pedro Reinel] finished the whole and marked these lands of Maluco, and on this pattern are constructed all the charts which Diogo Ribeiro makes'. Two of the cartographers here named were, like Magellan, Portuguese who had carried into the service of Spain the knowledge of the East Indies and the route thither learnt in the employment of the King of Portugal.[3]

The route of the *Vitoria* through the Eastern Archipelago, after Magellan's death off Cebu, is recorded in the sketch maps of Antonio Pigafetta, the chronicler of the

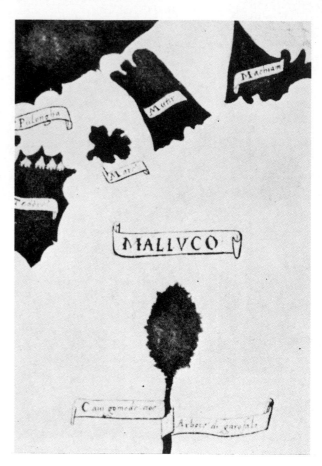

FIG. 86.—Sketch of the northern Moluccas, visited by Magellan's ships in 1521.
Drawn by Antonio Pigafetta.

expedition (Fig. 86); and her return in 1522, with a cargo of cloves picked up at Tidore in the Moluccas, awakened the Spaniards to the value of this trade.[4] The interest of the King of Portugal now lay in plotting the *raya* sufficiently far to the east to embrace the Spice Islands in his sphere. At a *junta* or conference held at Badajoz in 1524, the leading pilots and cartographers of the two countries, including (for Spain) Nuño García who had drawn Magellan's charts (Fig. 87), and Diogo Ribeiro, expounded their views on the longitude of the Moluccas in relation to the dividing line. By the Portuguese the islands were sited 43 degrees west of the anti-meridian, by the Spanish 3 degrees east of it—the position assigned in the official Spanish world map, the *padrón real*, after its revision in 1526.[5] In the absence of any method of determining longitude other than dead reckoning, and with national partisanship at work, no agreement was reached; but in 1529 Spain sold her claim and the *raya* was laid down, by consent, 17 degrees east of the Moluccas, which were thus (correctly) located within the Portuguese sphere.

During the middle decades of the 16th century Portugal's control of commerce

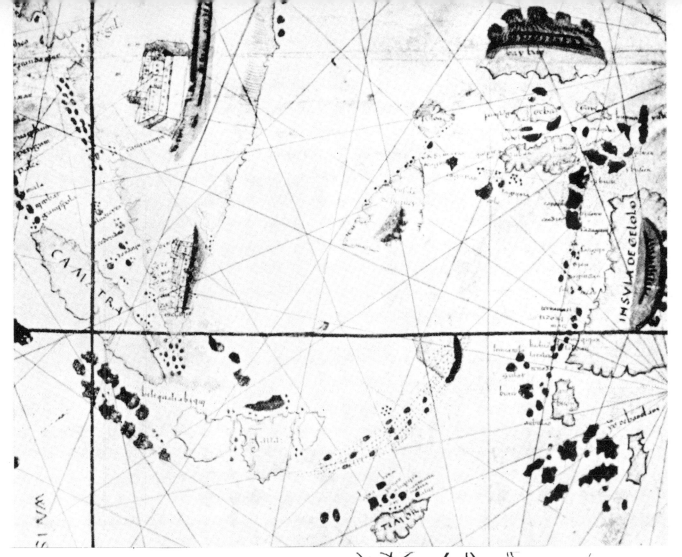

FIG. 87.—The East Indies, in a MS map by
Nuño García de Toreno, 1522.

FIG. 88.—A Spanish ship 'coming from
Maluco', drawn on a world map of 1529.

FIG. 89.—The East Indies, in a MS sea-atlas by Diogo Homem, 1558.

in the Indian Ocean and with south-east Asia was not challenged by any other European nation, and for the rest of the century Portuguese maps supplied the standard representation of the East Indies and neighbouring coasts and waters. The leading Portuguese cartographers of this period were Lopo Homem and his son Diogo, Fernão Vaz Dourado, who was born and worked at Goa, and Luiz Teixeira.[6] Their elaborately decorated charts and atlases (Figs. 25, 89), rich in place-names, showed the coasts frequented by the Portuguese ships, with their principal trading centres in the Archipelago on the islands of Celebes, Banda, 'Gilolo' (Halmahera), Ternate and Amboina in the Moluccas. The east coasts of Borneo and Celebes and the south coasts of Java and New Guinea were still unknown. To the north the Philippines remained in Spanish hands.[7]

The official policy of secrecy was no longer maintained by Portugal or at any rate did not extend to her eastern empire. Portuguese charts of the Far East and the route thither circulated freely abroad and were reproduced in the printed maps and atlases of Mercator and Ortelius. Netherlanders sailed as factors and pilots in Portuguese ships and were established as merchants in Goa and other Portuguese settlements overseas. Portuguese pilots entered the service of England after the union of Spain and Portugal in 1580. From such sources English and Dutch adventurers drew their information on the East Indian trade and navigation.

By 1580 English hopes of finding a passage to the Far East by the north of Asia had been disappointed.[8] The concentration of the Spanish and Portuguese colonial empires under the crown of Philip II, which closed the Lisbon spice market to English merchants, lent political support to projects for direct trade with the East Indies, both as a source for spices and as an 'ample vent of our wollen cloth, the naturall commoditie of this our Realme'. Drake, after his crossing of the Pacific, had in November 1579 visited Ternate, whose sultan sought his aid against the Portuguese and 'sent to our Generall with speciall message that . . . hee would yield himselfe and the right of his island bee at the pleasure and commandement of so famous a prince as we served' (Fig. 90). This 'message' could be, and was, later cited as a diplomatic justification for English commercial relations with the Spice Islands. Thomas Stevens, a Jesuit, had gone 'as a passenger in the Portugale Fleete' to Goa in 1579; he was the first Englishman to set foot in India, and his letter to his father, describing 'the whole course of the Portugale Caracks from Lisbon to the barre of Goa', was printed by Richard Hakluyt in 1589. Drake's raid on Cadiz in 1587 (the first expedition, says Hakluyt, 'that ever discharged Molucca spices in English portes') had acquainted 'the English Nation more generally with the particularities of the exceeding riches and wealth of the East Indies'. In 1591–3 the

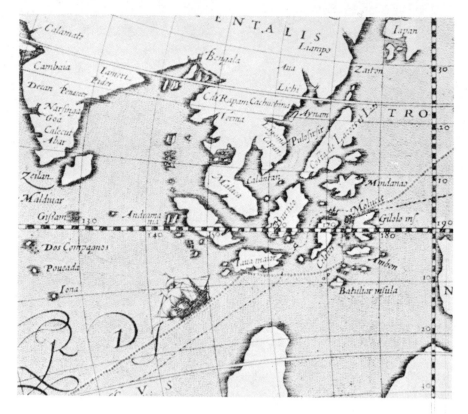

FIG. 90.—Drake's track through the Moluccas in 1579 (dotted line), in a world map engraved by Jodocus Hondius about 1590.

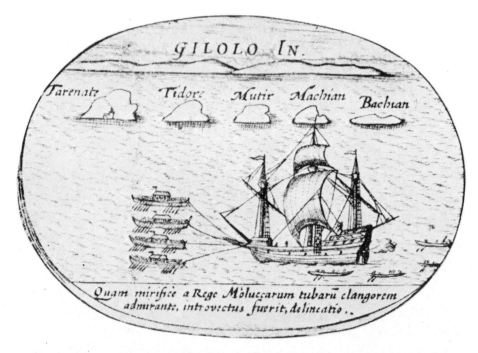

FIG. 91.—*The Golden Hind* towed into harbour at Ternate: an inset of Hondius's map.

Fig. 92.—Part of Linschoten's chart of the East Indies from Portuguese sources, published in 1595.

Edward Bonaventure, commanded by Captain James Lancaster, was the first English ship to pass the Cape of Good Hope and cross the Indian Ocean to the Malay Peninsula. In the second edition of his *Principal Navigations* (1598–1600) Hakluyt published the narrative of Ralph Fitch, who had travelled overland to India and visited Burma and Malacca, returning in 1591; and in 1600 a memorandum, probably written by Hakluyt, set out before the Privy Council 'Certaiyne Reesons why the English Merchants may trade into the East Indies'. At the end of the same year the English East India Company received its charter.

Among Dutch sources quoted by the author of 'Certaiyne Reesons' is 'John Huygen de Linschoten's worke, which lived about 7 yeres in India'. Linschoten, returning from Goa in 1592, had become the propagandist in Holland for Eastern trade.[9] His *Itinerario*, published at Amsterdam in 1595–6, described the trading stations of the Portuguese, the sailing routes of their eastern navigation, and the

Fig. 93.—Linschoten's illustration of an Indian market, with spices on sale.

commerce in spices (Figs. 13, 92, 93). Some of his material, derived from his friend Dirck Gerritsz, who had spent 26 years in India, had already been published in Waghenaer's sea-atlas *Het Thresoor der zeevaert* (1592).

The maps accompanying Linschoten's book were drawn by, or after, Peter Plancius, a preacher (like Hakluyt) and mapmaker of Amsterdam, who has been called 'the father of Dutch colonial cartography'. Plancius had in 1592 acquired a collection of charts and rutters at Lisbon from the Portuguese Bartolomeu Lasso, cosmographer to the King of Spain; and Linschoten's map of the East Indies (Figs. 13, 92), like the other charts in his book, was (as its title states) 'drawn from the most correct charts and rutters used today by the Portuguese pilots'.[10] This map, which derives from the charts of Vaz Dourado rather than those of Lasso, remained for many years the prototype for Dutch cartography of the Archipelago.

FIG. 94.—The first passage of the Cape of Good Hope by Dutch ships, August 1596.

The *Itinerario*, which was translated into English at Hakluyt's instance in 1598, provided valuable intelligence on the Portuguese empire in the East, 'where' (wrote Hakluyt in 1599) 'their strength is nothing so great as heretofore hath bene supposed', and it encouraged English and Dutch ventures. Linschoten himself sailed with Dutch expeditions for a North-East Passage in 1594 and 1595, and the Latin edition of the *Itinerario* (1599) contained Barents' polar chart recording his voyage to Novaya Zemlya in 1596-7 (Fig. 67).[11] The first Dutch expedition to the East Indies by the Cape (1595-7), under Cornelis Houtman, had opened up trade with Bantam, the great pepper port on the north coast of Java (Figs. 94-96). After sailing

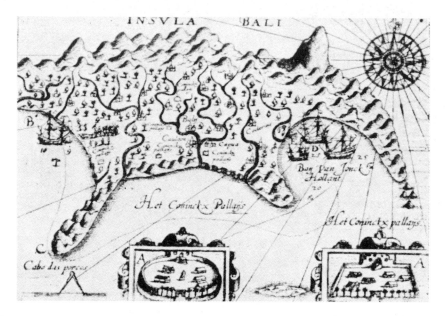

FIG. 95.—Bali, with the tracks and anchorages of Houtman's ships, 1597.

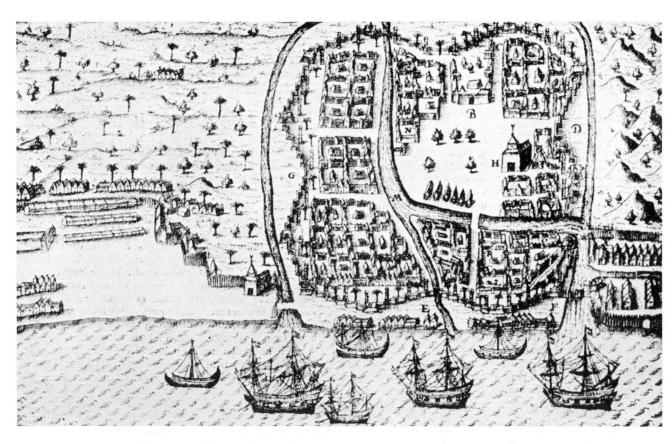

FIG. 96.—Plan of Bantam in Java, visited by Houtman in 1596.

3. 97.—The East Indies, in a world map by Houtman, engraved in 1600, showing the track of the first Dutch fleet.

E.M.—L

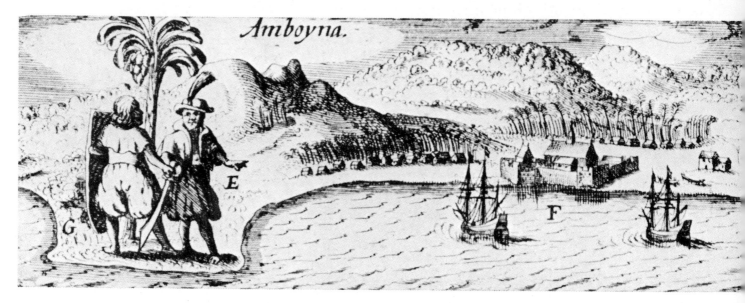

FIG. 98.—Amboina, after its capture by the Dutch in 1605.

FIG. 99.—The capture of a Portuguese carrack in the Malacca Straits by Dutch and English squadrons, October 160

east to Bali (Fig. 95), Houtman's squadron returned by the south of Java, which was thus shown to be an island, although no details of its south coast were put on the maps for many years. A second Dutch fleet, under Jacob van Neck and Wybrant Warwijck, whose pilots were instructed by Plancius, made a voyage to the Archipelago in 1598–1600 and established a factory at Bantam. The account of Houtman's voyage was written by Willem Lodewijcksz, a supercargo in the fleet; a map of the East Indies by Lodewijcksz and world maps by Houtman and van Neck commemorated these early Dutch enterprises (Fig. 97). Meanwhile the Dutch had attempted the westerly route to the Moluccas, that of Magellan; and in 1598–1601 Olivier van Noort made the first Dutch circumnavigation, without the loss of a ship, returning by the Philippines. In 1602 the Dutch United East India Company was formed by a merger of the various companies hitherto engaged, and Plancius was appointed cartographer to the new company.

The first voyage of the English company was made in 1601–3 by a fleet (Fig. 99) under the command of Lancaster. Lancaster reached Achin, in Sumatra, and Bantam where he loaded pepper and set up a factory—the first English trading post in the East. This became the centre of English trade in the Archipelago, where a period of commercial rivalry between the English and Dutch now began. Captain Thomas Middleton, commanding the English company's second venture (1604–6), reached Ternate; but the Dutch, by their capture of Tidore and Amboina (Fig. 98) from the Portuguese in 1605—in the presence of Middleton's ships—and by the foundation of their factory and settlement of Batavia on the north coast of Java (Fig. 100) in 1610, had soon won dominating positions on the trade routes between the Straits of Malacca and the Moluccas. The English company, lacking the government support enjoyed by the Dutch, had by 1623 been ousted from the Archipelago; but it found a new and profitable field for enterprise, at the expense of the Portuguese, in India, to which Captain Thomas Best led a fleet in 1612 and where commercial relations were established by Sir Thomas Roe's mission to the Great Mogul in 1615–18 (Fig. 102).

From Batavia and their other bases in south-east Asia the Dutch, following the Portuguese, had extended their trade into the China Sea and as far north as Japan; and in the 17th century they reached the north and west coasts of Australia. These advances and their Pacific explorations will be described later.[12]

In 1614 Hakluyt's incessant advocacy of instruction in the 'Art of Navigation' as a means of 'breeding up of skilfull Sea-men and Mariners' bore fruit in the appointment of a lecturer in navigation to the East India Company, with instructions to 'examine their journals and mariners and perfect their plots'.[13] Here the English

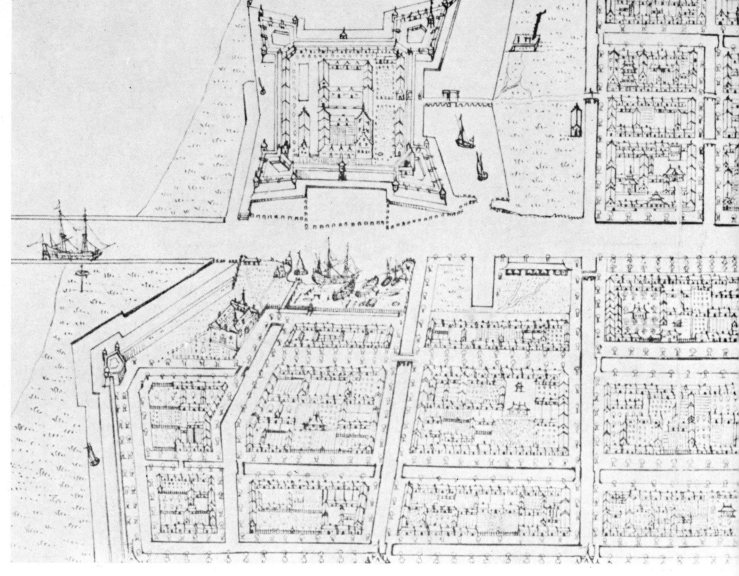

FIG. 100.—Part of a plan of Batavia, drawn about 1650.

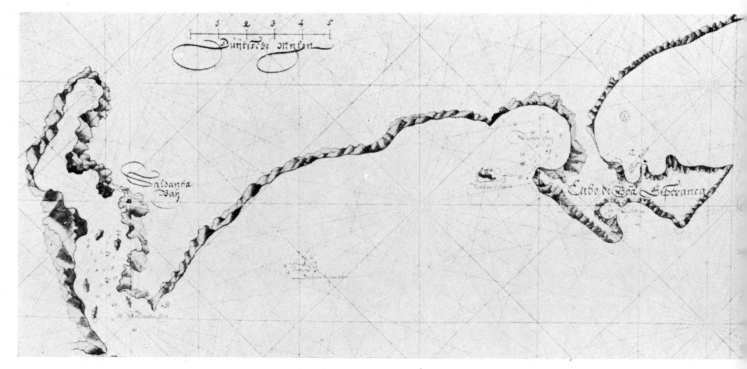

FIG. 101.—Dutch chart of the Cape of Good Hope, drawn about 1660.

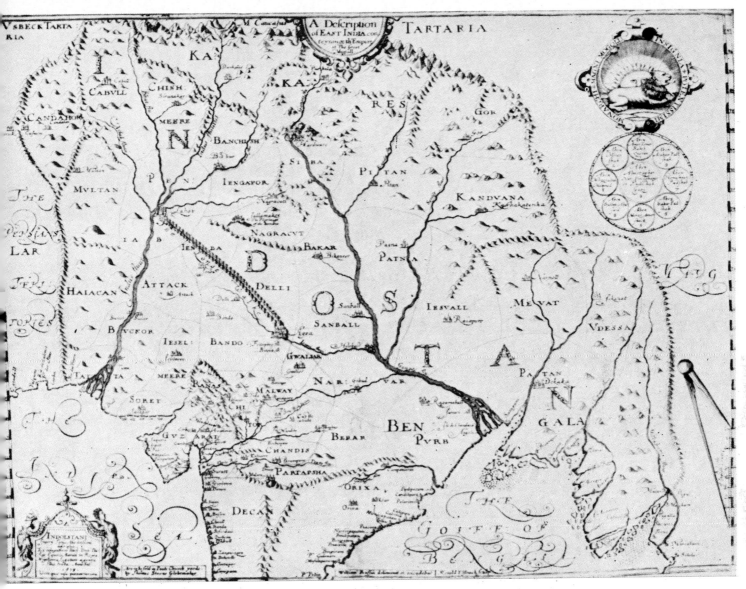

FIG. 102.—Map of the Mogul territories by William Baffin, engraved in 1619.

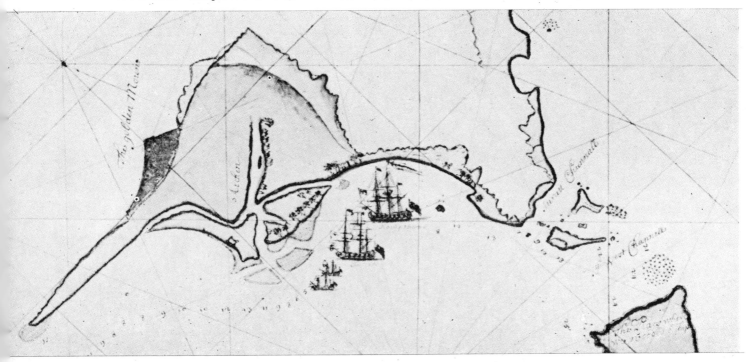

FIG. 103.—Chart of Achin in Sumatra, drawn by Captain John Kempthorne, 1687.

company was following precedents and an administrative procedure long established by the government of Spain, where the pilots of the Casa de la Contratación at Seville had these duties, and more recently by the Dutch companies. The English company's initiative produced few original charts before the end of the 17th century (Fig. 103), but the 'period of exploitation' which followed that of exploration of the East Indies by the Dutch yielded a rich harvest for cartography. Plancius was in 1619 followed as cartographer to the United East India Company by Hessel Gerritsz, and after his death in 1632 the post was held in succession by Willem Jansz Blaeu (1633–8) and by his son Joan.

The Dutch pilots and captains were supplied with charts of the eastern navigation drawn in Blaeu's workshop, and were required on their return to deliver the charts to Blaeu with their corrections. Thus a continuous revision and improvement of the prototype became possible. Charts were also drawn by pilots at Batavia (Fig. 100), the centre of government in the East, and these too were forwarded to Blaeu for information and copying.[14] In this way the coasts frequented by the Dutch East Indiamen, and the ocean bases—St Helena, the Cape (Fig. 101), Mauritius, Ceylon —which served as stages on their route to the East, were systematically covered by a regular hydrographic service over a century and a half before the supply of charts to ships' captains was organized by the British Admiralty.

Remarks on the Illustrations

Chapter VII

⟡⟡

86   The northern Moluccas, from sketches made by Antonio Pigafetta in his journal of the first circumnavigation (fol. 53r; see Fig. 43). These islands were visited in November–December 1521, after Magellan's death, by his two surviving ships, the *Vitoria* and *Trinidad*, and a cargo of cloves was taken aboard at Tidore. The right-hand sketch shows a clove-tree ('arbore di garofali').

87   The charts prepared at Seville by Nuño García de Toreño for Magellan's expedition were captured by the Portuguese in the *Trinidad* and are now lost. His chart of 1522 in the Biblioteca del Re, Turin, from which this detail is reproduced, draws the East Indian Archipelago from information brought back by the survivors of Magellan's squadron, and interprets its geography in the Spanish interest. The eastern *raya* or anti-meridian, here laid down for the first time on a map, passes through Sumatra—and thus assigns the Spice Islands and the Malay Peninsula to Spain. This is the earliest map (apart from Pigafetta's sketches) to name the various islands of the Moluccas: terranati, tidorj, maqujan, bachia, Insula de Gelolo.

88   This vignette in Ribero's world map of 1529 (see Fig. 122) depicts a three-masted Spanish ship, sailing before the wind, 'coming from Molucca'. The construction of the hull is clearly shown, with square stern and fore- and after-castles supported on open arches.

89   A typical Portuguese representation of the East Indies in the mid-16th century, in a finely illuminated portolan atlas drawn by Diogo Homem for King Philip II of Spain (British Museum, Add. MS 5415 A, ff. 17v–18).

90   The world map engraved by Jodocus Hondius, probably about 1590, depicts the circumnavigations of Drake (1577–80) and Cavendish (1586–8). Only two impressions of this map are known to have survived. Drake's route, here marked by the large ship and the line of dots, had led him across the Pacific to the Moluccas. At Ternate in 1579 he established friendly relations with the Sultan and took on board

a load of spices. This was regarded in Drake's day as one of the most notable events of his voyage.

91   An inset from the same map shows Drake's ship, the *Golden Hind*, towed into harbour by the war-canoes of the Sultan of Ternate, who was rowed alongside 'marvelling at the sound of trumpets' proceeding from the English ship. The islands are conventionally drawn in the background.

92   The chart of the East Indies engraved by Hendrik van Langren in the *Itiner-ario* of Jan Huyghen van Linschoten (Amsterdam, 1596) is said in its title to be drawn from Portuguese maps and rutters (see Fig. 13); and it has been suggested that Linschoten suborned Bartolomeu Lasso to prepare this and other charts for him. (East is at the top of the map.) The Portuguese knew the Philippines and Moluccas in detail, but not the east coasts of Borneo and Celebes or the south coast of Java. Java's width was considerably exaggerated (cf. Fig. 97).

93   An illustration of an Indian market, engraved by Baptista van Deutecum in Linschoten's *Itinerario* (1596), showing pepper, betel ('arecca') and night jasmine ('arbore triste') found in India and Malacca.

94   The first passage of the Cape of Good Hope by Dutch ships, under the command of Cornelis Houtman, in August 1596. This and the following illustration were published in *Diarium nauticum itineris Batavorum in Indiam Orientalem* (Amsterdam, 1598).

95   Bali, the most easterly island reached by Houtman (1597), with soundings and the anchorages and course of his ships.

96   This engraved plan of Bantam was perhaps drawn by Lodewijcksz, super-cargo in Houtman's squadron which called there in 1596. Here merchandise from China and the Moluccas was traded for Javanese pepper. Published in Lodewijcksz' *Historie van Indien* (Amsterdam, 1598).

97   The world map by Houtman, showing the track of the fleet under his com-mand (1596–7), was engraved in 1600. Passing through the Sunda Straits, Houtman traded at Bantam (Fig. 94) and sailed on to Bali (Fig. 95), to the east of Java. Return-ing westward, he cruised along the south coast of Java, which he found 'neither to be so broad nor to extend so far south as the chart draws it, otherwise we should have sailed through the middle of the island' (cf. Fig. 92). In the south is seen part of Terra Australis with the 'kingdoms' named on Mercator's chart of 1569 (Fig. 9). Houtman's track demonstrated that Java could not be a part of this supposed continent.

98   The view of Amboina, published in the *Oost ende West-Indische Spieghet* (Amsterdam, 1621), shows the Dutch fort taken from the Portuguese in 1605. This island, south of Ceram, became the centre of the Dutch-controlled spice trade in the eastern part of the Archipelago.

99　This engraving was published in *Het Journael van Joris van Speilbergen* (Delft, 1605). In September 1602 Captain James Lancaster, commanding three English ships, was joined at Achin in Sumatra by the Dutch squadron of Joris van Spilbergen, which had sailed by the Magellan Strait and the Philippines. In the Malacca Strait they met and captured the Portuguese carrack *São Antonio* of 1200 tons (wrongly called 'Ste Thome' on the plate). Above are the three English ships, with Lancaster's flagship the *Red Dragon* on the right; below are those of the Dutch, with Spilbergen's ship the *Schaep* on the left.

100　This finely drawn plan shows Batavia about 1650; it is in the British Museum (Add. MS 5027. A. 73), among a group of charts probably drawn at Batavia for Blaeu. After the first settlement in 1610 on the river Jacarta in north Java, this new city was founded by the Governor-General Jan Pietersz Coen in 1619.

101　This chart, drawn about 1660 for the use of Dutch East Indiamen, belongs to the·same group as Fig. 100 (British Museum, Add. MS 5027. A. 22). The technique is characteristic of Dutch hydrography in the 17th century.

102　This is the earliest English map of the Mogul territories, drawn from Sir Thomas Roe's information by William Baffin, master's mate of the ship in which Roe returned to England from India in 1619. Baffin had previously made four voyages for the North-West Passage (see Chapter VI), and was killed in 1621 in an engagement with the Portuguese in the Persian Gulf.

103　This chart of Achin, the pepper port of Sumatra, was drawn by Captain John Kempthorne, master of the East Indiaman *Kempthorne* (British Museum, Add. MS 3665, fol. 39v), and shows his ships riding at anchor. The chart is in Kempthorne's journal of his voyage in 1686–8.

Notes

Chapter VII

<hr>

[1] See Chapter IV.

[2] See Chapter II.

[3] Pedro Reinel (fl. 1485–1542) and his son Jorge (fl. 1519–72) both worked in Lisbon as official 'masters of maps and examiners in navigation'; Jorge was for a short time about 1519 in Spanish service at Seville. Diogo Ribeiro (fl. 1519–33), Portuguese by birth, entered the service of Spain at about the same time as Magellan and remained in Seville as royal cosmographer (see 'Remarks', Fig. 122).

[4] See Chapter III.

[5] For the *padrón real*, see Chapter IV.

[6] Lopo Homem (fl. 1517–54) and his son Diogo (fl. 1547–76) were both official chart-makers in Lisbon; Diogo was in London in 1547 and worked at Venice *c.* 1569–72. Fernão Vaz Dourado, born at Diu in 1520, worked in Goa until 1580; he was doubtless the 'expert master of navigation in Goa' by whom Linschoten's Amsterdam publisher, Cornelis Claesz, secured a 'map of Asia' about 1592. Luiz Teixeira (fl. 1564–1613) was a Portuguese cartographer whose representation of Japan was published by Ortelius in 1595.

[7] See Chapter IX.

[8] See Chapter V.

[9] Jan Huyghen van Linschoten, born at Haarlem about 1563, spent six years (1583–9) in Spanish service, sailing as a clerk in the East Indian fleets. (At this date the crowns of Spain and Portugal were united, and Spain controlled the Portuguese trade by the Cape.) Linschoten had his information on China from Dirck Gerritsz, who was to pilot the first Dutch fleet to the East in 1598. In 1592 Linschoten returned to Holland and wrote his *Itinerario*, which was published in 1595–6. In 1594–5 he accompanied Barents, as super-cargo, on his first two voyages for the North-East Passage (see Chapter V).

[10] See also note 6.

[11] See Chapter V.

[12] In Chapters VIII and X.

[13] For the Spanish practice, see Chapter IV.

[14] A number of Batavia-drawn charts, known as the 'Ruesta' collection, are in the British Museum (Add. MS 5027).

VIII

THE FAR EAST IN THE SIXTEENTH AND SEVENTEENTH CENTURIES

'WHOEVER IS LORD of Malacca has his hand on the throat of Venice.' This triumphant phrase, written soon after the fall of Malacca to the Portuguese in 1511, proclaimed the shift of mercantile power, from the Mediterranean to the Atlantic nations, accomplished by the advance of Portugal into the Indian Ocean.[1] Their occupation of Malacca opened to the Portuguese the gate into the Eastern Archipelago and the China Sea, and secured a pre-emption on the Far Eastern trade for which this port was the principal market. They knew little of the coasts beyond Sumatra and the Malacca Strait. To the east of the Malay Peninsula, contemporary maps still laid down another great horn of land curving southward from Indo-China—the last trace of the continental coastline within which Ptolemy's world-map had enclosed the Indian Ocean on the south and east (Fig. 104). Further north, the maps marked the provinces and cities of Cathay described by Marco Polo and Odoric of Pordenone.[2]

At Malacca and in the Spice Islands, to which they penetrated in 1512, the Portuguese gathered information on the navigation to the east from Chinese and Arab pilots. 'What I say of these islands [Amboina and Banda] . . . I have learnt from Moors, from their charts, which I have seen many times,' wrote Tomé Pires at Malacca in 1512. Francisco Rodrigues, who was in the expedition to the Spice Islands, copied 'a large map of a Javanese pilot, containing . . . the navigation of the Chinese and the Gores';[3] and the sailing directions from Malacca to Canton, with charts, which Rodrigues compiled about 1513 were doubtless taken from Chinese pilots (Figs. 7, 105). After the capture of Malacca Portuguese ships traded along the South China coast as far as Canton, first reached in 1513; and in 1517 Pires was

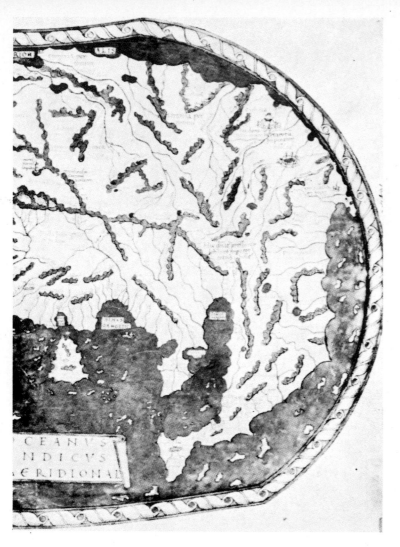

FIG. 104.—Eastern Asia in the world map drawn by
Henricus Martellus about 1490.

FIG. 105.—Sketch chart of the Gulf of Toṅgking by
Francisco Rodrigues, about 1513.

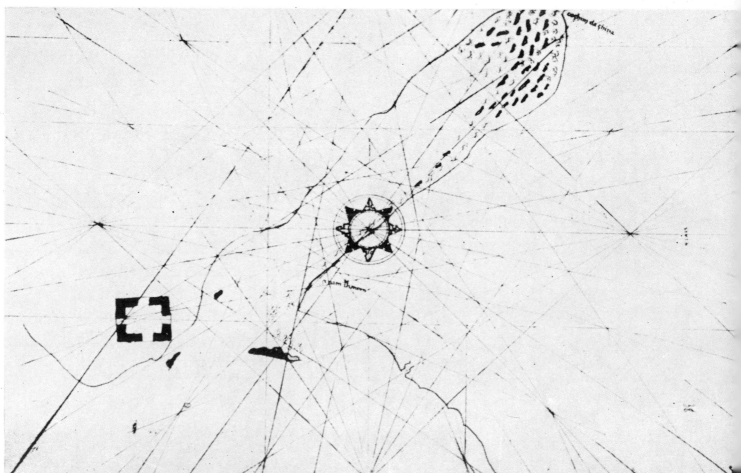

landed at that port as ambassador from the King of Portugal to the Emperor of India. The mission failed, for while he was at Peking, the Portuguese fell foul of the Chinese at Canton, where the members of the embassy ended their lives in captivity. The *Description of the Orient, from the Red Sea to China*, written by Pires before his mission, was the first European account of the Far East, of comparable fullness, since the Book of Marco Polo. In it we find the earliest use of the names Canton ('Quamtom'), Peking '('Peqim') and Japan ('Jampom'); the first European mention of the Philippines ('Luções'); and a description of the East Indies perhaps supplied by Rodrigues, whose charts and rutters are bound with the surviving manuscript of Pires' book.[4]

In 1521 Magellan's fleet, steering to the north of the Spice Islands 'as he had information that there were no provisions at Maluco', had discovered and sailed through the Philippines, where its commander was killed (Fig. 106).[5] The ensuing dispute between Spain and Portugal on the line of demarcation in the East has already been described.[6] From the agreement reached in 1529 Spain excluded the Philippines, which offered a terminal port for trading voyages from her colonial possessions in Central America, and in 1565 the islands were occupied by an expedition from Mexico under Miguel de Legaspi. A ship of this fleet, piloted by Andrés de Urdaneta, pioneered the return passage across the Pacific, sailing to 40° N to get out of the trade winds into the belt of westerlies; and the route established by Urdaneta was followed by the galleons which made the annual voyage between Manila and Acapulco, in New Spain, until the 19th century (Fig. 110).[7]

Meanwhile the Portuguese had extended their trade along the coasts of China, where about 1557 their trading settlement of Macao was founded. In 1542 they reached Japan, and in 1571 set up a factory at Nagasaki, on the southern island of Kyushu. Ralph Fitch, returning to England in 1592, brought back from Malacca news of the Portuguese trade 'from Mocao in China to Japan', in 'a great caracke which goeth thither every yere', bringing back Japanese silver in exchange for 'white silke, golde, muske, and porcelanes' of China.[8] St Francis Xavier. the 'Apostle of Japan', had landed on Kyushu in 1549, and the reports of Jesuit missionaries furnished the principal materials for European maps of Japan for nearly 100 years, until the expulsion of foreigners from the country in 1641. The maps of the Jesuits, drawn from their missionary journeys and depicting the Christian stations in perhaps over-sanguine extension, were reproduced by official Portuguese cartographers, notably Fernão Vaz Dourado who worked at Goa from about 1568. The earliest European map derived from this source gave the islands a 'turtle-backed' outline (Fig. 107). Towards the end of the century, probably under the influence of native Japanese maps, the representation of Luiz Teixeira published by Ortelius in 1595

FIG. 106.—Islands in the Philippines, including Mactan where Magellan was killed in April 1521: a sketch by Pigafetta.

FIG. 107.—Japan and the coast of South China, in a chart drawn by Vaz Dourado at Goa about 1573.

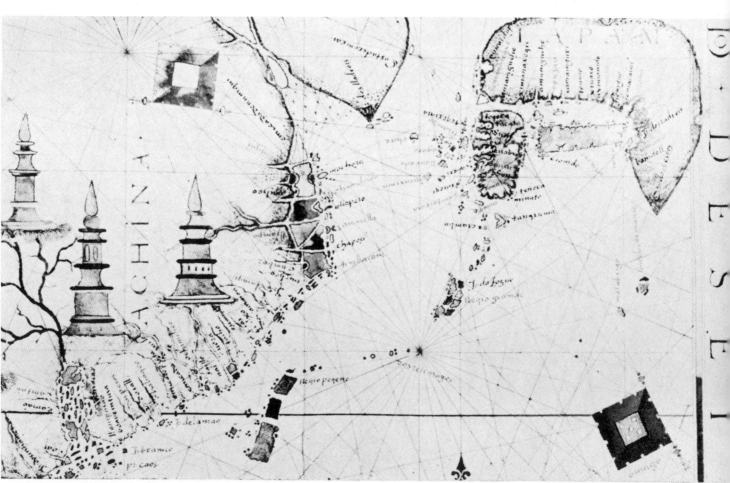

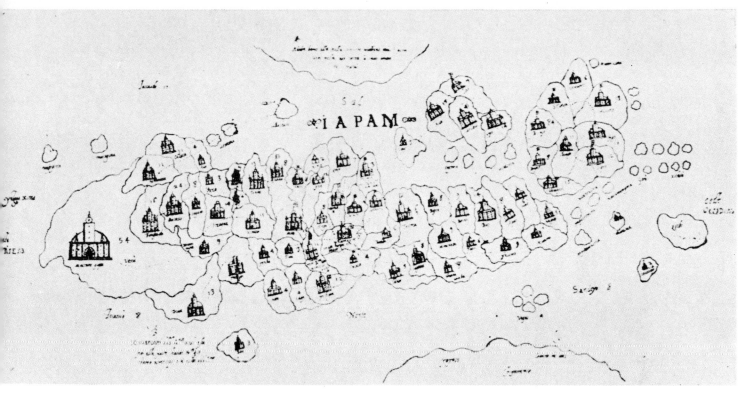

FIG. 108.—MS map of Japan, probably brought to Rome by an embassy of Japanese Christians in 1585.

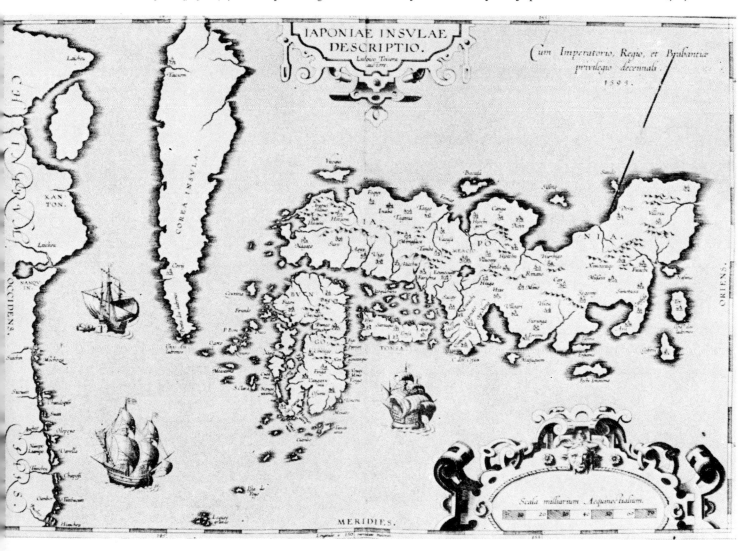

FIG. 109.—Map of Japan by Luiz Teixeira, published by Ortelius in 1595.

introduced a more correct outline for the main islands of Honshu and Kyushu but perpetuated their erroneous east-west orientation (Figs. 108, 109). Their relationship to the Chinese mainland and to Korea (often shown as an island) was not yet understood. The northern island of Yezo (now Hokkaido), inhabited by the Ainu, was first reported in a letter from India in 1548, but long remained unknown to mapmakers of the West and was not visited by a European until the Jesuit Girolamo de Angelis crossed from Honshu in 1615. The map of the island accompanying de Angelis' report (Fig. 111), however, had little influence on European cartography.

While the southern seaways to the East were dominated by Portugal and Spain, other nations sought alternative routes to the realm of the Great Khan. The instructions given in 1580 to Captains Pet and Jackman 'for search and discouerie of a passage by sea . . . Eastwards to the countries or dominions of the mightie Prince, the Emperour of Cathay, and . . . vnto the Cities of Cambalu and Quinsay' still recalled Marco Polo;[9] but Dr Dee's 'briefe advises' to them struck a more modern note, recommending that they 'saile ouer to Japan Island where you shall finde Christian men, Jesuits of many countreys . . . and perhaps some Englishmen'. After the failure of their search for northern passages, English and Dutch adventurers, supplied with fuller intelligence of 'the common and ordenary trade of the Spanyard

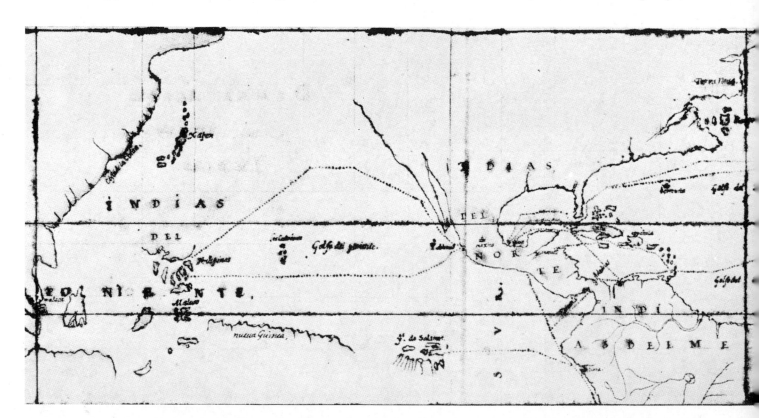

FIG. 110.—The Spanish trade routes in the Pacific, in a map drawn by López de Velasco about 1575.

and Portingall' to India, Molucca, China and Japan, turned to the routes already frequented by their rivals. In 1589 Juan González de Mendoza's work on 'the great and mightie Kingdome of China', translated at Richard Hakluyt's 'earnest request and encouragement', furnished Englishmen with their first authentic account of the country since Marco Polo.[10] Six years later came Linschoten's sailing directions for the China seas, taken from Spanish and Portuguese rutters and charts.[11] In 1588 Thomas Cavendish, returning from his voyage round the world, had brought home a 'large map of China', no doubt taken from a Portuguese ship, and the information on this map was published by Hakluyt in 1600, together with notes on the eastern navigation, 'such as hath not bene heard of in these parts', supplied by Cavendish, and with a dialogue 'of the kingdome of China' printed at Macao 'in China-paper' in 1590 and 'intercepted in the great Carack called Madre de Dios two yeeres after'.[12]

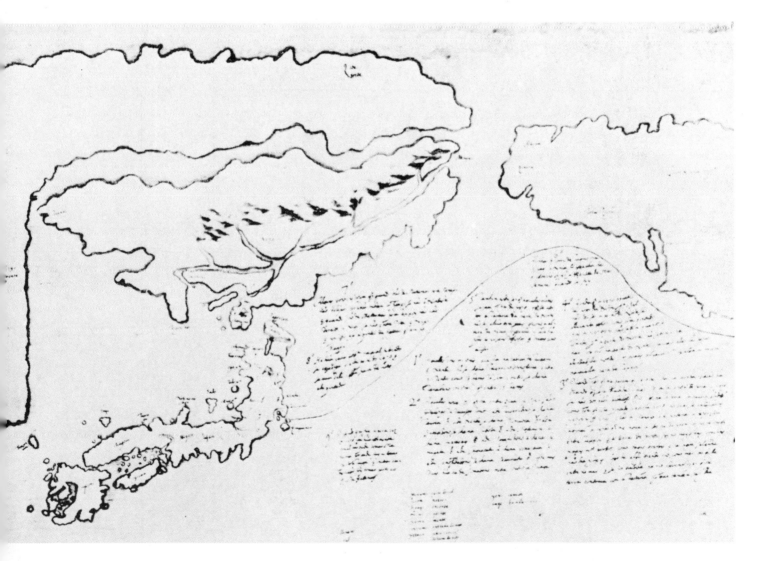

FIG. III.—Map of the Japanese islands drawn by Girolamo de Angelis about 1621.

The English East India Company, incorporated in 1600, believed that 'the countries of Cataia and China' would 'aforth a most liberall vent of English clothes and kersies', and woollen goods were carried in the Dutch ships that sought to extend their trade northward from the Archipelago into the China Sea. The first Dutch vessel to reach Japan, piloted by the Englishman William Adams, was one of a Rotterdam fleet that sailed in 1598 for the Moluccas by way of the Magellan Strait and was dispersed in the Pacific. The tale of the *Liefde*'s voyage was told in letters written by Adams from Japan in 1611. After leaving Chile, the captain steered for Japan, hoping to find there a better market for his 'woolen cloth', than in the 'hot countreyes' of the East Indies, and in 30° N (i.e. nearly six degrees south of the true position) 'sought the northernmost Cape [of Japan]; but found it not, by reason that it lieth faulce in all cardes, and maps, and globes'.[13] With the survivors of her crew disabled by scurvy, the ship was in April 1600 towed into a harbour of Kyushu and confiscated. Adams, a Kentishman who had served a shipbuilding apprenticeship at Limehouse, was employed by the Shogun in his craft, settled in the country, and married a Japanese wife. He became the intermediary through whom both the English and the Dutch opened up trade with Japan. A Dutch factory was set up in 1609 at Hirado on Kyushu, and in 1611 the English company, learning from its factors at Bantam and from the Dutch that Adams was 'in greate favour with the Kinge', directed its seventh and eighth voyages to Japan, with letters from King James I to the 'Emperor'. In June 1613 Captain John Saris in the *Clove* reached Hirado, where with Adams's help he established a factory and negotiated a trade treaty. Saris was not on good terms with Adams, whom he regarded as 'a naturalized Japanner' and as too friendly with the Dutch; and Adams cited his treatment by Saris as his reason for refusing the latter's offer to carry him back to England. In a letter to the Bantam factory in 1613, accompanied by a 'pattron [chart] of Japan' (now lost), Adams had reported that cloth had become as cheap there as in England, the market being flooded by the Dutch and by the 'ship from New Spain' (the Manila galleon). His forecast was justified by the failure of the English factory at Hirado, which was abandoned in 1623. Throughout the period of national isolation which, beginning in 1641, lasted into the middle of the 19th century, foreign trade with Japan, conducted through the port of Nagasaki (Fig. 112), was left in the hands of the Dutch and Chinese. It was in a Dutch ship that the German naturalist Engelbrecht Kaempfer in 1690 reached Japan, where he lived for two years collecting materials for his *History of Japan*, published in 1727 at London after his death (Fig. 116).

Along the China coast neither England nor Holland established a basis for regular trade until Portugal's stations on the Indian Ocean and in the Archipelago fell to

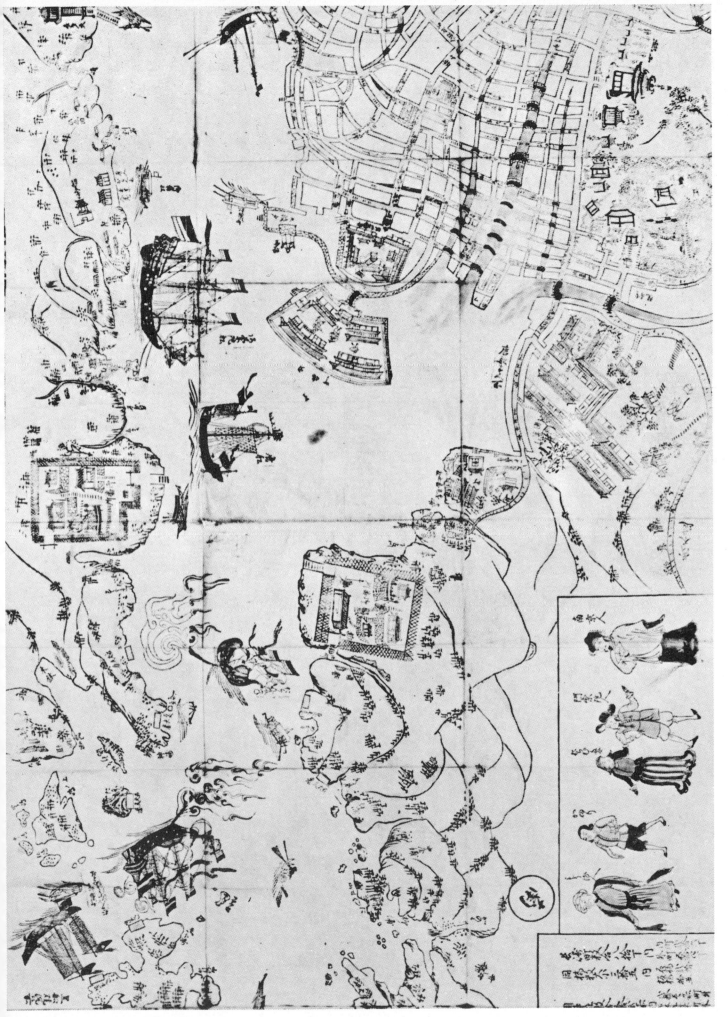

Fig. 112. —Nagasaki harbour.

the Dutch. There was no lack of projecting after 1600. The earlier material had not lost its value, and on his return voyage from Japan in 1613 Saris noted that 'wee found Ian Huijghen van Linschotens booke very true, for thereby we directed

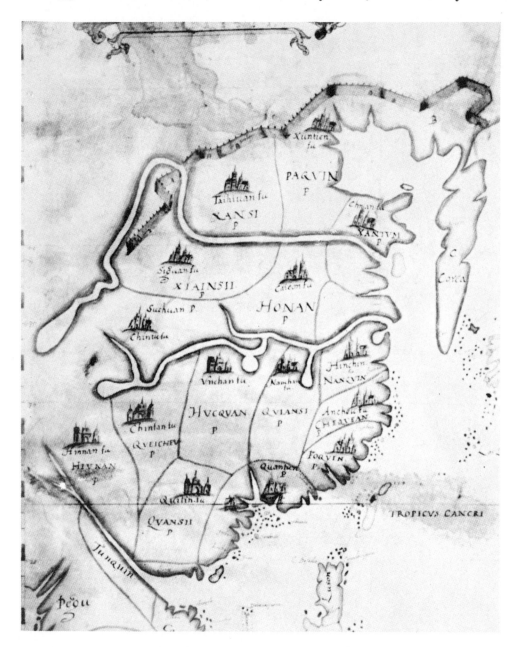

FIG. 113.—Map of China drawn by an Englishman in Madrid, 1609.

ourselues from our setting forth from Firando'.[14] English agents in Spain no doubt furnished new intelligence, such as the manuscript map of China dated from Madrid 1609 (Fig. 114). Samuel Purchas, editing in 1625 'Master Hakluyts many yeeres Collections, and what stock I received from him in written papers', added reports of the English and Dutch companies' voyages, with many documents on the East collected by them, including Adams's letters and a map of China 'in the Chinish language' (Fig. 114), the original of which 'was by Captain Saris . . . gotten at Bantam of a Chinese' and given to Hakluyt. From 1624 the Dutch had a factory on Formosa, and their capture of Malacca cut the communications between the remaining Portuguese bases of Goa and Macao. The English company saw the opportunity to take over the Portuguese carrying trade between India and China; but not until 1676 did it succeed in establishing a factory at Amoy, opposite Formosa (Fig. 115). Annual voyages were made along the coast to the north as far as Chushan.

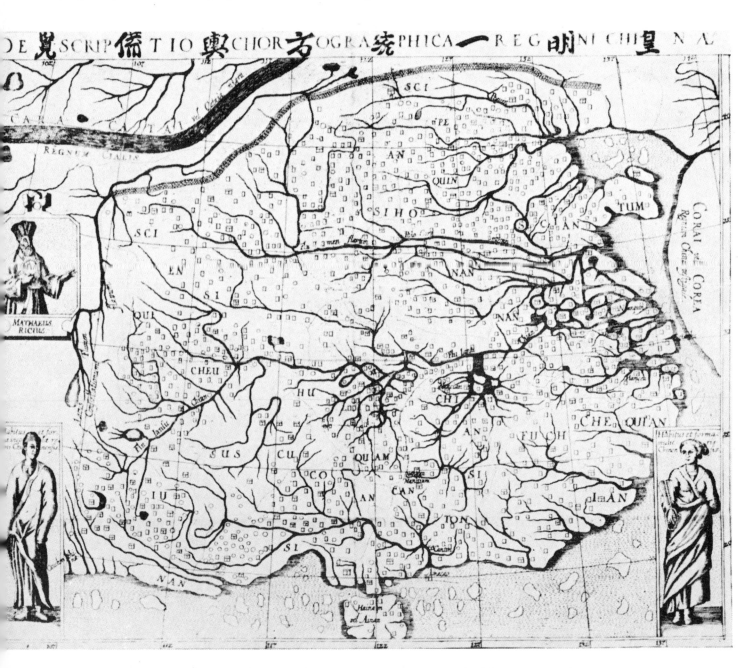

FIG. 114.—Map of China from a Chinese original, published by Purchas in 1625.

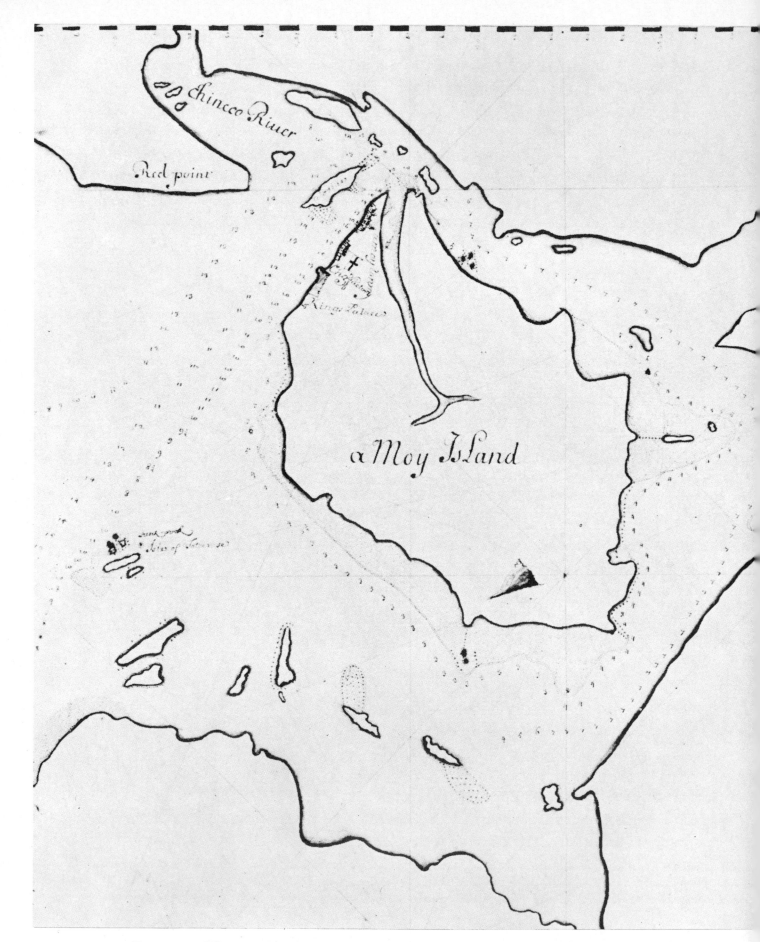

FIG. 115.—The island of Amoy, in a chart drawn by Captain John Kempthorne, 1687.

and the foundation of the great English tea trade with China was laid by the Canton factory established in 1762.

The geography of the lands to the north-east remained obscure alike to Chinese and Japanese and to European mapmakers until the 18th century. Yezo had been correctly described as an island by Saris, quoting a 'Japanner', and by de Angelis (Fig. 111); and it was so delineated in the maps of the Jesuit fathers Matteo Ricci, who established the Peking mission in 1601–10, and Martino Martini, whose atlas of China, drawn from native Chinese maps, was published by Blaeu at Amsterdam in 1655. Their Chinese sources knew nothing of Sakhalin, the Kuriles or Kamchatka. To the north of Yezo, or 'Jesogasima', Kaempfer described 'the Continent of Okujeso . . . that is upper or high Jeso'. By this he meant Kamchatka, of which he obtained vague reports from Japanese pilots; and he referred to Japanese as well as European ignorance regarding 'the full extent of the Eastern Coasts of Siberia, and the great Tartary' and the 'relation which they bear to the neighbouring continent which is probably that of Okujeso'. Geographers, he added, could not yet determine whether Okujeso 'confines on Tartary or America, consequently where they are to place the streight of Anian, or the so long wished for passage out of the North [i.e. Arctic] Sea into the great Indian Ocean'. This was no mere academic question, for on the answer depended the possibility of a northern sea passage from Europe.[15] As early as 1613 William Adams, in a letter sent home to the East India Company in the *Clove*, had recommended Japan as a base for 'discouerie to the northward . . . neuer hath bin better menes to discouer'.

The most fruitful voyage in these waters during the 17th century unhappily added to the confusion of mapmakers and led to a retrogression in the knowledge and interpretation of northern Pacific geography. Rumours of earlier landfalls to the north-east of Japan led the Dutch authorities in Batavia to despatch two expeditions, the first under Matthijs Quast and Abel Tasman in 1639, the second under Maarten Vries in 1643. Vries sailed along the east coast of Yezo, passed between the two most southerly Kurile Islands, which he named 'Staten Land' and 'Compagnies Land', and reached the southern end of Sakhalin, missing the strait to the south of it. The misunderstandings created by his reports and charts (Fig. 117) illustrate the errors into which an accurate but discontinuous coastal survey may betray cartographers. Yezo and Sakhalin were drawn as a continental promontory of Asia; and, although Kaempfer, writing of 'Jeso or Jesogasima . . . the most Northern Island', correctly concluded that 'the Country discovered by de Vries, to the north of Japan, was part of this Island', the misconception persisted well into the next

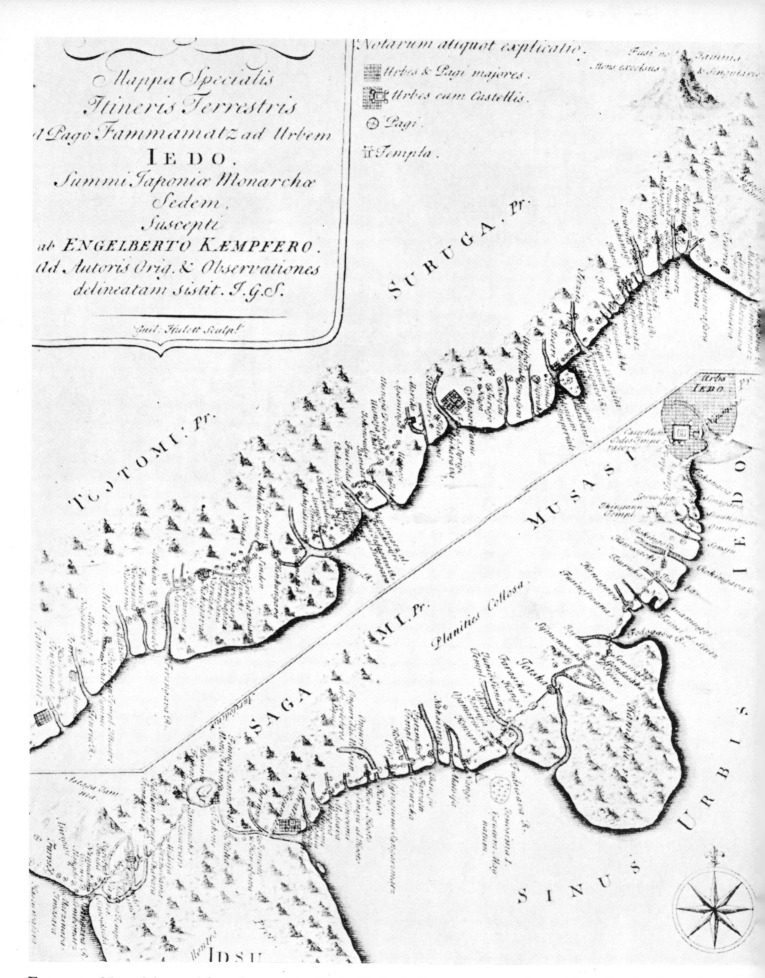

FIG. 116.—Map of the road from Nagasaki to Yedo (Tokyo), from the observations of Engelbrecht Kaempfer, 1690–
published in 1727.

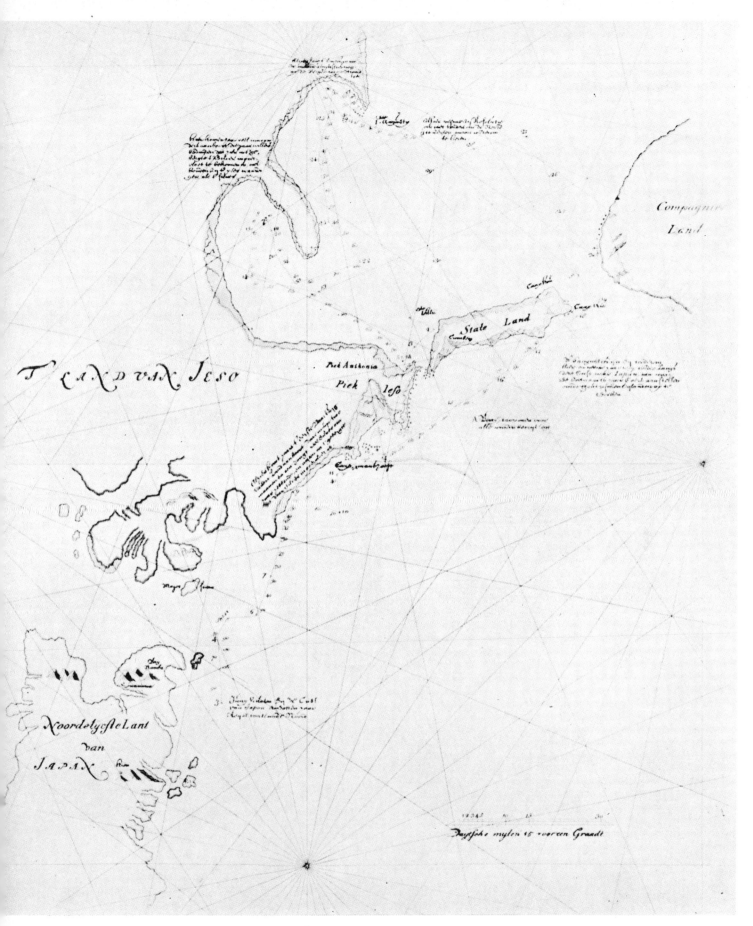

Fig. 117.—MS chart of the voyage of Maarten Vries to the north of Japan in 1643.

century. Moreover, Vries's representation of 'Compagnies Land', to the east of his track, suggested a continental connection with America.

These two errors made no small contribution to the often fantastic versions of the

FIG. 118.—North-east Asia, in a German map published about 1720.

geography of north-east Asia and north-west America found in maps during the first half of the 18th century (Fig. 118). The cloud of uncertainty was dispersed by the Russian expeditions of Bering (1725–9 and 1734–43), which established the positions of the Kamchatka and Anadyr Peninsulas and pointed to the existence of a strait dividing Asia and America (Fig. 119), and by the exploration of the waters between Japan and Kamchatka by the Frenchman La Pérouse in 1787. The results of

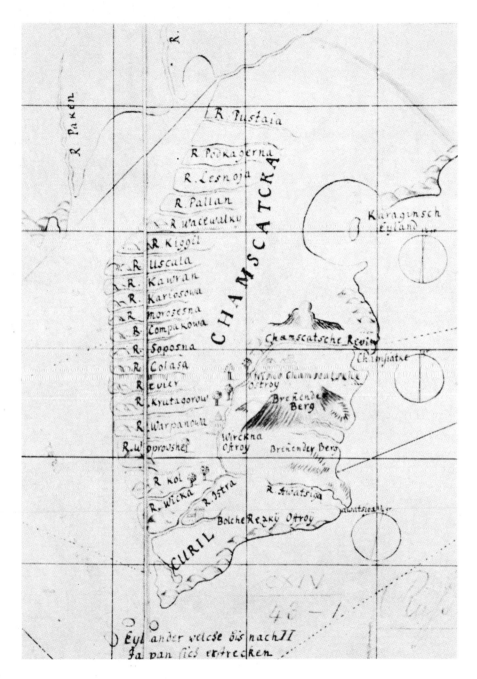

FIG. 119.—Kamchatka, in a map of Siberia, drawn in 1729 to illustrate Bering's first expedition.

Bering's explorations only became slowly known, but a map of his discoveries was published in 1737 by d'Anville in his *Nouvel Atlas de la Chine* (Fig. 120). D'Anville's maps of the Chinese provinces were derived from the great surveys extending over

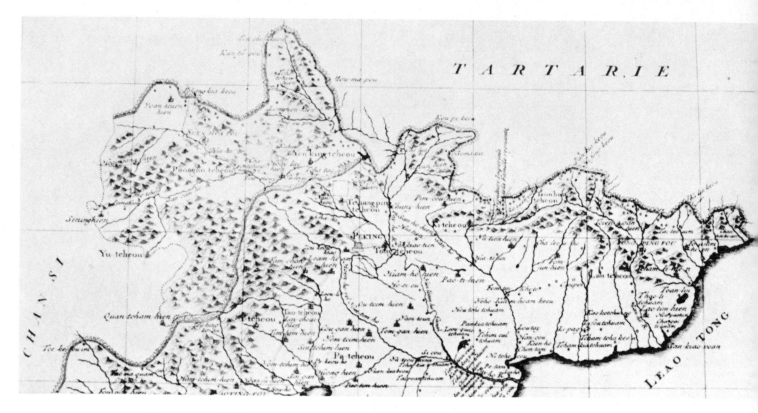

FIG. 120.—D'Anville's map of northern Hopeh, 1737; from the Jesuit surveys.

the whole Empire, made by Jesuit fathers for the Emperor Kang-hsi between 1708 and 1716; printed editions of their maps were produced by the Jesuits at Peking and brought to Europe. This atlas is a landmark in European knowledge of the Far East, and remained the standard authority on China during the 18th century.

Remarks on the Illustrations

Chapter VIII

◇◇◇

104 The eastern half of the world map drawn by Henricus Martellus about 1490 (British Museum, Add. MS 15760) illustrates European conceptions of Asia and the Far East before the Portuguese reached India. As in Ptolemy's maps, the size of Ceylon is exaggerated, and the peninsular form of India flattened. The Malay Peninsula has its Ptolemaic name 'Aureus Chersonesus'. To the east, beyond the 'Sinus Magnus', a great peninsula ('Catigara') curves southward. This feature is a remnant of the continuous coastline which in the world map of Ptolemy had linked south-east Asia to South Africa, enclosing the Indian Ocean to the south; the carto grapher, following the reports of travellers since Marco Polo, has indicated an open passage from the Indian Ocean into the China Sea. To the north lie 'India orientalis', with the realm of Prester John 'emperor of all India', and the provinces of Cathay ruled by the Great Khan, as described by Marco Polo. The geography of Central Asia derives partly from Ptolemy and partly from Marco Polo. (See also Fig. 18.)

105 From the MS description of the East by Rodrigues (see Figs. 12, 22). Rodrigues was never so far north as the Gulf of Tongking, and his information was doubtless gathered from Chinese pilots at Malacca. At the head of the Gulf, in the sketch, is marked 'Cochin da china', at its mouth Hainan island.

106 The islands of Bohol, Mactan, and Cebu in the Philippines, sketched by Antonio Pigafetta in his MS journal, fol. 53r (see Fig. 43). East is at the top. Magellan's crews were the first Europeans to reach the Philippines, which he named the Archipelago of San Lázaro. He concluded a treaty with the King of Cebu, and was killed in an attack on the island of Mactan in April 1521. The cross records his conversion of the people of Cebu to Christianity; and the legend on Mactan reads 'Here died the Captain General'.

107 The Japanese islands and coast of South China, in a chart drawn by Fernão Vaz Dourado at Goa about 1573 (British Museum, Add. MS 31317, ff. 27–28). At

the mouth of the Canton river (bottom left), Macao is not yet named; while further north lie the estuary of the Yellow River and Nanking. For Japan, the cartographer could consult nautical charts and the reports of the Jesuit missionaries, which provided lists of towns and provinces, with distances. The Portuguese knew only the southern islands of Kyushu and Shikoku, and southern Honshu; their ignorance of northern Honshu explains the 'turtle-backed' outline given to the group by Vaz Dourago and adopted by other mapmakers to the end of the century (cf. Figs. 9, 13).

108   In 1585 four Japanese Christians, from the Jesuit missions in Japan, visited the Pope. This manuscript map (in the Archivio di Stato, Florence) is thought to have been brought to Italy by the Japanese embassy. (South is at the top of the map.) It is presumed to have been drawn by a Portuguese or by a Japanese father from Japanese maps (G. Kish, in *Imago Mundi*, VI (1949), pp. 39-46); and the spelling of place-names is Portuguese in form. The two larger islands are Kyushu and Honshu. The boundaries of the feudal fiefs are shown, with the main roads (as dotted lines); and buildings with flags indicate the centres of Christianity. On the left (east) the name 'yehoga xima' denotes the northern island of Yezo or Hokkaido, which had not yet been visited by the Portuguese Jesuits (cf. Fig. 111).

109   The map of Japan by the Portuguese cartographer Luiz Teixeira was published by Ortelius in the 1595 edition of his *Theatrum*. The improved outline of the three principal islands (Kyushu, Shikoku, Honshu) may result from the use of Japanese maps obtained by the Portuguese. Honshu is still (as in Fig. 108) oriented E–W instead of NE–SW, and the southern point of Kyushu is laid down nearly two degrees too far south. Korea is represented as an island.

110   This map of the 'East and West Indies', embracing the Spanish territories on each side of the Pacific, is in the manuscript 'Demarcacion y diuision de las Indias' (*c*. 1575), by Juan López de Velasco, in the John Carter Brown Library, Providence, R.I. In the east, it draws the *raya* or demarcation line through the Malay Peninsula, as in the chart of 1522 by Nuño García (Fig. 87), thus placing the Moluccas within the Spanish sphere. The orientation of the Japanese islands is notably true. The map shows the trade routes between Manila and Acapulco (in Mexico) used by the Spaniards after their occupation of the Philippines in 1565 (see Chapter IX). The other Spanish trade routes, between Europe and the Caribbean and between Peru and Panama and Guatemala, are also indicated, together with the track of Mendaña from Peru to the Solomon Islands in 1567–8 (see Chapter IX).

111   The Jesuit father Girolamo de Angelis was the first European to cross the Tsugaru Strait and visit the northernmost Japanese island, Yezo or Hokkaido, on a voyage in 1618. His map, drawn about 1621, accompanies his report on Yezo, in the Jesuit archives in Rome. The island was at that date little known to the Japanese themselves, and is drawn on the map from de Angelis' own observations. Honshu is correctly oriented; Yezo is drawn on a much larger scale; Korea (on the left) is

depicted as a peninsula; a strait, with the name 'Anian' written on the American shore, separates Asia from America; and the Pacific coasts of America are drawn on a greatly reduced scale, the width of the ocean being shown as much less than the reality.

112　This woodcut plan of Nagasaki harbour was printed at Nagasaki between 1661 and 1672. During the period of national isolation, Nagasaki was the only Japanese port where foreign ships were allowed to trade; Dutch ships and Chinese junks are shown lying at their allotted anchorages in the harbour. The two panels at the bottom left-hand corner contain tables of distances by sea from Nagasaki and representations of foreign merchants (left to right: Arab, Dutch, Chinese).

113　This anonymous manuscript map of China (British Museum, Cotton MS Aug. I. ii. 45) is dated 'From Madrid, A° 1609'. Apparently drawn by an English agent from Spanish sources, the map points to English interest in China from the early days of the East India Company. The fifteen provinces of the Ming Empire are delimited and their chief cities ('fu') are marked; in the north is drawn the Great Wall 'of 300 Leagues'. The coastal outline is much more correct than is usual in contemporary printed maps, and Korea now appears as a peninsula.

114　The map of China published in *Purchas His Pilgrimes* (1625) was engraved from a Chinese original given to Hakluyt by Captain John Saris in 1614. The Chinese map (Purchas writes) 'was by Captain Saris . . . gotten at Bantam of a Chinese in taking a distresse for debts owing to the English Merchants'. This is perhaps the earliest map of China depending on Chinese sources to be published in Europe. Purchas inserts in a vignette a portrait of the Jesuit father Matteo Ricci; and, he adds, 'the names of the Provinces I have hunted out of the Jesuites Journeyes and other Relations'. Korea appears as a peninsula.

115　Captain John Kempthorne's chart of the island of Amoy off the coast of Fukien (British Museum, Add. MS 3665, fol. 71) was drawn on his voyage of 1686–8 (see Fig. 103). The chart shows the English factory established in 1676, between the 'Kings Palace' and the town, and soundings round the isle. Amoy, with its magnificent harbour, was a centre for Chinese trade with Formosa and the Malay Archipelago.

116　In 1690 Engelbrecht Kaempfer accompanied the annual embassy of the Dutch East India Company to Japan, where he remained for two years. The map shows the route by which the embassy travelled from Nagasaki to the Emperor's court, with (at the top) Fujiyama, which—wrote Kaempfer—'help'd me not a little in drawing and correcting the map'. Kaempfer's collections and manuscripts were acquired by Sir Hans Sloane and are now in the British Museum. Sloane employed a young Swiss, J. G. Scheuchzer, to prepare for publication in English Kaempfer's *Natural History of Japan* (London, 1727), in which his maps, redrawn by Scheuchzer, were printed.

117   In 1643, Maarten Gerritszoon Vries, commanding an expedition of the Dutch East India Company from Batavia, sailed north-east along the coast of Yezo, passed between the two westerly islands of the Kurile chain (here named 'State Land' and 'Compagnies Land'), and skirted the Sakhalin coast, which he wrongly thought continuous with that of Yezo. The manuscript chart on which his track is marked is in the Rijksarchief, The Hague; and this representation of the geography of the northern Pacific was diffused by printed maps from about 1650 (cf. Fig. 118).

118   This map by the German cartographer J. B. Homann, published at Nuremberg about 1720, illustrates the confused ideas on the geography of lands north of Japan that prevailed before the expeditions of Bering. Yezo is identified with Kamchatka, and west of the 'Canal de Pieck' and 'Fretum de Vries' lies Compagnie Land (cf. Fig. 117).

119   Bering's map drawn in 1729 (see Figs. 70, 71) is the earliest correct delineation of Kamchatka, which he crossed from east to west in the course of his first expedition (1725-9).

120   Between 1708 and 1716 the fathers of the Jesuit mission at Peking surveyed the Chinese Empire and Manchuria, and in 1716-20 they produced editions of their maps engraved on copper and wood; they first introduced copperplate engraving into China. The maps were carried to Europe by the French Fr J. B. du Halde, whose description of China, published in Paris in 1735, d'Anville's atlas was designed to accompany. In the illustration, the northern part of the province of Hopeh is shown, with Peking and sections of the Great Wall.

Notes

Chapter VIII

<><><><><><><><><><><><><><><><><><><><><><><><><><><><><><><><><><><><><><><><><><>

[1] See Chapter II.

[2] See Chapter I.

[3] The 'Gores' were the natives of the Ryukyu Islands. Rodrigues' copy of the Javanese chart was sent by the Viceroy Afonso d'Albuquerque to the King of Portugal, but is now lost.

[4] The *Suma Oriental*, written by Pires in 1512–15, was published in abridged form in Ramusio's *Navigazioni* (Venice, 1557). It was first edited in full from the original MS, with the rutter of Rodrigues, by Dr A. Cortesão for the Hakluyt Society (London, 1944)

[5] See Chapter IX.

[6] In Chapter VII.

[7] See Chapter IX.

[8] For Fitch, see Chapter VII.

[9] See Chapters I and V.

[10] For Mendoza, see Chapter I and Fig. 12.

[11] See Chapters I and VII; and Figs. 13, 92.

[12] The carrack *Madre de Dios*, from the East Indies, was taken by an English squadron off the Azores in 1592.

[13] E.g. in the Teixeira-Ortelius map of 1595 (Fig. 109).

[14] I.e. Hirado.

[15] See Chapter V.

PART FIVE

The South Sea

IX

THE SPANISH IN THE SOUTH SEA

16th and 17th centuries

THE DISCOVERY OF NEW LANDS adds little to the sum of geographical knowledge unless their position is determined with sufficient accuracy to enable later travellers to re-find them. The unfolding of the map of the Pacific from the early 16th century to the end of the 18th century is not a record of continuous growth. The plans for successive expeditions rested no less on conjecture, and on inference from evidence which seems flimsy enough today, than on solid knowledge. Until the age of Cook, the courage and seamanship of early navigators was not matched by their technical resources for the precise plotting of their landfalls. This defect in their equipment made itself sharply felt in a region with the great longitudinal extension of the Pacific, in which moreover sailing ships in passage between its eastern and western shores were forced by the steady wind systems into relatively narrow traffic lanes. The maps which explorers brought back, no less than their narratives, throw light on the illusions created by their discoveries, on the retreat of knowledge before fantasy, and on the diversion of enterprise to the pursuit of chimeras which nonetheless yielded new and fruitful discoveries. All these features characterize the history of Pacific exploration.

Columbus, identifying his lands and islands in the west with the Eastern Asia of Ptolemy and Marco Polo, never saw the intervening ocean whose existence was incompatible with his cosmographical ideas (Fig. 33). Other geographers, however, quickly became aware that many degrees of longitude must separate his discoveries from Cipangu and Cathay, and not long after his death in 1506 mapmakers were laying down a wide ocean in this space.[1] The first European to set eyes on the

185

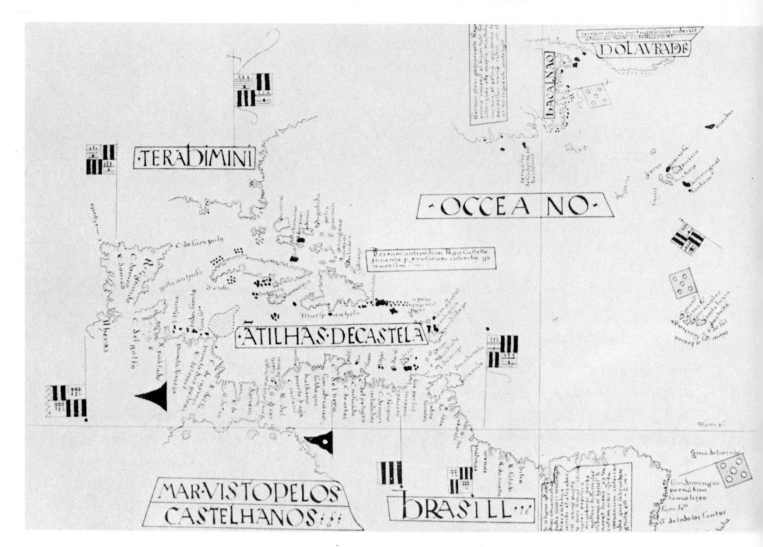

FIG. 121.—Central America, in a world chart probably drawn by Jorge Reinel in 1519, showing the Pacific coast dis covered by Balboa in 1513.

eastern shore of the Pacific was Vasco Nuñez de Balboa, who in 1513, crossing the isthmus from Darien, was shown by his native guides 'the great mayne sea heretofore unknowen to the inhabitants of Europe, Aphrike, and Asia' (Fig. 121).

To the King of Spain the 'South Sea' thus revealed offered a westerly route to the Spice Islands, reached by a Portuguese squadron a year before Balboa's discovery, as an alternative to the easterly sea-way used by Portugal.[2] The charts and globes which Magellan had seen in Portugal fostered belief in a strait, far to the south, connecting the Atlantic and Pacific Oceans; and when he sailed under the Spanish flag in 1519 he expected to show that this was the shortest route to the Moluccas and that they lay on the nearer, or Spanish, side of the eastern *raya*, the extension of the demarcation line agreed by Spain and Portugal in 1529.[3] These hypotheses rested on an underestimate of the length of a degree (rated by Magellan as $16\frac{2}{3}$

leagues) and consequently of the sailing time involved in crossing the Pacific. Only after a passage of ninety-eight days from the western end of his Strait did he reach the Ladrones in March 1521, and by then his starving and scurvy-ridden crew had been 'forced to eat the hides with which the main yard was covered'.

By bitter experience Magellan had demonstrated the width of the Pacific, but political expediency still determined its representation on the Spanish charts (Fig. 122). Before Spain surrendered her claim to the Moluccas in 1529, two abortive Spanish expeditions were sent out to open trade with them. The first under García de Loaysa, with Sebastian del Cano (who had brought Magellan's *Vitoria* home after his death in 1522) commanding a ship, sailed from Spain by the Magellan Strait in 1525. A relief squadron, under Alvaro de Saavedra who had with him charts by Magellan, was dispatched from Mexico in 1527. A survivor of Loaysa's expedition, Andrés de Urdaneta, reporting on it after his return to Spain in 1537, urged that 'a treaty be made with Maluco, for bringing all the clove, mace, and nutmeg harvest to Spain'. This advice came too late, but the Philippine Islands, discovered by Magellan and named by him the Archipelago of San Lázaro, had been exempted from the agreement of 1529, and it was here that the Spaniards sought a trading base in the western Pacific. Their conquest of Mexico and Peru had given them control of the Pacific seaboard of America, and the later Spanish expeditions were launched, not from Spain by the hazardous route pioneered by Magellan, but from the ports of Spanish America. Avoiding the belt of 'brave west winds' which in latitudes higher than 25° S were contrary for vessels entering the Pacific by Magellan Strait, they could make their westing with the steady south-east trade winds from Peru or north-east trades from Mexico.

The Philippines, named after Philip II by Ruy López de Villalobos who led an expedition from Mexico in 1542, were colonized for Spain by Miguel López de Legaspi in 1565, also from Mexico. Spain now had bases for trade on both shores of the Pacific, but the winds which carried her ships from east to west were adverse for the return voyage, as Saavedra and Villalobos had found to their cost. Urdaneta, Legaspi's chief pilot, and Arellano, one of his captains, independently pioneered the return passage by sailing north of the trade-wind belt into that of constant westerlies which in 42° N brought them to the Californian coast. Urdaneta's sailing directions were incorporated in the standard 'rutters' for the South Sea issued to Spanish pilots from the 16th to the 18th centuries, and for 250 years the annual Manila galleon, carrying silver from the mines of Peru and New Spain to the Philippines, where it was laden with spices and Chinese wares for the return voyage, plied on the routes thus established, sailing from Manila as soon as the south-west monsoon set in. In the galleon captured by Captain George Anson off the Philippines in June 1743

FIG. 122.—The Pacific Ocean, in a world chart drawn by Diogo Ribero in

POLVS MVNDI ARCTICVS:

TIERA DE LABRADOR

TIERA NOVA DE CORTEREAL

TIERA DE ESTEVA GOMEZ

TIERA DE AYLLON

TIERA DE GARAY

NVEVA ESPANA

GVATIMALA

OCCEANVS OCCIDENTALIS

MAR DEL SVR

CASTILLA DELORO

PERV

MVNDVS NOVS:

TIERA BRASILIS:

TIERA DE SOLIS

TIERA DE PATAGONES:

POLVS MVNDI ATARCTICVS:

the Magellan Strait, from a Spanish chart of 1527, also probably by Ribero.

'there was found a chart of all the Ocean . . . which was what was made use of by the galleon in her own navigation', with other 'draughts and journals'.[1] From these the chronicler of Anson's voyage was able to describe the seasonal Manila trade:

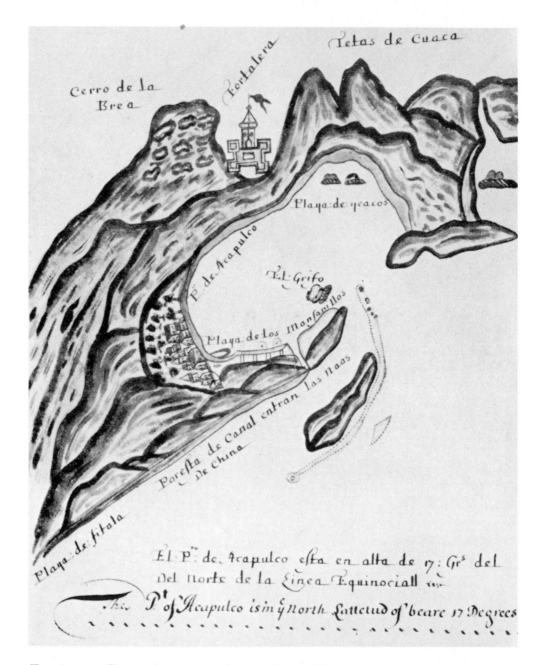

FIG. 123.—Chart of the port of Acapulco in Mexico, copied by William Hack
in 1681 from a MS Spanish rutter drawn at Panama in 1669.

'This trade from Manila to Acapulco [in Mexico] and back again, is usually carried on in one or at most two annual ships, which set sail from Manila about July, and arrive at Acapulco in the December, January or February following,

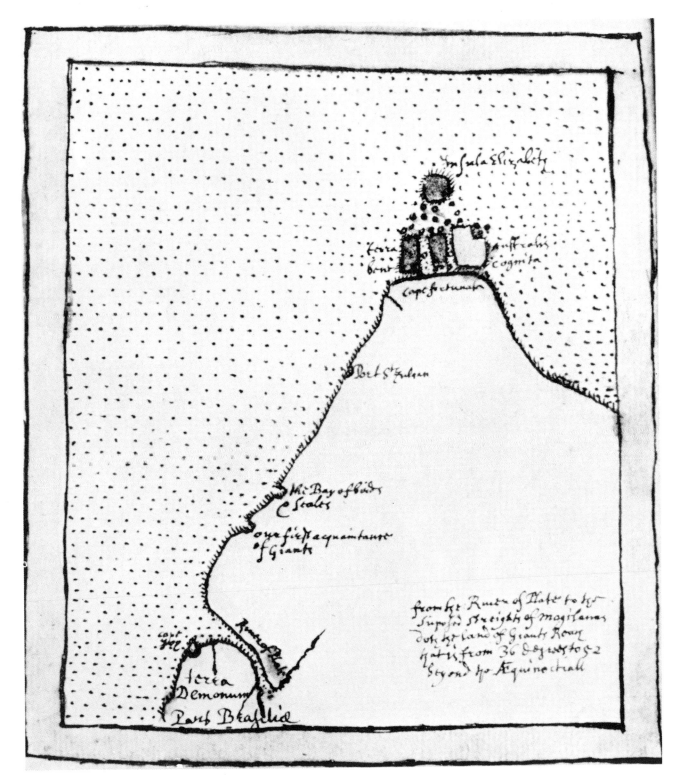

FIG. 124.—Sketch map of Patagonia and Magellan Strait by Francis Fletcher, chaplain on Drake's voyage in 1577–80.

and . . . return for Manila some time in March, where they generally arrive in June'
(Figs. 110, 123).

In the 16th century the Portuguese, developing their trade in the Malay Archipelago, had made no attempt to carry their discoveries further south or east, although
they touched at New Guinea in 1526 and a Portuguese discovery of Australia in the
first half of the century has been inconclusively inferred from the evidence of
certain manuscript maps (Fig. 126). The main island groups of the Pacific lie within
the zone of the south-east trades, to the south of the Spanish sailing route between
Mexico and the Philippines; only Hawaii, in 20° N, lay near the track of the Manila

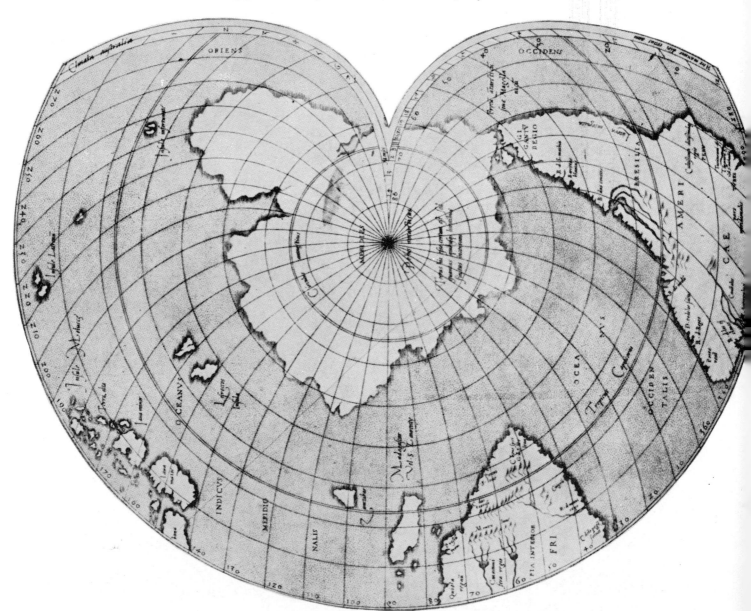

FIG. 125.—The Southern Hemisphere, in an engraved world map by Mercator, 1538.

galleon, but its reputed discovery in 1542 by a pilot of Villalobos is now discredited.[5] Many of these groups were to be discovered by expeditions sailing from east to west —the Spanish from Peruvian ports, the Dutch and English by Magellan Strait or Cape Horn.

By the middle of the 16th century the Pacific had become an objective for exploration and not merely a trade route; and nearly all these enterprises were inspired by one of the most persistent geographical illusions. The concept of a vast inhabited continent, extending from the South Pole into the Tropics and bounding to the south the Atlantic, Pacific, and Indian Oceans, was inherited by Renaissance geographers from the cosmography of the Christian Middle Ages[6] (Figs. 125–7). Seeking a scientific basis for this belief, they held that, if the earth were to remain in equilibrium, the land-masses of the northern hemisphere must be balanced (as Mercator wrote on his world chart of 1569) 'under the Antarctic Pole [by] a continent

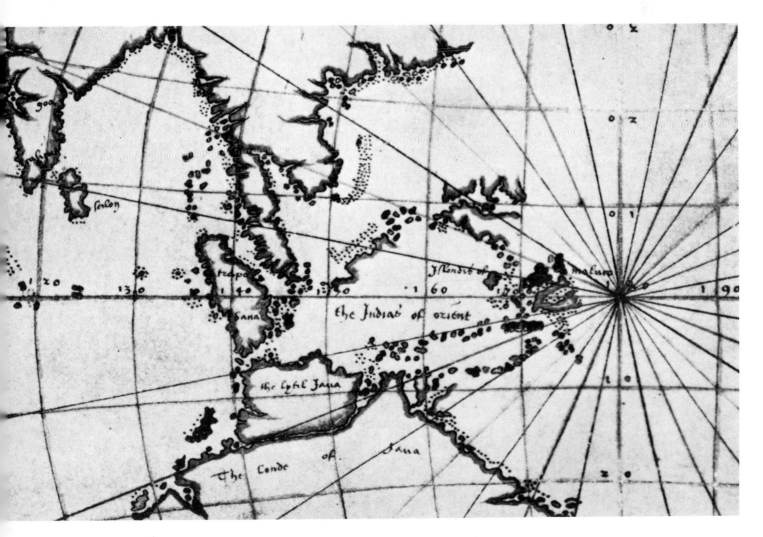

FIG. 126.—South-east Asia, in a world chart drawn by Jean Rotz in 1542.

so great that, with the southern parts of Asia, and the new India or America, it should be a weight equal to the other lands'.[7] For two and a half centuries after Magellan geographers laid down Terra Australis, the Southern Continent, on their maps and anxiously gathered evidence for its existence and outline.

There were sceptics among the explorers themselves. Magellan's men took Tierra del Fuego to be an island; passing through the strait 'they thought the land to the left to consist of islands, for on that side they sometimes heard the beating and roaring of the sea, as if upon some farther shore'. Drake in 1578, blown south from the western end of Magellan Strait, 'plainly discovered that the same terra australis, left or sett down to bee terra incognita before we came there, to bee no Continent . . . but broken Islands and large passages amongst them', where 'the Atlantic Ocean and the South Sea meet in a most large and free scope' (Fig. 124). In 1681 the buccaneer Captain Bartholomew Sharp sailed from Panama south to 60° round Cape Horn, and the narrator of his voyage inferred 'that there is no such continent

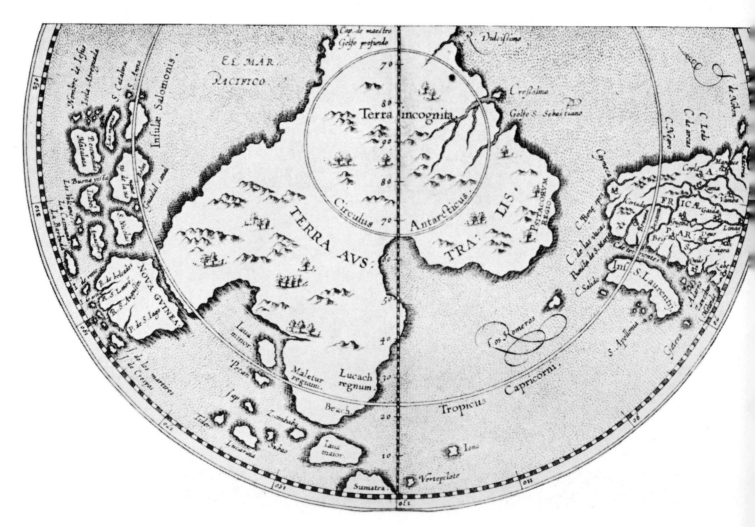

FIG. 127.—Part of the Southern Continent, by Cornelis Wytfliet, 1597.

as Terra Australis incognita, as is named and described in all the ancient maps'.[8]

Yet from the time of Magellan to that of Cook the search for Terra Australis led to almost every notable discovery in the Southern Pacific, and mapmakers confidently plotted new landfalls and signs of land reported by navigators as details of a continental coast. Nor could the existence of the Southern Continent be wholly demonstrated or disproved by expeditions sailing from the east with the trade winds. These left unexamined, to the south of the tropic, a vast area within which a ship could not make head against the westerlies and a continent might still be conjectured to lie. Only to ships entering the Pacific from the west was this area open for exploration.

The first Spanish expedition from Peru, provoked by tales of an Inca voyage to islands to the west (perhaps the Galapagos) and 'fitted out for the discovery of certain islands and a continent', sailed from Callao in 1567 under Alvaro de Mendaña, with Hernan Gallego as chief pilot and Pedro Sarmiento de Gamboa in command

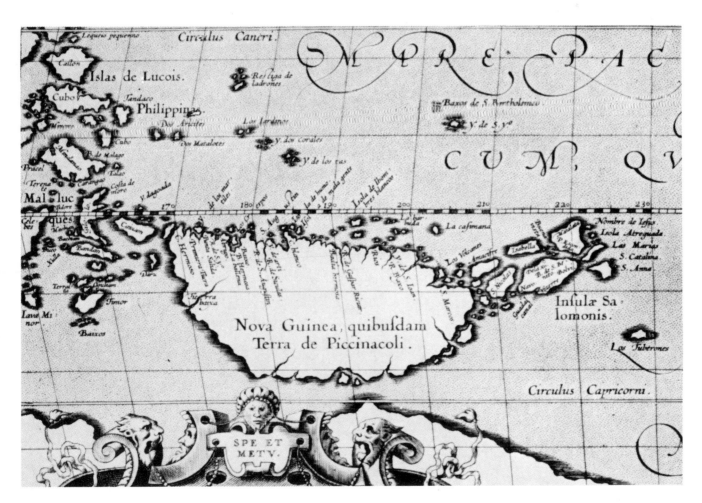

Fig. 128.—Islands of the western Pacific, in a map by Ortelius published in 1587.

of the flagship. Mendaña, following a course to the north of Magellan's, missed all the Polynesian islands; and the Solomon Islands, which he discovered and explored, were certainly not Terra Australis, which Sarmiento asserted to lie to the south-east, vainly advocating 'a south-east course in search of the other land which he wished to discover, lying opposite Chile'.

The Solomons were the first of the great Pacific island groups to appear on the maps (Figs. 110, 128, 129), in a form doubtless derived from the now lost charts of Mendaña. Their location, however, laid down by Gallego by dead-reckoning 1700 leagues (85 degrees) west of Peru, that is some 25 degrees short of their true position, was long to perplex cartographers and explorers. Maps of the 16th century (e.g. Figs. 127–9) drew them—more or less correctly—off the eastern tip of New Guinea, though still displaced far to the east; Robert Dudley in 1646 identified them with the Marquesas, Mendaña's discovery of 1595, 70 degrees east of their longitude;[9] and in the 18th century the Solomons were still laid down some 20 to 25 degrees too far east. Alexander Dalrymple identified them with Dampier's discovery, New Britain (Figs. 134, 148). Their very existence was doubted, and they were sometimes

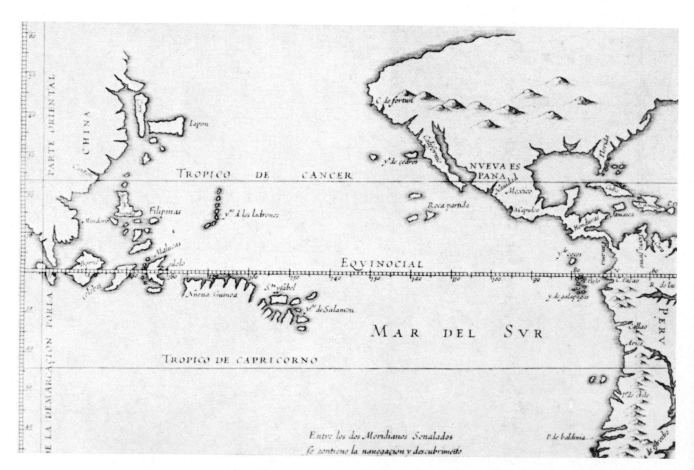

FIG. 129.—The Pacific, in a map by Herrera published in 1602.

removed from the chart altogether. 'Although the group included eight large islands stretched like a net across the course of navigators in an almost unbroken line for 600 miles,'[10] it was sought in vain for two centuries. In the years 1767, 1768, and 1769 three expeditions passed through the islands and gave new names without recognizing them as Mendaña's discovery. Bougainville in 1768 concluded that 'if there were any such islands, their situation was erroneously laid down'.[11]

Two more Spanish voyages were to be made from Peru to colonize the Solomons and the continent of which they might be outliers. On his expedition in 1595–6, with Pedro Fernández de Quiros as chief pilot, Mendaña discovered the Marquesas (Fig. 131)—the first Polynesian archipelago to become known—and reached the Santa Cruz group, four degrees east of the Solomons, which he failed to find. Quiros himself, a visionary and an expert navigator, had (as the Spanish Council of State was later to note) 'got it into his head to be a second Columbus', whose mission was the annexation of Terra Australis for Spain and the conversion of its natives.

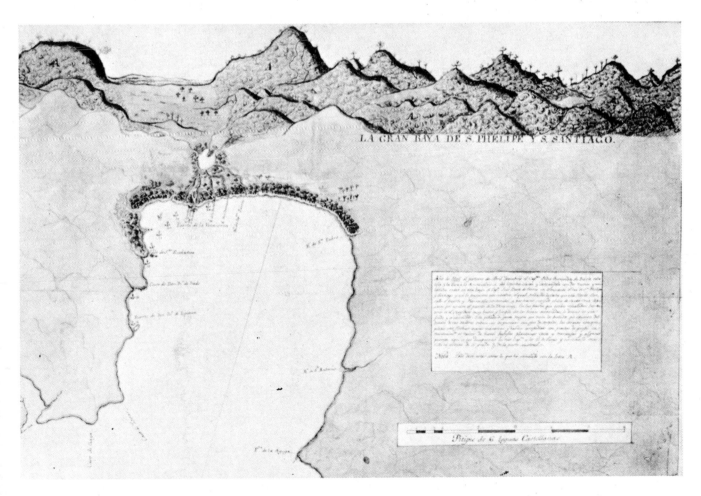

FIG. 130.—Prado's chart of the Bay of St Philip and St James, in the New Hebrides, discovered by Quiros in 1606.

E.M.—O

Sailing in 1605, on a course to the south of those taken by earlier navigators, he passed through the Tuamotu Archipelago and, missing the Santa Cruz islands, reached the New Hebrides, which he recognized as the continent 'sought for so long'. Here, with solemn ceremony, he took possession 'of this bay named the Bay of St Philip and James . . . and of the site on which is to be founded the city of New Jerusalem . . . and of all this region of the south as far as the Pole, which from this time shall be called Austrialia del Espíritu Santo' (Figs. 130, 131). The supposed longitude of Quiros' new discovery, like that of the Solomons, ascertained by dead reckoning, gave geographers wide scope for individual judgment. On their maps (Fig. 133) Australia del Espíritu Santo and New Jerusalem were ultimately located

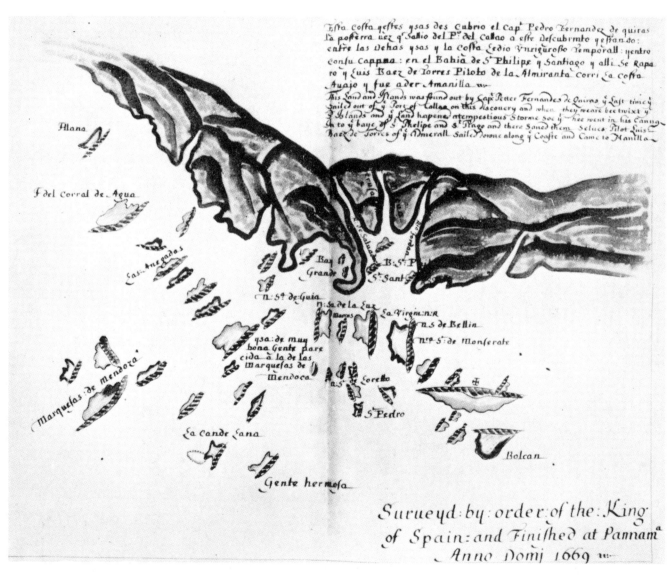

FIG. 131.—The discoveries of Mendaña and Quiros in the Pacific. Copied by Hack in 1681 from a Spanish map of 1669.

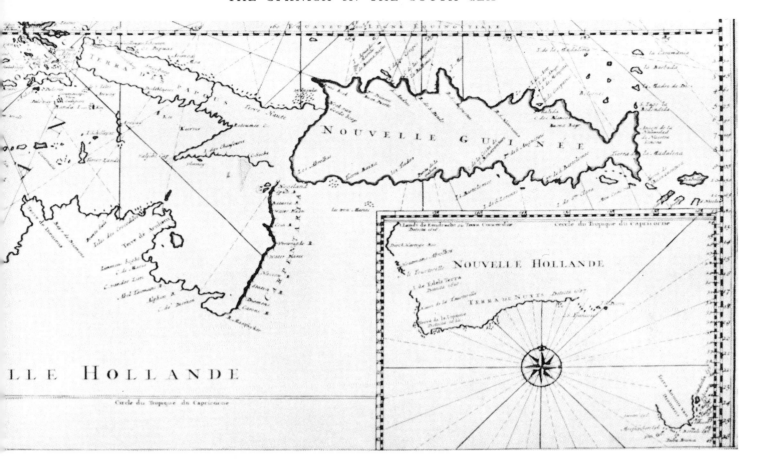

з. 132.—Chart of New Guinea and the north coasts of New Holland (Australia), published at Amsterdam in 1700.
Inset, the south-east coasts of New Holland, as discovered by the Dutch.

on the north-east coast of New Holland (Australia), 350 leagues west of the correct position; and the error was not rectified until Bougainville sailed west from the New Hebrides in 1768.[12]

At the Bay of St Philip and St James, Quiros was separated from his second ship, in which were Captains Diego de Prado y Tovar and Luis Váez de Torres. While Quiros returned to New Spain by the northern route, Prado and Torres sailed south-west and then north-west. This brought them to the eastern point of New Guinea, from which they ran along the south coast, passing through Torres Strait and making for Manila. The north coast of New Guinea had been examined in 1528 by Saavedra and in 1545 by one of Villalobos' captains, Ortiz de Retes, who named it;[13] Prado and Torres were the first navigators to ascertain that it was an island. Although evidence of their passage through Torres Strait found its way on to printed maps (Figs. 132–3), the reports and charts which they forwarded to the King of Spain remained secreted in the Spanish archives, and their discovery was not published. When Cook sailed through the Strait in 1770, he was able to claim the

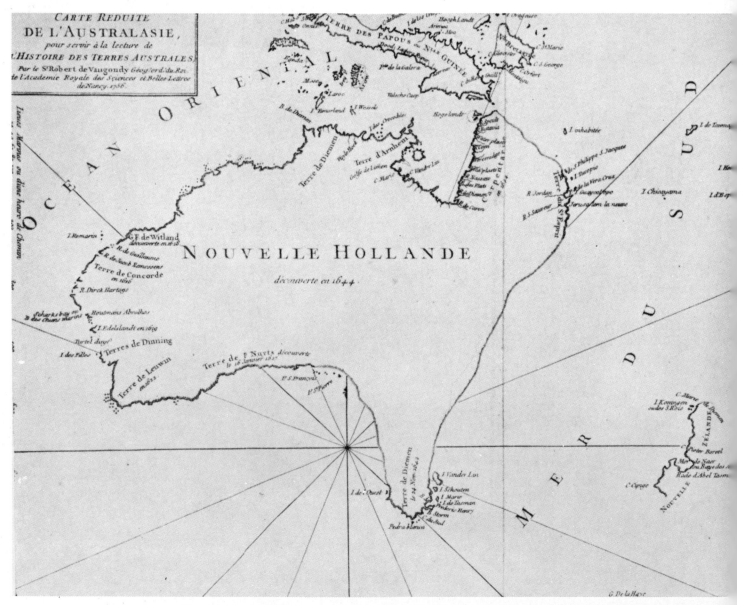

FIG. 133.—Map of Australia and the south-west Pacific by Robert de Vaugondy, published in 1756. *Inset:* Quiros' discoveries in the New Hebrides are located on the north-east coasts of Australia.

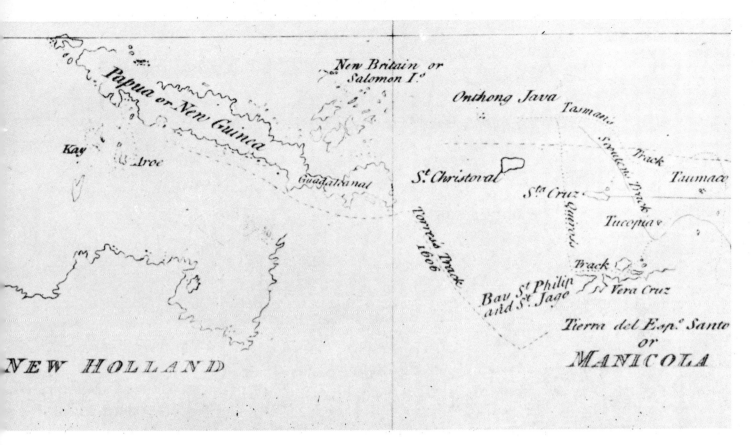

FIG. 134.— Torres' track in 1606 through the strait between Australia and New Guinea, as laid down in an engraved chart by Alexander Dalrymple, 1767.

satisfaction of 'being able to prove that New-Holland and New-Guinea are two Separate Lands or Islands, which untill this day hath been a doubtfull point with Geographers'.[14]

To Quiros' importunate petitions for royal support of further voyages to Terra Australis, the King of Spain's advisers were indifferent. They recommended that his services should be retained lest he offer them elsewhere but that he should not be re-employed in discovery or colonization. Spain's interest was now seen to lie in the sealing off of the Pacific as a Spanish lake, within which her established commercial routes would be secure and no other power would have the opportunity to attempt the further discoveries which she denied herself. This policy partly explains the relative poverty of the cartographic records of the Spanish voyages, by comparison with those of the Dutch and English. The raids of Drake in 1577–80 and of Cavendish in 1588–90 had already betrayed the weakness of the Spanish empire in the South Sea; but it was the Dutch who were to add the next chapter in the exploration and mapping of the Pacific.[15] Their effort, prompted by policy of a very different kind, was nevertheless dominated by the shade of Quiros.

Remarks on the Illustrations

Chapter IX

◇◇

121   In 1519 the Portuguese cartographer Jorge Reinel was employed in the Spanish service at Seville where he drew charts for Magellan's expedition (see Chapter VII). This world chart was probably drawn by him at that time; sometimes known as 'Kunstmann IV', it was preserved in the Armeebibliothek, Munich, until the war of 1939–45, but has since disappeared. Balboa's discovery of the Pacific in 1513 ('Mar visto pelos Castelhanos') is depicted, with the sections of its coast which he explored in 1517. Yucatan, discovered in 1518, is already correctly shown as a peninsula; Florida is named 'Tera Bimini' (see Chapter IV, note 4).

122   Diogo Ribeiro, a Portuguese by birth, was working at Seville from about 1519 and became 'cosmographer and chartmaker' in the Casa de la Contratación. The three world maps from his hand which have survived (one of 1527, two of 1529) may be regarded as copies of the Spanish *padrón real* (see Chapters IV, VII). The reproduction is taken from his chart of 1529 in the archives of the Propaganda Fide, Rome; the inset from that of 1527 in the Grossherzogliche Bibliothek, Weimar. Magellan's track in 1519–20 is marked by drawings of his two ships, the *Vitoria* and *Trinidad*; and the place-names in the inset record his passage along the coast of Patagonia and through his strait, here named 'Estrecho de Fernam de magallanes'. The length of Magellan's crossing of the 'Mar del Zur' had already impressed cartographers, and Ribeiro represents the width of the Pacific, from Peru to the Moluccas ('Gilolo'), as 125 degrees of longitude. This is 25 degrees more than the width shown by Agnese in 1536 or Velasco in 1575 (Figs. 46, 110); but it is still 25 degrees short of the true width (150 degrees), and the underestimate was perhaps prompted by the political exigency which required the Moluccas to be laid down on the Spanish (or eastern) side of the demarcation line on the east.

123   In 1681 the English buccaneer Captain Bartholomew Sharp, cruising off the coast of Chile, took from a Spanish prize a manuscript copy of the standard *derrotero* (rutter, i.e. set of charts and sailing directions) used by Spanish pilots in

their navigation of the Pacific coasts of America. On Sharp's return to London King Charles II ordered the rutter to be transcribed and translated 'with all possible secrecy'; this was undertaken by William Hack, who set up at Wapping as a maker of charts and sea-atlases. The original Spanish manuscript, drawn at Panama in 1669, is now in the Huntington Library, California; Hack's transcript and translation, from which this plan of the port of Acapulco is reproduced, is in the British Museum (MS Harl. 4034); and the 'Wagoner of the Great South Sea', drawn by Hack and presented by Sharp to the King in 1682, is also in the British Museum (K. Mar. VIII. 15). Acapulco, in Mexico, was the American terminal of the Manila trade route, and Hack's chart marks the channel by which 'the ships from China' (i.e. the Manila galleons) entered the port.

124   The 'scheame' or crude sketch of Patagonia and the Magellan Strait, drawn by Francis Fletcher, Drake's chaplain on his voyage of circumnavigation, has been preserved in a copy of his journal made in 1680 by the apothecary John Conyers (British Museum, MS Sloane 61). After his passage of the Strait in August–September 1578, Drake was blown to the south by a storm with his one remaining ship, the *Golden Hind*, and took refuge in a group of islands 'bearing triangle-wise one from another'; the southernmost of these he named Elizabeth Island, and it has been suggested that it lay in the position of the shoal now called Burnham Bank. Fletcher's sketch ironically names the 'islands' to the south of the Strait 'Terra australis bene cognita', indicating scepticism concerning the identification of Tierra del Fuego with the Southern Continent. Patagonian giants are again recorded on a map (cf. Fig. 56).

125   The double-cordiform world map of 1538 by Mercator, from which the Southern Hemisphere is here reproduced, was derived from a similar map by Oronce Finé engraved in 1531 (Fig. 197). Finé's is perhaps the second map to depict the supposed continent surrounding the South Pole (the first being that of Franciscus Monachus, Fig. 45); and it was the earliest to use the name Terra Australis. In Mercator's map the Continent bears the modest legend: 'That land lies here is certain, but its size and extent are unknown.' Its coastline, the northernmost point of which reaches about 35° S in the Pacific, is shown as conjectural, with the exception of Tierra del Fuego, which appears as a headland of the Continent. A similar representation of Terra Australis, with detail added from Marco Polo, appeared in Mercator's world chart of 1569 (Fig. 8).

126   Jean Rotz was a native of Dieppe who, as hydrographer to King Henry VIII, dedicated to the King in 1542 a manuscript 'Boke of Idrography' (British Museum, Royal MS 20. E. IX). In this atlas, as in other charts by Dieppe cartographers (see Fig. 51), the outline of the north coast of Terra Australis ('the londe of Jaua') resembles the configuration of Australia and bears Portuguese names. This has been held to prove a Portuguese discovery of Australia by the Portuguese

before 1550. In the detail reproduced from Rotz's world chart, Sumatra is named 'Trapobana' (Ptolemy's name for Ceylon, transferred after the Portuguese reached Sumatra); and 'the lytil Jaua', to the south, represents Java, separated by a narrow strait from the Continent.

127   Later mapmakers delineated the outline and interior of the Continent with greater assurance, giving it wider extension and more detail. This map is in Cornelis Wytfliet's *Descriptionis Ptolemaicae augmentum* (Louvain, 1597), the first printed atlas devoted entirely to America. Wytfliet, following Mercator's world chart of 1569 (Fig. 8), lays down two promontories, separated by a gulf, to the south of New Guinea and 'Iaua maior'; to one of these are transferred kingdoms of south-east Asia recorded by Marco Polo. The Solomon Islands are drawn as outliers of Terra Australis.

128   The map of the Pacific published by Ortelius in 1587 represents the Solomon Islands, discovered by Mendaña in 1568, with approximate correctness in relation to New Guinea, but locates them some 40 degrees too far east.

129   The maps in the *Descripcion de las Indias occidentales* of Antonio de Herrera (Madrid, 1601) were based on those of Velasco (cf. Fig. 110). This map of the Pacific, like that of Ortelius, lays down the Solomons 40 degrees east of their true position, and the Moluccas 110 degrees (instead of 150) west of Peru.

130   This is a 19th-century copy, in the British Museum (Add. MS 17642. f.), from the original chart by Diego de Prado y Tovar in the Spanish archives at Simancas. It shows 'the great bay of St Philip and St James', with the 'Puerto de la Vera Cruz', in the island of Espiritu Santo, New Hebrides, discovered by Quiros. Here Quiros in May 1606 took possession 'of all the lands in sight, and of all this part of the south as far as the Pole'. Prado's chart reflects Quiros' belief that his land formed part of the continent which he sought.

131   This is the last chart in Hack's copy from the Spanish rutter of the South Sea brought back by Sharp in 1681 (British Museum, MS Harl. 4034; see Fig. 123). It displays, in a conventional pattern, the discoveries of Mendaña in 1595 and of Quiros in 1606. As in Prado's chart (Fig. 130), the Bay of St Philip and St James is drawn on the coast of a mountainous mainland.

132   The chart of south-east Asia in the sea-atlas *Suite du Neptune François* (Amsterdam, 1700) shows the south coast of New Guinea, as charted by Torres in 1606 and with the names given by him, side-by-side with the older Dutch representation of New Guinea ('Terra des Papous') connected by land with Australia (cf. Figs. 110, 138, 147).

133   This map by the French cartographer Robert de Vaugondy was published in the *Histoire des navigations aux terres australes* by C. de Brosses (Paris, 1756). Its delineation of New Guinea is based upon the chart of 1700 (Fig. 132), but the

discoveries of Torres are more successfully assimilated to the older representation. 'Nouvelle Guinée' has been moved some 20 degrees to the east and is in a recognizably modern form; all trace of a land connection with Australia has disappeared. Ignorance of the longitude of the New Hebrides, reached by Quiros in 1606 and supposed by him to be a part of a continent, has led the cartographer to locate Quiros' discoveries on the unknown east coast of Australia (inset), where we see his Australia del Espíritu Santo ('Terre du St Esprit'), New Jerusalem, Bay of St Philip and St James, and Port of Vera Cruz. This was one of the maps carried by Cook in the *Endeavour*, and he wrote in his journal in 1770: 'I all ways understood before I had a sight of these Maps that it was unknown whether or no New-Holland and New Guinea was not one continued land . . . but as I believe it was known before tho' not publikly I clame no other merit than the clearing up of a doubtfull point.'

134   Alexander Dalrymple's 'Chart of the South Pacifick Ocean', engraved in 1767, was also carried by Cook in the *Endeavour*. It shows Torres' track in 1606 along the south coast of New Guinea, based on a memorial addressed to the King of Spain in 1614, a copy of which had come into Dalrymple's hands. The chart was designed to support Dalrymple's hypothesis of a continent lying to the south of explorers' tracks, and he represents the 'Tierra del Esp° Santo' discovered by Quiros as part of a continental coast. The Solomon Islands are identified with New Britain (discovered by Dampier in 1700; see Fig. 148), but Guadalcanal is joined to the eastern point of New Guinea.

Notes

Chapter IX

[1] See Chapter III, and Figs. 38, 42.

[2] See Chapter II.   [3] See Chapter VII.

[4] This chart, engraved for the account of Anson's voyage published in 1748, marked the routes of the annual galleons, as established in the 16th century and regularly followed until the early 19th century.

[5] The westerly track of the galleons lay between 13° and 14° N. The representation of an island group ('Los Monges'), in about the latitude of Hawaii, by Ortelius (1570) and later cartographers also suggested that Hawaii was already known to the Spaniards; but 'Los Monges' were in fact the northern Ladrones, discovered in 1522 by the *Trinidad*, of Magellan's squadron, on her unsuccessful attempt to return to America by the northerly route. Cook was in fact the first European discoverer of the Hawaiian islands, in 1778 (see Chapter XI).

[6] See Chapter I.   [7] See Chapter XI.

[8] The comment from Drake's voyage is that of his chaplain Francis Fletcher (see 'Remarks', Fig. 124); that on Sharp's is from an account by an anonymous buccaneer (one William Dick) inserted in the second edition of *The Buccaneers of America*, by John Exquemelin (London, 1684).

[9] Sir Robert Dudley's *Dell'arcano del mare* (Florence, 1646) was the first sea-atlas by an Englishman.

[10] Quoted from *The Discovery of the Solomon Islands . . . in 1568*, ed. Lord Amherst and B. Thomson (Hakluyt Society, 1901).

[11] See Chapter XI, note 10.

[12] See Chapter XI, and Fig. 150.

[13] New Guinea, which may have been seen by Abreu in 1511 (see Chapter II), received the name of 'Os Papuas' from the Portuguese captain Jorge de Meneses who touched there in 1526, off route from Malacca to the Spice Islands. Charts of Portuguese origin (e.g. Fig. 92) show this name, while those of Spanish origin (e.g. Figs. 128, 129) call the island 'Nova Guinea', or variants. In the 18th century both names came to be used in a single chart (cf. Figs. 132, 133).   [14] See Chapter XI.   [15] See Chapter X.

X

THE DUTCH QUEST OF THE SOUTH-LAND

17th century

◇◇

IN THE PACIFIC OCEAN, wrote William Dampier in 1697, 'the Spaniards have more than they can well manage. I know yet, they would lie like the Dog in the Manger; although not able to eat themselves, yet they would hinder others.' This negative policy had been forced on Spain nearly a century earlier, less by the failure of her expeditions from Peru to find and colonize Terra Australis—the Southern Continent —than by the establishment of the Dutch in the Indian Ocean and Eastern Archipelago. For the exploration of the Mar del Zur[1] and for the oceanic voyages which it entailed, Dutch seamen were better equipped than the Spanish. The ports of south-east Asia and its islands, in which they had supplanted the Portuguese, furnished bases from which the South Sea could be entered by the west—the only course on which sailing ships could navigate in latitudes higher than 40° S. 'No European colony', observed the Council at Batavia in 1642,[2] '[is] better fitted for initiating these promising discoveries than the city of Batavia, which is as it were the centre of East India, both known and unknown.' Trained in the narrow waters of north-west Europe, the pilots of the Netherlands were not afraid of the inshore navigation necessary in charting a strange coast; they were skilled in the dead reckoning of the day and quickly became familiar with the wind-systems of the south-west Pacific. Their technical skill in navigation and hydrography and the elaborately organized chart service centred in Amsterdam ensured that the experience of the Dutch pilots was faithfully recorded and filed in cartographic form for use by successive expeditions sent out on discovery.[3] Unlike most of the Spanish voyages in the Pacific, which generated copious written records but few charts, the course of nearly every Dutch expedition was clearly and precisely laid down on charts, which indeed for a few voyages provide the only, or almost the only, documentary evidence.

In the fitting and manning of the ships employed on long cruises the Dutch had a further advantage over the Spanish. The complement of Spanish and English ships in the previous century had been relatively large, with a general ratio of not less than one man to two tons of burden. Thus Magellan's flagship the *Trinidad* (130 tons) had a crew of 62, and Drake's five ships in 1577, with a total tonnage of about 260, carried 164 men. Many of these were soldiers, 'gentlemen', colonists, or others not responsible for working the ship; of the 150 persons in Mendaña's two ships which made the Solomon Islands voyage in 1567-8, one-half were soldiers. The Dutch and English were interested in discovery as a means to trade rather than colonization; their ships were cargo-carriers, manned by smaller crews of seamen only. The complements of the vessels in which they made the eastern navigation and explored the South Pacific in the 17th century averaged about one man to three

FIG. 135.—A Dutch fleet westward bound in the Pacific, from the 'Great Chart of the South Sea' drawn by Gerritsz in 1622.

tons or more of burden, and by the end of the century this proportion had fallen even lower, as the ratio of one to four in Dampier's *Roebuck* (1699–1701) shows.

The earliest Dutch fleets to enter the Pacific followed Magellan's track (Fig. 135);[4] but the factories in Java and the Moluccas founded by the Dutch East India Company after its incorporation in 1602 gave its officers easier access to the southern Pacific and to the 'Great South-land' generally believed to fringe it.[5] Between 1606 and 1628 landfalls were made on the northern, western, and southern coasts of Australia by Dutch vessels either sailing with instructions for exploration or (more commonly) running on recognized shipping routes. These discoveries of chance or design were recorded on the charts drawn by the pilots or compiled at Amsterdam

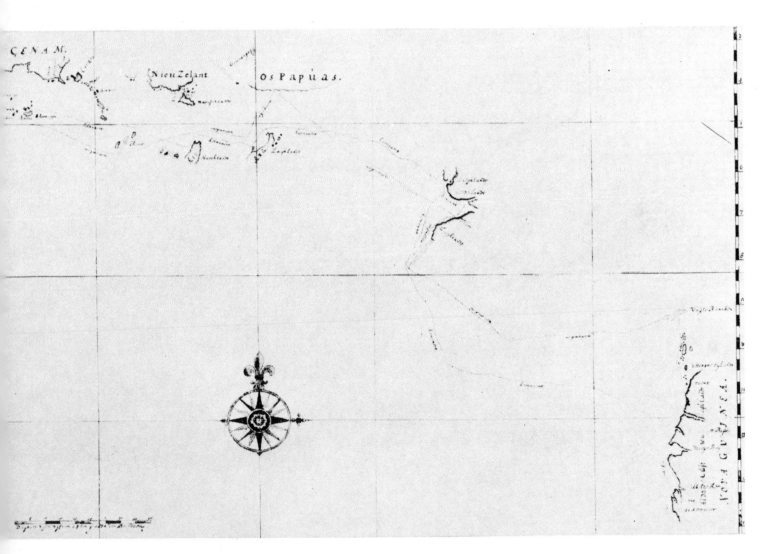

FIG. 136.—The *Duyfken*'s chart, showing her track from Banda in 1606 and the first discovery of Australia ('Nova Guinea').

by the Company's hydrographers—Peter Plancius from 1602 to 1619, Hessel Gerritsz from 1619 to 1632, and from 1633 W. J. Blaeu and his son.

Whether Torres had sighted the Australian coast on the passage through his strait in June 1606 is doubtful.[6] Three months earlier Willem Janszoon in the pinnace *Duyfken*, dispatched from Bantam in November 1605 'for the discovery of the land called Nova Guinea', had sailed south across the western entrance of Torres Strait, which he took to be a deep bay although his chart shows open water, and down the west coast of Cape York Peninsula to Cape Keerweer ('turn back') in 13° 40′ S (Fig. 136). Captain John Saris, at Bantam in June 1606, picked up a report that 'the Flemmings Pinasse, which went upon discovery for Nova Ginny, was returned to Banda, having found the Iland'.[7]

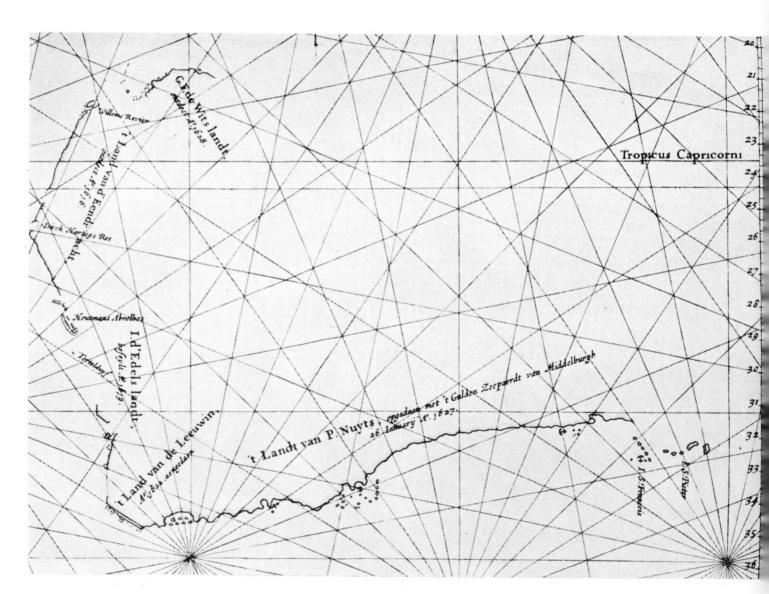

FIG. 137.—The Australian coasts, in a chart of Hessel Gerritsz, engraved in 1618 and revised to 1627.

The discovery of the west coast of Australia which followed was more fortuitous. The earlier Dutch fleets in passage from the Cape of Good Hope to Java had sailed with the monsoon by way of the African coast and India; but from 1611 Dutch captains were laying an easterly course, with the steady west winds, from the Cape to the longitude of Java before turning north. On this new and faster route the uncertainty with which the easting could be determined by dead reckoning led inevitably to unforeseen landfalls on the Australian coast. The instructions given to Tasman in 1644 noted that 'in the years 1616, 1618, 1619 and 1622, the west coast of the great unknown South-land from 35° to 22° was unexpectedly and accidentally discovered by the ships *d'Eendracht, Mauritius, Amsterdam, Dordrecht,* and *Leeuwin,* coming from the Netherlands'.

In 1616 the ship *Eendracht,* commanded by Dirk Hartog, came upon land between 22° and 28° S. Practically the only contemporary records of this first landfall on the west coast are the charts of Hessel Gerritsz (Fig. 137), which show the 'Land van d'Eendracht discovered in 1616', 'Dirck Hartogs Ree [road]', and to the north 'Willems Revier' visited by the ship *Mauritius* in 1618. In the following year Frederik Houtman, commanding the *Amsterdam* and *Dordrecht,* 'suddenly came upon the South-land of Beach in 32° 20″, naming it D'Edelsland after his super-cargo; coasting north by west he came upon the dangerous shoal subsequently known as Houtman's Abrolhos (i.e. 'Keep your eyes open'), and in 27° he identified Hartog's Eendrachtsland. The chart by Gerritsz (Fig. 137), engraved in 1618 and revised after 1627, displays these and other chance landfalls on the west and north-west coasts, and provides almost the sole record of the striking Dutch discoveries along the south coast. In 1622 the ship *Leeuwin* found land running south-east to 35°, and five years later the *Gulden Zeepaerdt* followed this shore, to which the name Pieter Nuyts Land was given, eastward to the Isles of St Francis and St Peter.

The difficulty of fixing a ship's position on the easterly run from the Cape, especially when plotted on the plane charts generally used by seamen, was remarked by the Company's Governor-General Jan Pieterszoon Coen, who was himself nearly cast ashore in 1627. 'In $28\frac{1}{2}$ S we came upon the land of d'Eendracht. In the plane chart the reckonings of our steersman were still between 300 and 350 miles from any land . . . although the reckoning of the chart with increasing degrees [the Mercator chart] showed only 120 miles, and the reckoning by the terrestrial globe only 50 miles distance from the land.' Coen drew the conclusion that in reckoning distance sailed 'in the plane charts most in use' allowance should be made for the decreasing value of a degree of longitude in higher latitudes and that 'the true bearing and configuration of the said land' must be ascertained. Already in 1623, after the wreck of an English ship in 20° 10′ S, two ships, the *Pera* and *Arnhem,* had been sent from

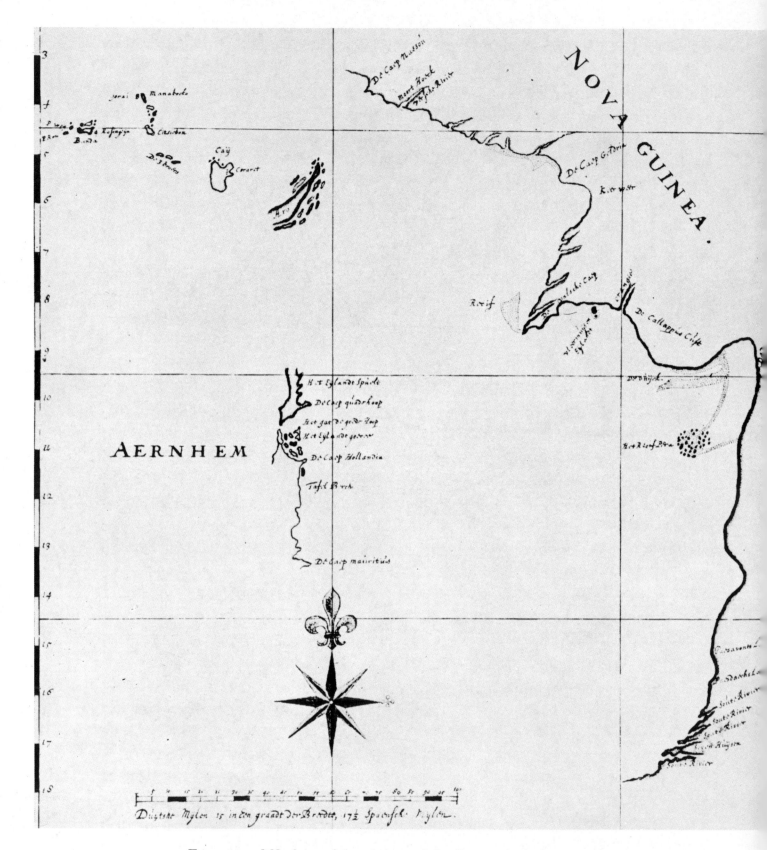

FIG. 138.—MS chart of the voyage of the *Pera* and *Arnhem* in 1623.

Amboina under Jan Carstensz to continue the *Duyfken's* examination of 'Nova Guinea', that is the west coast of the Cape York Peninsula, as far (if need be) as 50° S, thus determining its relation to Leeuwin Land. Caught among the reefs at the western end of Torres Strait, which they charted as a shallow bay ('Drooge Bocht'), they sailed south on the *Duyfken's* course beyond Cape Keerweer to about 17° S. From here the *Pera* returned along the same track, but the *Arnhem* sailed north-west to discover 'islands' which were named Speultland—perhaps Groote Eylandt—and Arnhems Land (Fig. 138).

Meanwhile, in competition with the Company, an expedition from Hoorn in Holland, led by Jacob Le Maire (as 'president') and Willem Schouten (as senior captain), had entered the Pacific from the east in search of 'new lands and islands towards the south'—the Southern Continent heralded by Quiros. Avoiding the routes by the Indian Ocean and by Magellan Strait reserved to the privileged Company, they sought and found 'a new passage' through the Strait of Le Maire and round Cape Horn into the South Sea (Fig. 139, inset). The land on their left as they traversed the strait was taken to be a part of Terra Australis and named Staten Land. Sailing north to catch the trades, they passed through the Tuamotu Archipelago and reached the Hoorn Islands, north-west of Fiji (Figs. 139, 140). Le Maire, who took these to be part of the Solomon Islands or of the New Hebrides discovered by Quiros (Fig. 140), proposed to sail west for the continent, but was overruled by Schouten's more cautious advice to run north 'in order not to drop too far below New Guinea'. A north-west course took them north of the Solomons to New Ireland, and they made their way along the north coast of New Guinea to the Moluccas and Batavia (Fig. 139, inset).

By 1627 the Dutch could piece together their Australian landfalls to make the almost continuous coastline shown in the chart by Gerritsz (Fig. 137) from De Wits Land to Pieter Nuyts Land and the Isles of St Francis and St Peter. The identity or connection of this 'known South-land' with the 'unknown South-land' —*Terra Australis incognita*—of the 16th-century cartographers remained obscure. Failure to penetrate Torres Strait from its western end, and indeed to recognize that the strait existed, sustained the belief that north-east Australia was a southward extension of New Guinea (Figs. 141, 146-7). Whether 'Nova Guinea', thus enlarged, had a land connection with the known South-land or was divided from it by a strait was the subject of speculation. Some maps, such as that published by Hondius in 1630 (Fig. 141), still laid down 'Beach'—the imaginary gold-bearing province of Terra Australis shown in 16th-century maps[8]—in juxtaposition with the coasts painfully observed and plotted by Dutch seamen since 1606. Such an association of

E.M.—P

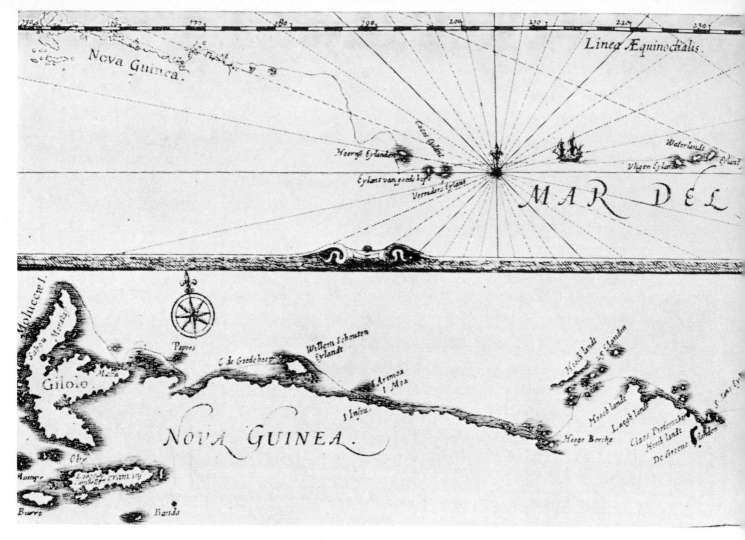

FIG. 139.—The track of Schouten and Le Maire across the Pacific in 1616. The two insets below show the

fact and fancy, not yet dispelled by the discouraging reports of pilots who had visited the Australian coasts, continued to nourish the Company's confidence that the South-land embraced 'rich countries or regions . . . profitable to the Company'. Exploration was expected not only to yield prospects of gold or of trade with the South-land but also 'to prepare the way for afterwards finding a short route to Chile' within the latitudes of the brave west winds. Two possible routes into the zone of westerlies called for investigation. If open sea lay to the south of Leeuwin Land and Nuyts Land (i.e. of the 'known South-land'), the Pacific might be entered from the Indian Ocean; but a much shorter passage from Batavia would be offered by a strait, if it existed, between 'Nova Guinea'—the Cape York Peninsula—and Eendrachtsland, the known westerly portion of the South-land. To answer these questions was the purpose of the two voyages made in 1642–3 and 1644 by Abel Janszoon Tasman for the Governor-General Anthony van Diemen.

Tasman's instructions were drawn up from plans submitted by Frans Jacobszoon Visscher, who accompanied him as chief pilot. They charged him to sail south from

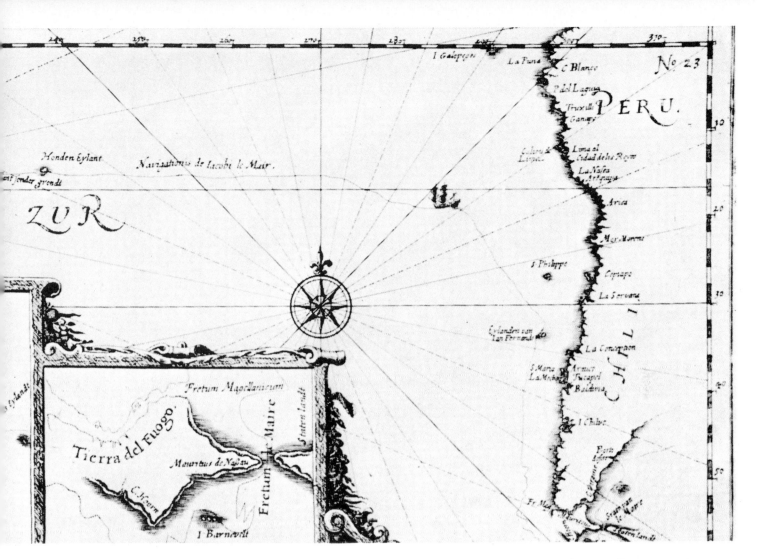

...ssage of Le Maire Strait and Cape Horn (*right*) and their course along the north coast of New Guinea (*left*).

Mauritius 'until you get into the western trade wind, with which you will sail nearly south ward until you come upon the unknown South-land or as far as 52° or 54° S'; thence eastward to the longitude of New Guinea 'or of the Salomonis Islands situated in about 220 degrees longitude, or until you should meet with land':[9] Tasman was offered the alternative of sailing north to Nuyts Land and following its coast eastward to ascertain 'whether this discovered South-land joins Nova Guinea near Cape Keerweer, or whether it is separated from the same by channels or passages'. If he took the first course, he was to sail with the south-east trades to the Solomon Islands and thence to New Guinea. Rounding its west point, he was to run south to Cape Keerweer and follow the coast west to Willems River. The Governor-General and Council expected that his voyage would be 'rewarded with certain fruits of material profit and immortal fame'.

Tasman sailed from Mauritius in October 1642 with two ships, the *Heemskerck* and *Zeehaen* (Fig. 145). In 49° S he was forced by rough weather to bear up east, and in November he discovered 'the first land we had met with in the South Sea'.

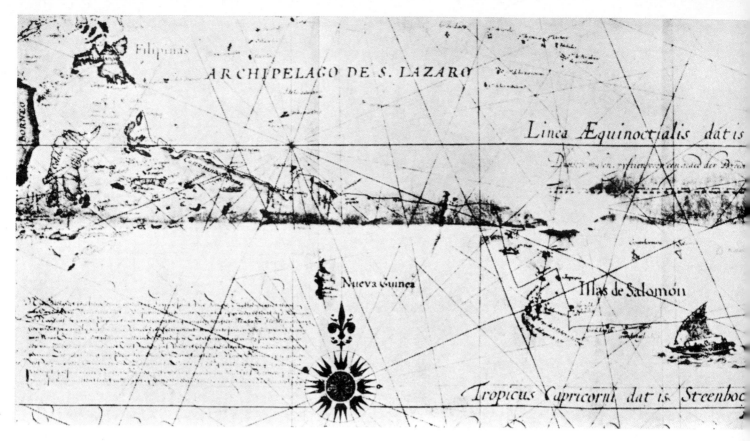

FIG. 140.—Part of Gerritsz' 'Chart of the Great South Sea' drawn in 1622 and carried by Tasman.

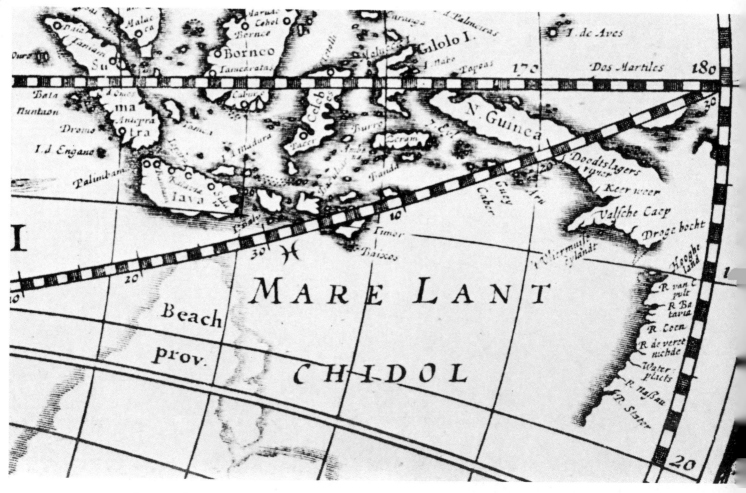

FIG. 141.—Part of a world map by Hondius, published in 1630.

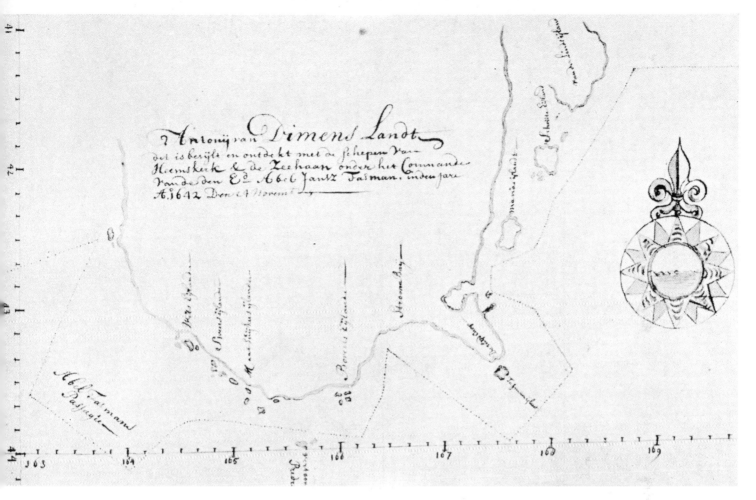

FIG. 142.—Tasman's chart of his track along the coasts of Tasmania, November–December 1642.

This was the coast of Tasmania, which he called Anthony van Diemens Landt (Fig. 142). Sailing east, he made his second discovery of land early in December, that of the west coast of New Zealand (Fig. 143), named 'Staten Landt, since we deemed it quite possible that this land is part of the great Staten Landt [discovered by Le Maire and Schouten], though this is not certain. . . . We trust that this is the mainland coast of the unknown South-land.' After losing four men in an attack by the Maoris (Fig. 144), Tasman sailed into the entrance of Cook Strait, coasted the North Island to Cape Maria van Diemen, and, satisfied that open sea lay between him and Chile, set his course north-east. Tasman thus missed two opportunities of resolving his doubt whether New Zealand were part of the South-land: he did not sail east through Cook Strait, although he suspected its existence and a chart drawn by Visscher marked an opening, and he did not turn south from Cape Maria van Diemen, a course which would have demonstrated that his Staten Land was insular.

217

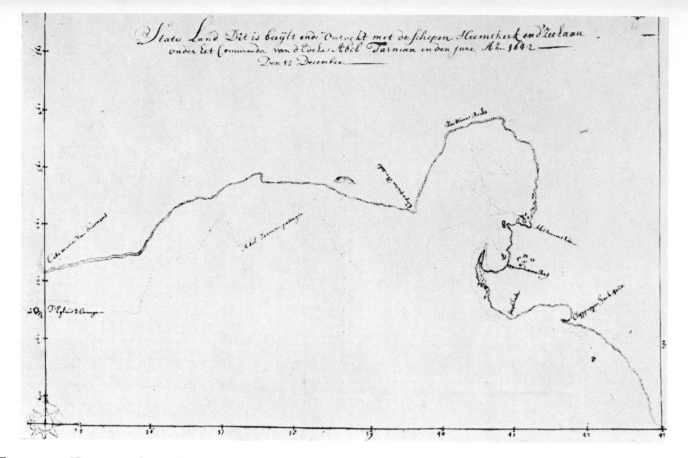

FIG. 143.—Tasman's chart of the west coast of New Zealand, with the opening of Cook Strait, December 1642.

FIG. 144.—Tasman's ships with Maori canoes in 'Murderers Bay', New Zealand, December 1642.

Tasman's north-east course was set, as he supposed, for the Hoorn Islands. He had on board the journal and charts of Le Maire and Schouten and the 'Great Chart of the South Sea', drawn by Hessel Gerritsz in 1622, on which their track was laid down (Figs. 139, 140). The difficulty in relating his own longitude to that of the islands on his charts prevented him from picking up the discoveries of Le Maire and Schouten. Instead, he sailed through the Tonga Group (Fig. 145) and, turning west, nearly came to disaster among the coral reefs of Fiji, which he named Prins Willem's Islands. In spite of Tasman's own doubts, these were surmised 'to form part of the Insulis Salomonis'. The 'Islas de Salomon' marked on Gerritsz' chart just west of the Hoorn Islands were in fact Quiros' New Hebrides, but the true Solomon Islands discovered by Mendaña in 1568 were believed to lie close under the lee of New Guinea. Like Schouten in 1616, Tasman accordingly decided to steer north and then west and to return in the track of Le Maire and Schouten by the north coasts of New Ireland and New Guinea. He

FIG. 145.—Tasman's ships lying at anchor off the island of Amsterdam (Tongatabu), January 1643.

reached Batavia in June 1643, leaving the last part of his orders unexecuted.

Tasman's 'circular tour' of the South-land known to the Dutch, and hereafter called New Holland ('Nova Hollandia'), had lopped the whole of it from Terra Australis, whose conjectural coasts he had pushed far to the south and east (Fig. 147). His second expedition, in 1644, was designed to investigate two possible short passages from Batavia into the South Sea, which would open up the route to Chile by the north of New Zealand: the 'shallow bay' (Torres Strait) charted by Carstensz in 1623, and the coast of 'Nova Guinea' (the Cape York Peninsula) beyond Carstensz' farthest south in 17°. If neither strait existed, he was to follow the coast of the South-land to the west and south as far as Houtman's Abrolhos. Tasman's

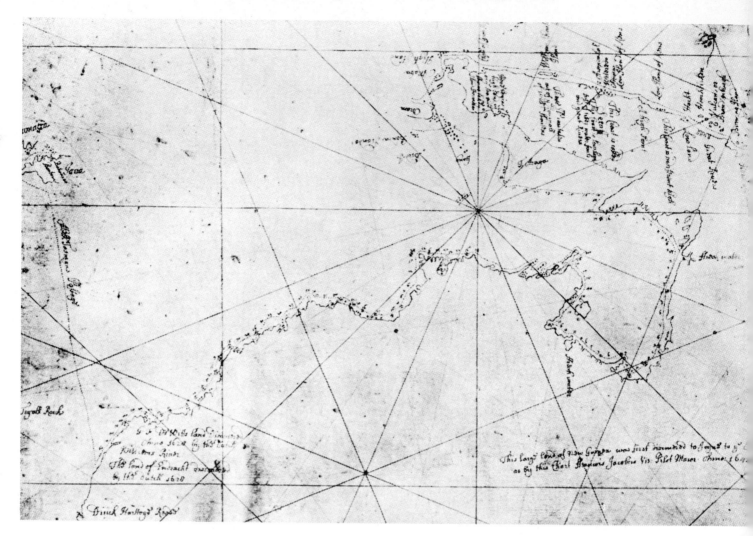

FIG. 146.—The course of Tasman's voyage in 1644, in a copy of a MS chart by Visscher.

journal has not survived, but his track is drawn on two charts derived from those of the voyage (Fig. 146). The chart and the Governor-General's reports show that he 'found no open channel between the half-known Nova Guinea and the known land of D'Eendracht or Willem's River; they found however a large spacious Bay or Gulf'—the Gulf of Carpentaria. The coast was traced continuously westward from Arnhem Land and the Van Diemen's Land of the north (so named in 1636) and south to Willem's River. Thus (wrote the Governor-General) 'this vast and hitherto unknown South-land has, by the said Tasman, been sailed round in two voyages'. This was no small achievement, but the poverty of the country and of its 'naked beach-roving' inhabitants convinced the Company that it offered no prospect of 'material profit' by trade, and further exploration was discouraged. To the geography of New Holland and its adjacent waters, as established by Tasman

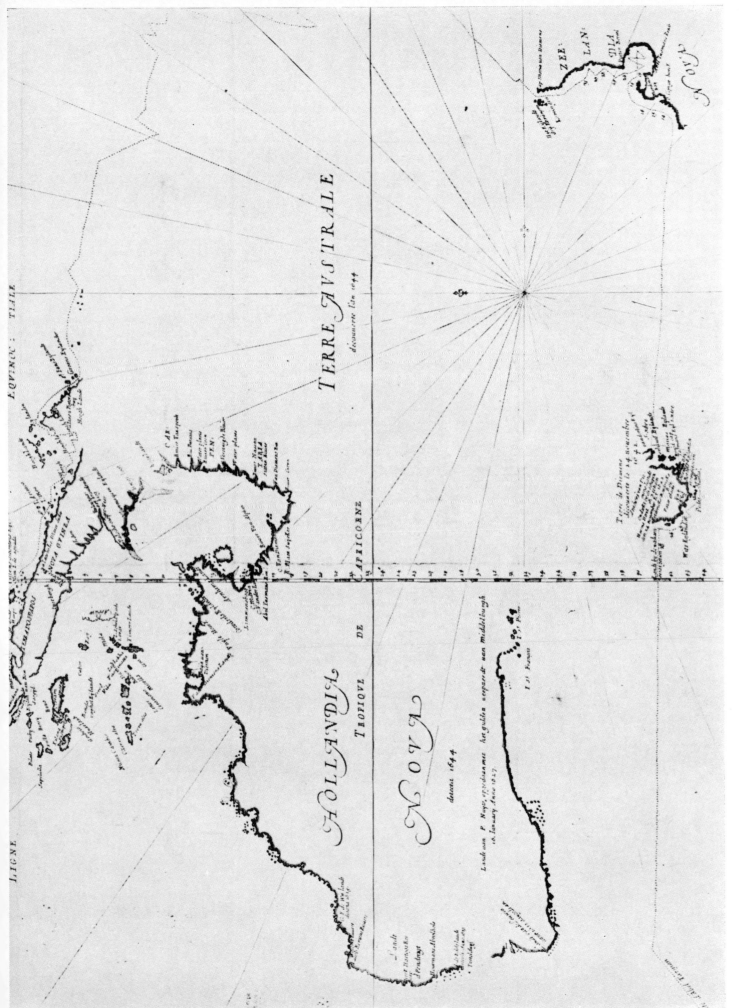

FIG. 147.—Map of the South-land by M. Thévenot, published in 1663.

and displayed in Thévenot's map (Fig. 147), few and minor additions were made until the voyages of Carteret, Bougainville and Cook, a century and a quarter later.[10]

The belief that New Holland was dissected by a strait or passage from north to south was not destroyed by Tasman's voyage of 1644. William Dampier, an Englishman of inextinguishable curiosity,[11] had in his *New Voyage round the World*, published in 1697, pointed to the need for further exploration of New Holland. In 1699, commanding H.M.S. *Roebuck*, he sailed with the intention of circumnavigating New Holland and exploring the islands to the north. Crossing the Indian Ocean, he reached the coast of Eendrachtsland and sailed north by Sharks Bay (so named by him) and along the islands fringing the north-west coast. The strength of the tides

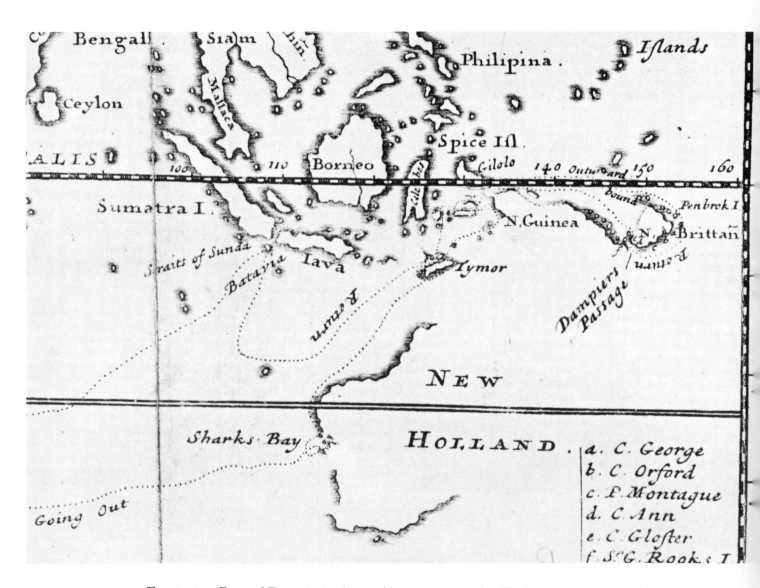

FIG. 148.—Part of Dampier's chart of his voyage in the *Roebuck* in 1699–1700

gave him 'a strong Suspicion that here might be a kind of Archipelago of Islands, and a Passage possibly to the S. of N. Holland and N. Guinea into the great S. Sea Eastward'. He was 'afterwards confirmed in the Opinion, when by coasting New Guinea, I found that other parts of this great Tract of Terra Australis, which had hitherto been represented as the Shore of a Continent, were certainly Islands; and 'tis probably the same New Holland'. This refers to Dampier's discovery, later in his voyage, of the passage separating New Guinea and New Britain, hitherto supposed to be one land (Fig. 148). In 1705 a Dutch expedition re-examined Van Diemen's Land (west of Arnhems Land) and, failing to penetrate Van Diemen's Gulf, to the .south of Bathurst and Melville Islands, concluded 'that this inlet runs right through to the south side of New Holland'. From this they drew, like Dampier, the inference 'that the South-land in a great measure consists of islands'; and Swift could locate his Lilliput, with open sea to the east, where the modern maps show the interior of South Australia. Nearly a century was to pass before Matthew Flinders, charting the Australian coasts, dispelled this geographical fantasy.[12]

Remarks on the Illustrations

Chapter X

❖❖

135   This drawing, in the chart by Gerritsz in the Bibliothèque Nationale (see Fig. 140), showing Dutch ships under shortened sail, may represent the squadron commanded by Joris van Spilbergen which crossed the Pacific from the Straits of Magellan in 1615–16.

136   The manuscript chart of the *Duyfken*'s voyage in 1606 is in the so-called 'Atlas of Prince Eugene' (vol. XLI, no. 31), in the Nationalbibliothek, Vienna. Her track is drawn from Banda to landfalls on the south and south-east coasts of New Guinea ('Os Papuas'), and thence on a SE and easterly course to the reefs at the entrance of Torres Strait ('Vuyle Bancken', i.e. horrid reefs). She then sailed south along the west coast of Cape York Peninsula before turning back at Cape Keerweer.

137   The chart by Hessel Gerritsz, engraved in 1618 and revised to 1627, names and dates the Dutch landfalls on the west and south coasts of Australia to the latter year. This chart is the principal authority for the discovery of the south coast: 'the land of P. Nuyts, come upon by the *Gulden Zeepaerdt* of Middelburgh, 1627'.

138   This manuscript chart, in the Rijksarchief at The Hague, shows the coasts discovered on the voyage of the *Pera* and *Arnhem* in 1623, under Jan Carstensz. From False Cape ('De Valsche Caep') they ran along the south coast of New Guinea and were caught in the reefs 'as in a trap' at the western end of Torres Strait, to which, although shown as open water in the *Duyfken*'s chart (Fig. 136), 'we gave the name Drooge Bocht (shallow bay) in the new chart'. The land to the south— Cape York Peninsula—was therefore laid down and named in Carstensz' and later charts as part of New Guinea. The discoveries of the *Arnhem* after her separation from the *Pera* are also shown.

139   The track chart of the east–west voyage across the Pacific by Schouten and Le Maire in 1615–16 was published in Schouten's *Iournal ofte beschrijvinghe* (Amsterdam, 1618). The inset on the right shows the first passage of the Strait of Le Maire

and round Cape Horn; that on the left the course along the north coast of New Guinea to the Moluccas.

140   The 'Great Chart of the South Sea', drawn in 1622 by Gerritsz, as hydrographer of the Dutch East India Company, attempted to reconcile the discoveries of Quiros and the Dutch in the south-west Pacific. The track of Schouten and Le Maire is drawn, and a legend identifies 'the north coasts of the Papuas navigated by Le Maire', the south-west coasts of New Guinea, and the Australian coast discovered by the *Duyfken* (called on the chart 'Nueva Guinea') as one and the same land. The suggestion of a strait, i.e. Torres Strait, shown 'in the Spanish maps' to the south of New Guinea is explicitly rejected by Gerritsz. The 'Islas de Salomon' on his chart comprehend the Hoorn Islands of Schouten and Le Maire and Quiros' discoveries in the New Hebrides. Gerritsz gives no indication of Terra Australis. This chart was carried by Tasman in 1642–3, and accounts for the course of his voyage after leaving the coast of New Zealand.

141   The world map published by Henricus Hondius in 1630 delineates the Dutch discoveries southward from New Guinea in 1606 and 1623; but in place of those along the west coast of Australia appears only the conventional 16th-century delineation of Terra Australis under the old name of Beach (cf. Figs. 8, 127).

142   This and the three following illustrations (143–5) are reproduced from an 18th-century copy of Tasman's journal in the British Museum (Add. MS 8946). The original journal, containing his charts and views, is in the Rijksarchief, The Hague. After his first sight of land on the west coast of Tasmania in November 1642, Tasman was blown off by unfavourable winds. After rounding Cape Pillar (the south-east point of Tasmania) he anchored off the bay now called Blackman's Bay, and when he left he was compelled by north-west winds to turn east, i.e. in the direction in which he supposed the Solomons to lie.

143   Tasman's chart of the west coast of New Zealand, from Cape Foulwind to Cape Maria van Diemen, marks his tracks along the coast and into the mouth of Cook Strait, December 1642–January 1643. (East is at the top.) After making his landfall on the South Island, Tasman rounded Cape Farewell and anchored in 'Murderers Bay' (Golden Bay). His chart shows Cook Strait as a 'bight' closed by land; but the corresponding chart by the pilot Visscher admits the possibility of a lead to the east (into the South Sea) by drawing the head of the 'bight' in dotted line.

144   Tasman's ships, the yacht *Heemskerck* and the flute *Zeehaen*, are represented at anchor in Murderers Bay, with Maori canoes; a double canoe in the foreground. Here the Maoris killed a boatload of Tasman's men.

145   In January 1643 Tasman watered at the island of Amsterdam (Tongatabu), where the *Heemskerck* (left) and *Zeehaen* are seen lying off the watering place.

146   The principal evidence for the course of Tasman's voyage of 1644 is contained in two manuscript charts: one ascribed to Tasman (now in the Mitchell Library, Sydney), the other copied, probably by Thomas Bowrey at Madras in 1687, from a lost chart by Visscher (British Museum, Add. MS 5222.12). The reproduction from Bowrey's (?) copy of Visscher's chart draws the tracks of Tasman's ships —the *Limmen*, *Zeemeeuw*, and *Bracq*—along the south coast of New Guinea and southward across the entrance of Torres Strait, marked by the words 'Shoal water' and a dotted line, which represents a hazardous coast (not a doubtful passage). The track, with numerous soundings, indicates Tasman's vain search for a sea lead to the southward as he coasted the Gulf of Carpentaria, Arnhem Land and the north coast of Australia as far as Eendrachtsland before turning north to Batavia. In the bottom right-hand corner is Visscher's conclusion on the geography of the Southland (translated into English): 'This large land of New Guinea [i.e. the Cape York Peninsula] was first discovered to joyne to yᵉ Southland [i.e. the western coasts of Australia] by yᵉ Yot Lemmen as by this Chart François Jacobus Vis: Pilot Maior Anno 1643 [a mistake for 1644]'.

147   The results of Tasman's discoveries were first published in a world map by Blaeu in 1648. The finely engraved map in M. Thévenot's *Relation de divers voyages curieux* (Paris, 1663) gave general currency to the Dutch discoveries on the coasts of New Holland and in the south-west Pacific. It shows the earlier Dutch landfalls from the Isles of St Francis and St Paul, on the south coast, to Eendrachtsland; and the coasts of northern Australia and the Gulf of Carpentaria are laid down from Tasman's voyage of 1644 (cf. Fig. 146). Torres Strait is left open, with the legend 'Droge bogt'. Tasman's track in 1642–3 is marked.

148   Dampier's chart was published in his second book, *A Voyage to New Holland* (1703). His doubts about the continental character of New Holland sprang in part, by analogy, from his discovery that New Britain was not (as generally believed) part of New Guinea but a separate island. His intention to circumnavigate New Holland was frustrated by the 'rottenness' of the *Roebuck*, and he returned by Timor to Batavia.

Notes

Chapter X

[1] The Spanish name for the South Sea or Pacific (see Chapter III, note 15) continued to appear on Dutch charts throughout the 17th century.

[2] In their instructions to Tasman.

[3] See Chapter VII.

[4] In 1598, when two Dutch fleets passed the Cape of Good Hope for the Moluccas (see Chapter VII), two other squadrons, under Jacob Mahu and Olivier van Noort, sailed from Holland and passed Magellan Strait into the Pacific. William Adams sailed with Mahu (see Chapter VIII).

[5] See Chapters VII and IX.

[6] The track followed by Torres through the strait is not precisely known.

[7] For Saris, see Chapter VIII.

[8] See Chapters I and IX, and Figs. 8, 125–7.

[9] The longitude was reckoned by the Dutch eastward from the meridian of Teneriffe.

[10] See Chapter XI.

[11] 'The farther we went [wrote Dampier], the more Knowledge and Experience I should get, which was the main Thing that I regarded.'

[12] See Chapter XI.

XI

JAMES COOK
AND THE MAPPING OF THE PACIFIC

18th century

◇◇

THE LAST DUTCH VOYAGE of exploration across the Pacific, that of Jacob Roggeveen who sailed in 1721 under the flag of the Dutch West India Company (and therefore by Cape Horn), had no more success than its predecessors in running down the illusory continent which Quiros thought he had found in 1606. Roggeveen followed the wake of earlier navigators, and his only important discoveries were Easter Island and part of the Samoa group. Meanwhile other European peoples with oceanic ambitions were turning their eyes to the South Sea and its geographical problems and to the opportunity for commercial expansion offered by this 'unknown area in which may be situated a continent greater than any of the other four'.[1]

Dampier's *New Voyage round the World*—a best-seller from its publication in 1697—had kindled his countrymen's interest in the Pacific; but English and French 'projecting' activity was slow in bearing fruit, and the South Sea promoters in 1711 were able to 'float a company without floating a ship'. Nor had the strategy of Pacific exploration, dictated by the steady wind systems, yet been learnt. A century and a quarter after Tasman's voyage of 1642–3, no other European ship had entered the South Pacific from the west; and, south of the Tropic of Capricorn, the map showed a vast empty space stretching from Tasman's west coast of New Zealand almost to Patagonia. Cartographers have always abhorred a vacuum, and they regarded this 'perfect and absolute blank' with less favour than the Bellman's crew accorded his chart.[2] Along its fringes they laid down the lands and islands sighted, in fact or imagination, by the explorers of two centuries—Staten Land, Juan Fernandez,

228

'Davis Land', Easter Island, atolls of the Tuamotu Archipelago, the Tonga group, the west coast of New Zealand. These could be interpreted as sections of the coastline, or as outliers, of the Southern Continent whose existence was 'wanting on the South of Equator to counterpoize the land on the North, and to maintain the equilibrium necessary for the earth's motion' (Fig. 149).[3]

The author of these words, Alexander Dalrymple, writing in 1767,[4] summed up the arguments which, in the eyes of academic geographers, pointed to Terra Australis. To the theory of equipoise he added an argument from islands (those discovered in the South Sea were 'derived from, or have an intercourse with, a Continent to the South')[5] and an argument from wind-systems; he believed the seasonal westerly winds found by explorers in the tropical belt of the Pacific to be monsoon winds (like those of south-east Asia), denoting the proximity of 'extensive chains of land'. To these general—and fallacious—arguments Dalrymple added the supposed indications of land noted on the fringes of an area outlined by the tracks of Quiros (1605), Schouten and Le Maire (1616), and Tasman (1643).[6] In 26° S for instance Quiros had in 1606 seen 'to the Southward very large hanging clouds and a very thick horizon, with other known signs of a Continent'; and in 1616, in 20° S, Schouten and Le Maire 'perceived they approached the land by some branches of trees floating in the Sea'.

The theoretical arguments of the 'continent mongers' encouraged projects for the commercial and political exploitation of the South Sea. The possibility of extensive inhabited lands, lying in temperate latitudes and unknown to Europeans, could not be ignored by the rival mercantile powers of England and France. The British 'siege' of Spain's *mare clausum* in the Pacific opened with authorized raids on the Spanish trade routes and ports, culminating in the spectacular voyage of Anson in 1740–4.[7] It was more systematically developed, in the second half of the century, by projects for establishing trading stations in the East Indies, by political manœuvring for the naval bases necessary to the exploration of the Pacific from the east, and by a series of expeditions which eventually traversed the ocean throughout its longitudinal width and from the Antarctic to the Arctic Circle.

The first voyage promoted by the British Admiralty after the close of the Seven Years' War in 1763 had similar objectives to those of Drake in the *Golden Hind* in 1577.[8] The Lords Commissioners had 'reasons to believe that Lands and Islands of great extent hitherto unvisited by any European Power may be found in the Atlantick Ocean between the Cape of Good Hope and the Magellanick Strait, within Latitudes convenient for Navigation, and in climates adapted to the produce of Commodities usefull in Commerce', and 'that a Passage might be found between the

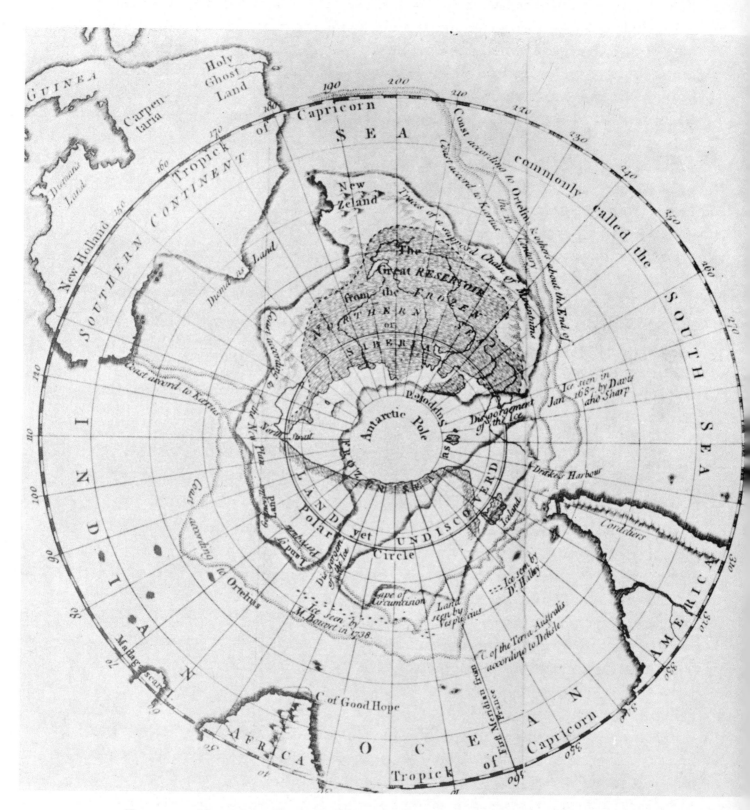

FIG. 149.—Map of the Southern Hemisphere, south of the Tropic, published in 1763.

Latitude of 38° and 54° [N] from that coast [Drake's New Albion, or California] into Hudson's Bay'. Commodore Byron, sailing in 1764 in the frigate *Dolphin*, was accordingly to discover Terra Australis, by a cruise between the Falkland Islands and the Cape of Good Hope, and the North-West Passage by its Pacific entrance. Byron passed the Magellan Strait and, showing little respect for his orders and an unlucky aptitude for missing islands, crossed the Pacific to the Ladrones by a course, north of the Tropic, which added little to knowledge. In 1767–8 the *Dolphin* made her second circumnavigation, this time under Captain Samuel Wallis, who sailed in company with the *Swallow*, Captain Philip Carteret. Wallis's instructions confined him to the search for Terra Australis 'in the South Hemisphere between Cape Horn and New Zeeland'; after entering the Pacific by the Magellan Strait or Cape Horn, he was to 'stretch to the Westward about One Hundred or One

FIG. 150.—The *Dolphin*, Captain Samuel Wallis, lying in Matavai Bay, Tahiti, 1767; a sketch by George Pinnock.

Hundred and Twenty degrees of Longitude from Cape Horn, losing as little South-ing as possible'. The two ships parted company on debouching from the Strait. Wallis's orders had taken little account of the 'brave west winds', and his only considerable discovery—a significant one—was that of Tahiti (Fig. 150). Carteret, in an ill-found ship, made a spirited voyage, in the course of which he crossed the South Pacific in a higher latitude than any earlier navigator, reached the Solomon Islands (for the first time since their discovery by Mendaña exactly 200 years before), and found the strait—overlooked by Dampier—between New Britain and New Ireland.[9] A French expedition under Louis Antoine de Bougainville, crossing the Pacific in 1768, penetrated into the unexplored triangle between the New Hebrides, the Australian coast, and the Solomons (Fig. 151). After touching at Tahiti and Samoa, Bougainville sailed resolutely westward (rejecting the safer north-westerly course of all previous voyages) to the New Hebrides and onward till he found the breakers of the Great Barrier Reef under his bows. Thus narrowly failing to discover

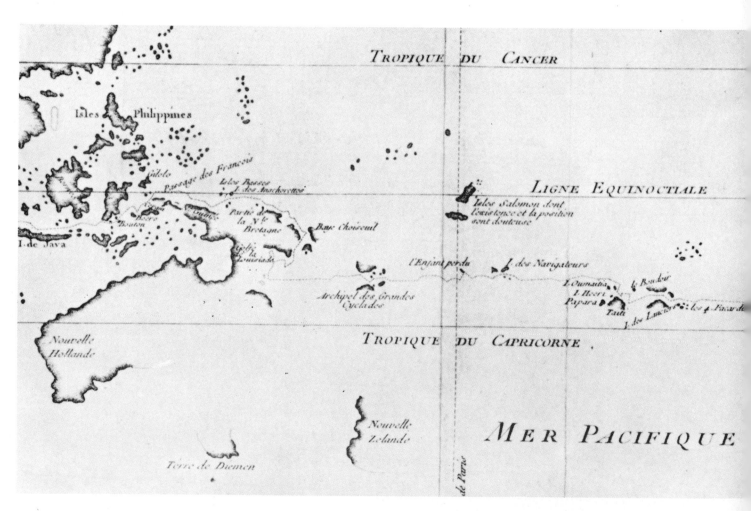

FIG. 151.—Bougainville's track in the south-west Pacific in 1768.

the east coast of Australia, he hauled off north and passed through the Solomons, which he (like Carteret) did not identify, on his way to Batavia.[10]

Both Carteret and Bougainville had sailed over ocean where contemporary maps laid down the solid land of a continent; but there was still ample room for a great land-mass extending along the south of the Atlantic and Indian Oceans and (in the South Sea) almost as far north as the Tropic (Fig. 149). The main question remained unanswered, and the Admiralty's choice of the commander who was to answer it, and of his ship, was unusual but illuminating. In place of the senior naval officers who had led the earlier British expeditions, they pitched upon a warrant officer whose only previous command had been a 60-ton brig employed on coastal survey —but who was already the most accomplished surveyor of his day in the British naval service. James Cook, master R.N., reputed 'a good mathematician, and very expert in his business', was in 1768 selected to command H.M. Bark *Endeavour*, sent out by the Admiralty to carry the Royal Society's scientists to Tahiti, where the transit of the planet Venus across the sun was to be observed. Cook's additional secret instructions required him to search for the continent which 'there is reason to imagine . . . may be found to the Southward of the Tract lately made by Captⁿ Wallis . . . or of the Tract of any former Navigators in Pursuits of the like kind'.

Earlier explorers in the South Pacific had been frustrated by deficiencies in their knowledge and technical equipment. It had not been appreciated that the westerly winds of the forties closed the higher latitudes to sailing ships entering from the east; and Cook's own first voyage was directed by Cape Horn. Determination of longitude by dead reckoning, on an east–west course across the great width of this ocean, was often at fault in fixing the position of landfalls, which were generally plotted too far east because of the common underestimate of distance sailed. When Cook sighted New Zealand in October 1769, his dead reckoning placed him about four degrees east of his true longitude; yet he possessed, in the tables of the newly founded *Nautical Almanac* and in the chronometers which he carried on his second and third voyages, means for determining longitude greatly superior to those of his predecessors. Finally, the science of hydrography was little developed. 'No Branch of practical Geometry [wrote an eminent surveyor in 1773] has been so little considered by Men of Science as Maritim Surveying.'[11] In 1768 Cook had just spent five years on a survey of the coasts of Newfoundland, and in his view the explorer's task was to bring home a trustworthy chart of his discoveries.

The construction of charts was a neglected discipline in the seaman's education during the 18th century, particularly in the British Navy. Anson had in 1748 urged that the complement of men-of-war on long cruises should include 'a person, who with the character of an engineer should be employed in drawing such Coasts, and planning such Harbours, as the Ship should touch at', and he complained 'how very imperfect many of our accounts of distant countries are rendered, by the relaters being unskilled in drawing and in the general principles of surveying', without which 'navigation is at a full stand'. Yet in 1770 Cook could still write of 'the few [seamen]

FIG. 152.—A north-country collier leaving Whitby harbour.

I have known who are capable of drawing a Chart or Sketch of a sea coast'; and not until after the establishment of the Hydrographic Office of the Admiralty in 1795 was any regular provision made for the compilation and correction of charts and their issue to H.M. ships. But Cook's survey of Newfoundland had been made by trigonometrical methods adapted from those employed by military engineers in land survey, and he approached his task of discovery in the spirit of a hydrographer.

234

Chart and journal he considered as complementary—and equally important—records of a voyage and, unlike Wallis who had (in common with most naval captains of his time) left the surveying to his master, Cook was evidently himself responsible for most of the chartwork on his first voyage and for the close supervision of that of his officers on the later voyages. His three expeditions not only revealed the geography of the Pacific but also set new standards in the survey and hydrography of unknown coasts.

Some of the credit for Cook's success must go to his ships. The warships employed by previous naval expeditions, whether British or French, were ill-adapted to the task of geographical discovery. The frigates in which Byron, Wallis, and Bougainville sailed had a burden (some 600 tons) equal to that of the largest merchant ships, yet they were too weak in construction to lie ashore. These qualities were likely to induce caution in commanders whose duty was to 'keep the coast aboard'; and such ships were not of a kind in which (as Cook wrote) 'the officers may, with the least hazard, venture upon a strange coast'. After his first voyage Cook specified the qualities required in a ship employed on discovery: she must be of shallow draught, 'yet of a sufficient burden and capacity' to carry stores for a long voyage, she must be 'of a construction that will bear to take the ground; and of a size, which . . . may be safely . . . laid on shore'. These properties, Cook concluded, 'are not to be found in ships of war of forty guns, nor in frigates, nor in East India Company's ships, nor indeed in any other but North-country-built ships, or such as are built for the coal-trade'. In these ships Cook had served as a merchant seaman in the North Sea and had learnt to 'view a shoal with equanimity'.[12] The ships which he commanded on his Pacific voyages were all 'cat-built' colliers from Whitby shipyards, ranging in burden from 300 to 462 tons, roomy ships of strong construction and almost flat-bottomed.

In August 1768 Cook sailed from Plymouth in the *Endeavour* with a complement of eighty-four and a 'suite' of scientists and their servants numbering eleven. Earlier captains had preferred the passage by Magellan Strait, where antiscorbutic plants could be found; but Cook, noting the difficulties experienced by Wallis in his four months' passage of the Strait, and confident in his resources for the prevention of scurvy, chose the Cape Horn route. At Tahiti he remained three months for the astronomical observations and for refitting (Figs. 153–4), and then sailed south and west to discover the east coast of New Zealand. New Zealand was circumnavigated and 2400 miles of coast were charted in six months (October 1769–March 1770; Fig. 156). Reaching across the Tasman Sea, Cook made his second great discovery, that of the east coast of New Holland, which he traversed from April to August

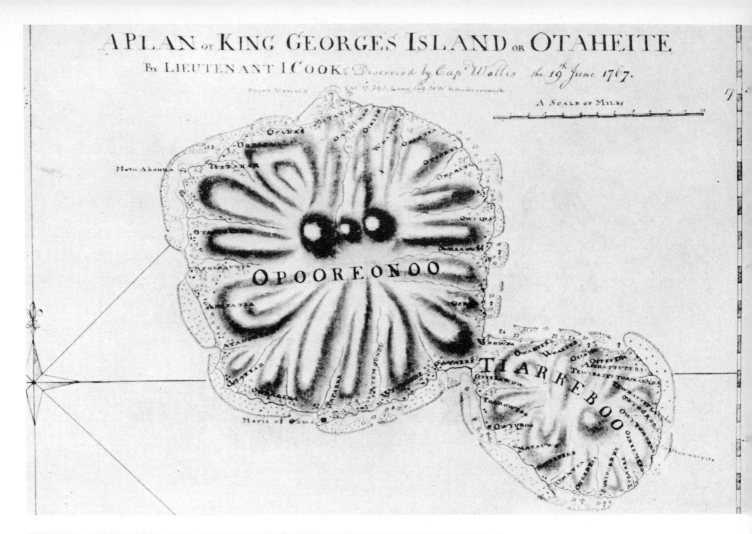

A PLAN of KING GEORGES ISLAND or OTAHEITE

By LIEUTENANT I. COOK. Discovered by Cap.t Wallis the 19.th June 1767.

A SCALE OF MILES

OPOOREONOO

TIARREBOO

A PLAN of ROYAL or MATAVAIE BAY in GEORGES ISLAND

A Scale of One Mile

FIG. 153.—Cook's chart of Tahiti 1769.

FIG. 154.—Cook's chart of Matavai Bay, Tahiti, 1769.

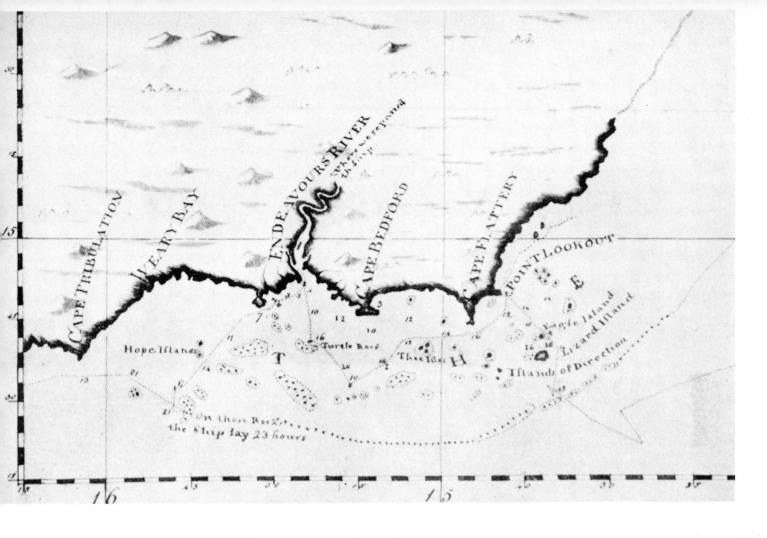

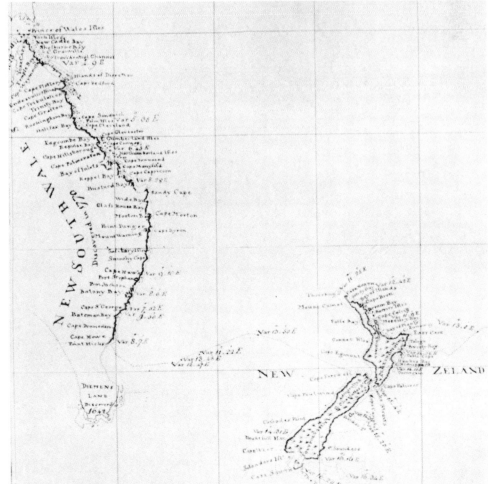

FIG. 155.—Part of Cook's chart of the coast of New South Wales, 1770.

FIG. 156.—The charting of New Zealand and the east coast of Australia by Cook, 1769–70.

1770, sailing '360 Leagues without having a Man out of the cheans heaving the Lead . . . a circumstance that I dare say never happen'd to any ship before'. Although the *Endeavour* was three times near disaster among the reefs, Cook's charting of 2000 miles of coast in four months produced an astonishingly good outline (Figs. 155–6).

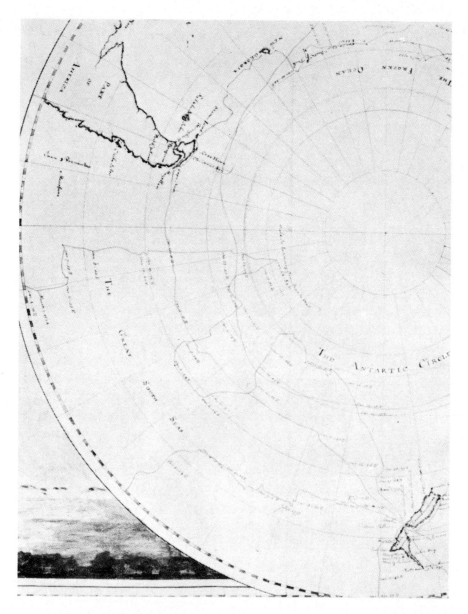

FIG. 157.—Part of a general chart of Cook's second voyage, with the tracks of the *Resolution* in the South Pacific and Antarctic, 1773–4.

On August 17, 1770, the *Endeavour* was being driven towards the coral reef, 'not above 80 or 100 yeards from the breakers . . . so that,' wrote Cook, 'between us and destruction was only . . . the breadth of one wave'—yet the three men taking observations for longitude remained at their instruments, and Green the astronomer commented 'these observations were very good'. Cook made his way to Batavia by Torres Strait, which was thus passed for the first time by a European ship since Torres and Prado in 1606.[13]

Reflecting on this voyage, Cook outlined at the end of his Journal the plan to be followed in examining the diminished but still immense expanse in which Terra Australis might lie. He recommended 'that the most feasable Method of making further discoveries in the South Sea is [from the Cape of Good Hope] to enter it by the way of New Zeland . . . and . . . with the prevailing Westerly winds, run to the Eastward in as high a Latitude as you please and . . . if after meeting with no Continent & you had other Objects in View, than haul to the northward . . . after which proceed with the trade wind back to the Westward'. This was the pattern for his second expedition (July 1772–July 1775), in the *Resolution*, another Whitby bark, with the *Adventure*, Captain Tobias Furneaux, as consort.

In the course of this voyage (Fig. 157) he three times crossed the Antarctic Circle (never before passed by a European ship; Fig. 158), reaching the high latitude of 71° 10′ S; he demonstrated that no continental land lay north of 60° S in the Indian or Atlantic Oceans; and he made three extensive cruises in the South Pacific which

FIG. 158.—The *Resolution* among 'ice islands' in the Antarctic, January 1773.

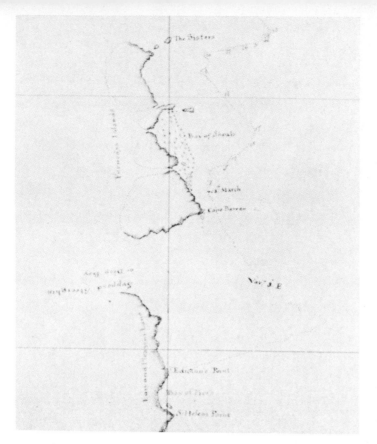

FIG. 159.—Chart of the north-east coast of Van Diemen's Land (Tasmania), with the track of the *Adventure* under Furneaux in February 1773.

FIG. 160.—Chart of the Marquesas drawn in the *Resolution*, April 1774.

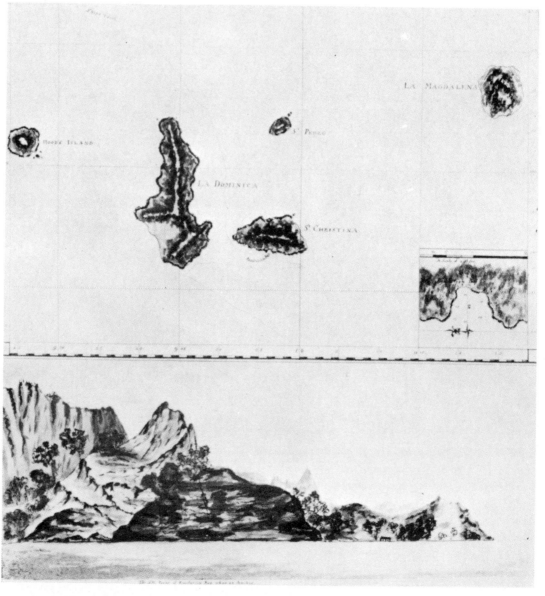

satisfied him 'that the greatest part of this southern continent (supposing there is one) must lie within the polar circle'. The 'savage and terrible' aspect of South Georgia (Fig. 161) indeed led him to affirm that 'to judge of the bulk by the sample, [the continent] would not be worth the discovery'. The principal surveys of this voyage were those of Tasmania (visited by Furneaux in the *Adventure* while separated from Cook), the Friendly Islands, the Marquesas, the New Hebrides, and New Caledonia (Figs. 159, 160).

In July 1776 Cook sailed on his last voyage, again in the *Resolution*, this time accompanied by the *Discovery*, Captain Charles Clerke. His objective was that

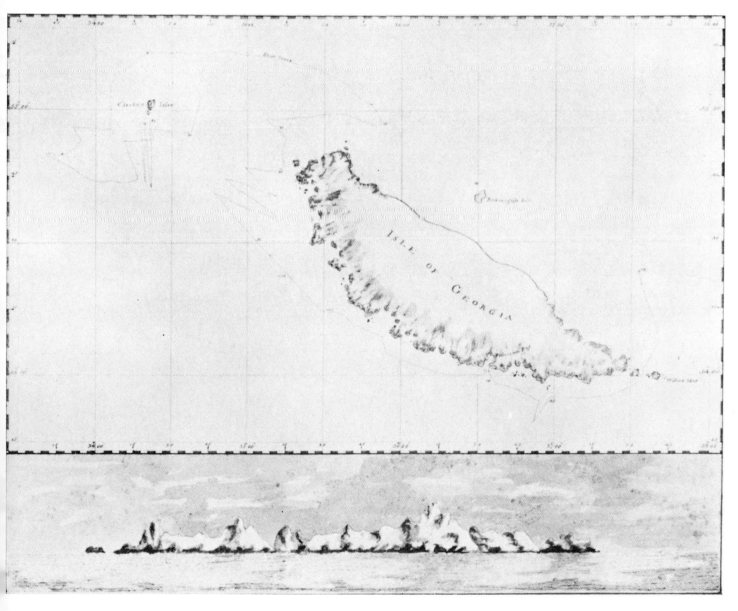

FIG. 161.—Chart of South Georgia, with the track of the *Resolution*, January 1775.

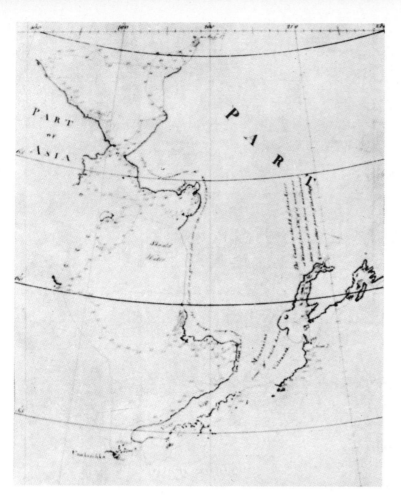

FIG. 162.—The coasts of Alaska and Bering Strait, is
a chart drawn by Cook, October 1778.

FIG. 163.—The *Resolution* and *Discovery* lying is
Prince William Sound, Alaska, May 1778; a drawing b
John Webber.

defined in the second part of Byron's instructions, 'to find out a Northern Passage by sea from the Pacific to the Atlantic Ocean'. Taking once more the eastward route by the Cape of Good Hope, he touched at Tasmania (which, relying on Furneaux's report and chart of 1773, he took to be part of the Australian coast; Fig. 159), New Zealand and Tahiti. At the end of 1777 he sailed north to discover Hawaii and, early in 1778, north-east to the Pacific coast of North America. Running along this in search of a strait and charting as he went, he sailed from $44\frac{1}{2}°$ N through Bering Strait, both shores of which were examined, and along the Alaskan coast to his farthest north in 70° 44' (Fig. 162). During this part of the voyage, 3000 miles of coast were surveyed and charted in little over four months. Returning to refit, Cook was killed by natives of Hawaii on 14 February 1779.

Cook's may without exaggeration be called the first scientific voyages of discovery.[14] They mark an epoch no less in the mapping of the world than in its exploration. The accurate methods of coastal survey, by triangulation from shore stations, which he had applied in Newfoundland, were not possible in the Pacific, where the charts had generally to be drawn by a continuous running survey from the ship, with compass bearings or sextant angles taken on shore features, and a good deal of masthead sketching. Cook's hydrographic work in the Pacific, although it stood the test of time, was necessarily a compromise between his standards and his opportunities. While making a sketch survey in the New Hebrides in 1774, he commented: 'The word survey is not to be understood here in its literal sense; surveying a place, according to my idea, is taking a Geometrical plan of it, in which every place is to have its true situation, which cannot be done in a work of his Kind.' But this very consciousness that the finished work fell short of his standards itself distinguishes him from his predecessors. In a rare moment of self-analysis, he wrote of himself as one 'whose ambition leads me not only farther than any man has been before me, but as far as I think it possible for man to go', and he described 'the pleasure which naturally results to a Man from being the first discoverer, even was it nothing more than sands and Shoals'. To the bold spirit of earlier navigators he added his own qualities of leadership and critical method. This 'good mathematician, very expert in his business' drew the modern map of the Pacific.

When Cook's voyages were over, only a handful of Polynesian islands remained undiscovered (the Gambier group, the northern Marquesas, and isolated islands of the Cook group and Tuamotus). English naval surveys were to complete his own work on the Pacific coasts of North America and along the Australian coasts. From 1792 to 1794 Captain George Vancouver, who had sailed with Cook on his last two voyages, carried out 'perhaps the most arduous survey that it had fallen to any

FIG. 164.—The tracks of Cook's ships on his three voyages of discovery.

navigator to undertake',[15] that of the intricate north-west coast of America from 39° N to Cook Sound 61° N. Running surveys of almost the entire coastline of Australia were made between 1797 and 1822 by naval vessels based on Sydney. The strait between Tasmania and the mainland was discovered in 1797–8 by the surgeon George Bass on a 600-mile voyage in a whale-boat. In 1802–3 Captain Matthew Flinders charted the south and west coasts from Cape Leeuwin (in the south-east) to Torres Strait, in the *Investigator*, 'a north-country-built ship', which 'in form, nearly resembled the description of vessel recommended by Captain Cook as best calculated for voyages of discovery'. Flinders's work was completed by Captain Phillip Parker King, who, in the course of his 'survey of the inter-tropical and western coast of Australia', between 1817 and 1822, three times circumnavigated the continent in the little cutter *Mermaid*.

Remarks on the Illustrations

Chapter XI

◇◇◇

149   The 'Chart of the Antarctic Polar Circle . . . according to the new hypothesis of M. Buache', published at London in the *Gentleman's Magazine* in 1763, was based on maps of 1757 by the French geographer Philippe Buache. Buache, an active seeker of system in physical facts, believed in the 'continuity of the continents with the lands thought to surround the South Pole', and identified islands as peaks of submarine mountain chains. He also noted the preponderance of land in the northern hemisphere, and one of his maps represents the north polar lands as if seen through those about the South Pole. Both these concepts are embodied in the English map here reproduced, in which the Arctic lands are shaded. The coasts of Terra Australis are drawn according to the various conjectures of mapmakers— Ortelius at the end of the 16th century, Petrus Kaerius at the beginning of the 17th, and J. N. Delisle and the 'New Plan' (of Buache) in the 18th. Its links with the southern tips of America, Africa and Tasmania are represented by 'lands' sighted by explorers, e.g. Drake's Harbour; and the icebergs reported on voyages of the 17th and 18th centuries were believed by Buache to have been 'disgorged' by rivers or gulfs flowing from the mountains of Antarctica.

150   Bougainville's track in the south-west Pacific is laid down in the general chart published in his *Voyage autour du monde* (Paris, 1771). Sailing west from Tahiti, he made landfalls in the Tonga islands ('I. des Navigateurs'), New Hebrides ('Grandes Cyclades'), and Solomon Islands ('Baye Choiseul'). On the Equator, some 25 degrees east of their true position, the chart lays down the 'Isles Salomon'—'whose existence and position are doubtful'.

151   This drawing by George Pinnock, a midshipman in the *Dolphin*, depicts Captain Wallis's ship lying in Port Royal (Matavai Bay), Tahiti, in June–July 1767 (British Museum, Add. MS 15499). It is taken looking south, and may be compared with Cook's plan of the bay (Fig. 154). On the sandspit leading to Cook's Point

Venus (outside the view to the left) is a Tahitian 'long-house'; on the right is One-Tree·Hill.

152   The cat-built bark shown in a painting by the Whitby artist Thomas Luny (in the Commonwealth National Library, Canberra) is of the same type as those in which Cook made his Pacific voyages. The vessel in Luny's picture has been (wrongly) identified as the collier *Earl of Pembroke*, which was renamed *Endeavour* after her purchase by the Admiralty in 1768.

153   Cook's chart of Tahiti, laid down from his boat journey round the island in May–June 1769 (British Museum, Add. MS 7085.6). This is in a set of manuscript charts drawn by Cook on his voyage in the *Endeavour*.

154   Cook's chart of his anchorage in Matavai Bay (B.M., Add. MS 7085.8) may be compared with Pinnock's drawing (Fig. 151). One-Tree Hill is shown on the right; and Dolphin's Bank is the reef on which Wallis's ship struck when entering the bay. The position of Point Venus, where the astronomical observations of the transit of the planet Venus were made in June 1769, was determined by Cook and Green, the astronomer, correctly for the latitude and with an error of no more than one minute of longitude. Cook was the first explorer to run his longitudes from the prime meridian of Greenwich.

155   This detail of Cook's chart of the coast of 'New South Wales' (B.M., Add. MS 7085.34) shows the reef on which the *Endeavour* struck in June 1770, Endeavour River where she was careened and repaired, and her perilous passage through the reef in August. (West is at the top.)

156   Cook's charting of New Zealand and the east coast of Australia, between October 1769 and August 1770, is shown in this detail of his 'Chart of the Great South Sea or Pacifick Ocean' (B.M., Add. MS 7085.1), on the Mercator projection. This displays the remarkable accuracy of his outline and his general correctness in latitude. The track of the *Endeavour* illustrates the pertinacity with which her commander 'kept the coast aboard'; and on shooting his ship through the Great Barrier Reef for the second time he admitted that 'we have ingaged more among the Islands and shoals upon this coast than may be thought with prudence I ought to have done with a single ship . . . but if I had not we should not have been able to give any better account of the one half of it than if we had never seen it'.

157   This general chart of Cook's second voyage (British Museum, Add. MS 15500.1) is in a set drawn by one of his men, perhaps Henry Roberts, midshipman in the *Resolution*. The detail reproduced shows the tracks of the *Resolution* in the South Pacific and Antarctic, 1773–4 (cf. the sketch map, Fig. 164). On his second cruise from New Zealand Cook twice crossed the Antarctic Circle (in January and February 1774); his farthest south, in 71° 10' S, is noted on the chart with the legend 'Field Ice Extending from East to West'. Cook rightly concluded 'that this ice

extended quite to the pole, or perhaps joined on some land'. He admitted that he saw no evidence of land, yet he added 'I think that there must be some to the south beyond this ice'. His intuition was correct, for he was little more than 50 miles from the Antarctic Continent. Cook's track in this area is crossed by another line (blue in the original) showing the northern limit of ice-bergs encountered by him.

158 The engraving, from a drawing by William Hodges, official artist of the second expedition, shows the *Resolution* among 'ice islands' in the Antarctic, January 1773. The boat's crew are breaking off blocks of ice to be melted for drinking water.

159 This chart by an officer of the *Adventure*, perhaps James Burney, shows her track off the north-east coast of Van Diemen's Land (Tasmania) in March 1773 (British Museum, Add. MS 31360.62). Following in Tasman's track along the south coast and round Cape Pillar (see Fig. 142), Furneaux was, like him, blown offshore and so failed to discover the strait between Tasmania and the Australian mainland. In his report to Cook he expressed the opinion 'that there is no straits between New Holland and Van Diemen's Land, but a very deep bay'. The author of this chart was more sceptical and marks, in the position of Banks Strait, 'Suppos'd Streights or Deep Bay'.

160 The chart of the Marquesas (B.M., Add. MS 15500. 8), perhaps by Roberts, marks the *Resolution*'s track in April 1774, with (inset and view) her anchorage in Resolution Bay, on Santa Christina island.

161 On his way homeward in January–February 1775, Cook sailed through waters, south-east of Cape Horn, where Ortelius and later cartographers had drawn sections of a continental coast. This part of his voyage, in the course of which he discovered South Georgia and the South Sandwich Islands, enabled him to 'assert that the extensive coasts laid down in Mr Dalrymple's chart of the ocean between Africa and America, and the Gulf of Saint Sebastian, does not exist'. The chart and view reproduced (B.M., Add. MS 15500.16), also perhaps by Roberts, show the course of the *Resolution* along the north coast of South Georgia, which he recognized as an island. (South is at the top of the chart.) Cook was impressed by 'the inexpressibly horrid aspect of the country: a country doomed by nature . . . to lie buried in everlasting snow and ice'; and concluded that 'the greatest part of this southern continent (supposing there is one) must lie within the polar circle'.

162 This manuscript chart, 'hastily copied', was enclosed in the letter dated 20 October 1778, which Cook wrote to the Secretary of the Admiralty from Unalaska in the Aleutian Islands and sent home by way of Russia; it was received in London on 6 March 1780, a year after Cook's death. It is in the Public Record Office (Adm 1/1612, M.P.I. 83). The track of the *Resolution* and *Discovery* is shown from Prince William Sound and Cook Inlet (May–June 1778), west to the Aleutians

and then north through Bering Strait. On the American coast he reached 70° 44′ N (17 August 1778) before being stopped by ice and returning south to Unalaska.

163   This drawing by John Webber, the official artist of Cook's third voyage, shows the *Resolution* and *Discovery* lying in Snug Corner Cove, Prince William Sound, May 1778 (British Museum, Add. MS 17277.37). By now Cook, searching for a sea passage into the Atlantic, had found the American coast 'to trend very much to the west'. He sent two boat parties to examine the arms of the Sound; their report and 'the circumstance . . . of the floodtide entering the Sound from the south rendered the existence of a passage this way very doubtful'.

Notes

Chapter XI

◇◇

[1] The quotation is from John Callander, *Terra Australis cognita* (Edinburgh, 1766–8).

[2]   'He had bought a large map representing the sea,
           Without the least vestige of land;
           And the crew were much pleased when they found it to be
           A map they could all understand.'
                       (Lewis Carroll, *The Hunting of the Snark.*)

[3] Cf. Mercator's hypothesis, quoted in Chapter IX.

[4] In *An account of the discoveries made in the South Pacifick Ocean previous to 1764* (printed 1767; published London, 1769). A copy of this was carried in Cook's ship the *Endeavour* on his voyage of 1768–71.

[5] Geographers had long ascribed the origin of all islands to marine erosion: 'the Rocks [in the sea] haue beene parcell of the mayne lande . . . long agone, and by the often souffing of the . . . waues of the sea . . . the other substaunce or stuffe is beaten and consumed away' (William Bourne, 1578). In 1605 Quiros took the coral atolls of the Tuamotus to be signs of a mainland, 'the mother of all those islands'.

[6] Roughly in the space bounded by the meridians of 90° W and 175° W (of Greenwich) and the parallel of 20°–25° S.   [7] See Chapter IX.

[8] Although Drake, with the private support of the Queen, envisaged his voyage as a raid against Spanish overseas power, the original and official plan provided for a search for Terra Australis in the South Pacific. (Cf. Chapter IX.)

[9] For Dampier, see Chapter X, and Fig. 148.

[10] Not until 1781 did Jean-Nicolas Buache, noting the constant underestimate of distance sailed (estimated from dead reckoning) in east-to-west crossings of the Pacific, identify Mendaña's Solomons as the islands found by Carteret, Surville, and Bougainville.

[11] Murdoch Mackenzie, *A Treatise of Maritim Surveying* (London, 1773).

[12] The phrase is that of Cook's editor, Dr. J. C. Beaglehole.

[13] See Chapter IX.

[14] This leaves out of account (as not strictly serving 'discovery') the voyages made by Edmond Hailey in 1700–1 to determine magnetic variation in the Atlantic Ocean.

[15] Edward Heawood's judgment.

PART SIX

The Continents and the Poles

XII

NORTH AMERICA FROM SEA TO SEA

17th and 18th Centuries

◇◈◇

DRAKE'S RETURN from the Pacific in 1580 and the failure of expeditions to discover northern passages to Cathay[1] revived English interest in 'western planting', or settlement in the temperate lands of America to the north of the Spanish colonies. In the propaganda writings of Richard Hakluyt this was advocated as an export market for the 'utterance' of English woollen goods, as an outlet 'for the manifolde imploymente of nombers of idle men', as 'a great bridle to the Indies of the Kinge of Spaine', and as a base from which 'the Northwest passage to Cathaio and China may . . . be searched oute as well by riuer and ouerlande, as by sea'.[2] Hakluyt rested the English 'title which we haue to that part of America which is from Florida to 67 degrees northwarde' on the Cabot voyages; and to Raleigh, who in 1584 succeeded to Sir Humphrey Gilbert's patent for colonization, he therefore suggested 'y^{or} best planting wilbe aboute the bay of the Chesepians'. While Gilbert's expedition of 1583 had been directed to Norumbega, Raleigh in 1585 planted his colony further south, on the coast of the present state of North Carolina, called by the English 'Virginia' (Fig. 165).[3] Here, on Roanoke Island, in Currituck Sound, the settlers under Ralph Lane maintained themselves for a year before being repatriated in Drake's fleet. Raleigh's second colony established itself at Roanoke in 1587, but when its governor John White eventually returned to the site in 1590 he found the colonists vanished and, among the remains of their fort, he recovered three of his chests with 'my bookes torne from the couers, the frames of some of my pictures and Mappes rotten and spoyled with rayne'.

The Roanoke enterprise produced a noble graphic record of the land and its people. In the colony of 1585–6 John White, who may with little doubt be identified

253

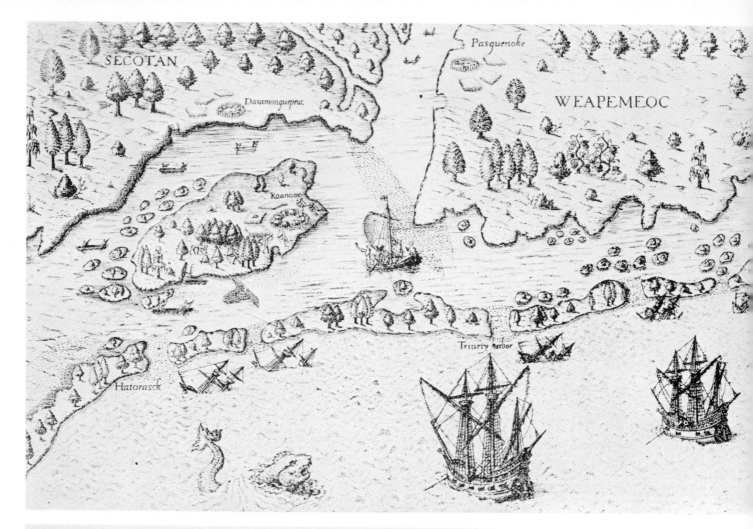

SECOTAN

Pasquenoke

WEAPEMEOC

Dasamonquepeuc

Roanoac

Trinitty harbor

Hatorasck

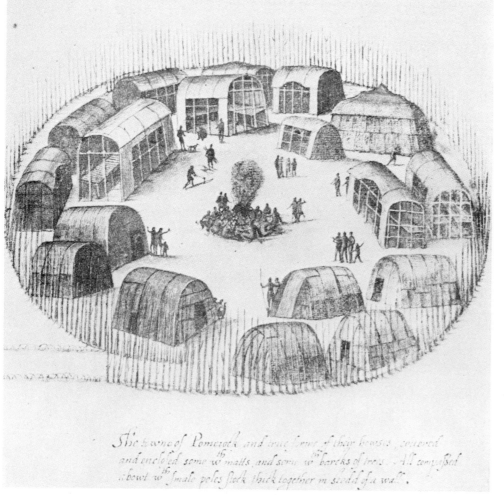

The towne of Pomeiock and true forme of their howses, covered
and enclosed some w[i]th matts, and some w[i]th barcks of trees. All compassed
abowt w[i]th smale poles stuck thick together in steed of a wall.

FIG. 165.—'The arriual of the
Englishemen in Virginia', 1585; an
engraving by T. de Bry.

FIG. 166.—An Indian village,
drawn by John White.

with the governor of the second colony,[1] seems to have had instructions similar to those given in 1582 to Thomas Bavin, apparently the surveyor, artist and scientific observer in Gilbert's expedition: 'drawe and sett downe the distinct places & countries by drawen plott [map] as also by writing', 'specially sett down in figures the iust latitude of euery Notatious place', 'also drawe to life all strange birdes beastes fishes plantes hearbes Trees and fruictes . . . also drawe the figures and shapes of men and women in their apparell'. Raleigh had indeed been advised in 1585 to send out 'a skilfull painter . . . which the Spaniards vsed commonly in all their discoueries to bring the descriptions of all beasts, birds, fishes, trees, townes, &c.'; this was John White's task. Although the colonists complained that, embarking in Drake's ships, 'all our Cards, Books, and writings were by the Sailers cast ouer-boord', the water-colour drawings which White brought home in 1587 depict in precise and vivid detail the Algonkian Indians, their villages and daily life, and the

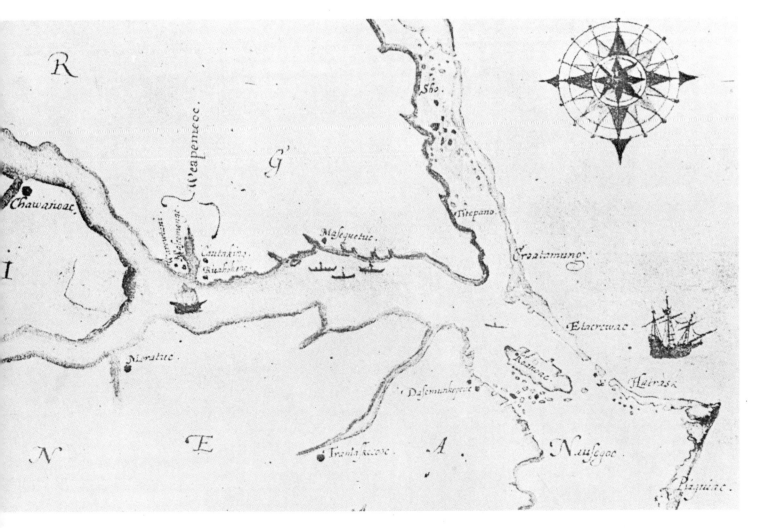

FIG. 167.—Part of a map drawn by White from the explorations by the colonists of 'Virginia', 1585–6.

flora and fauna of their country (Fig. 166). Of the two maps of the coast between Florida and Chesapeake Bay, found among White's surviving drawings, that on the larger scale, representing the region explored by the colonists (Fig. 167), is the most accurate map of any part of the coast of north-east America made during the 16th century.[5]

Raleigh's colonies failed, but they were the prototype of the 'western planting' which bore fruit in the colony successfully founded in 1607 on the James River, 120 miles north-west of Roanoke. The 'new Virginia', the first permanent English settlement on American soil, became a self-supporting community sustained by the natural resources of the country (Fig. 168). Yet its charter granted the colony rights of expansion 'into the land throughout from sea to sea west and north-west', and the colonists were instructed to seek a river by which 'you shall soonest find the other sea'. Captain John Smith, governor of Virginia in 1608–9 and the first historian of

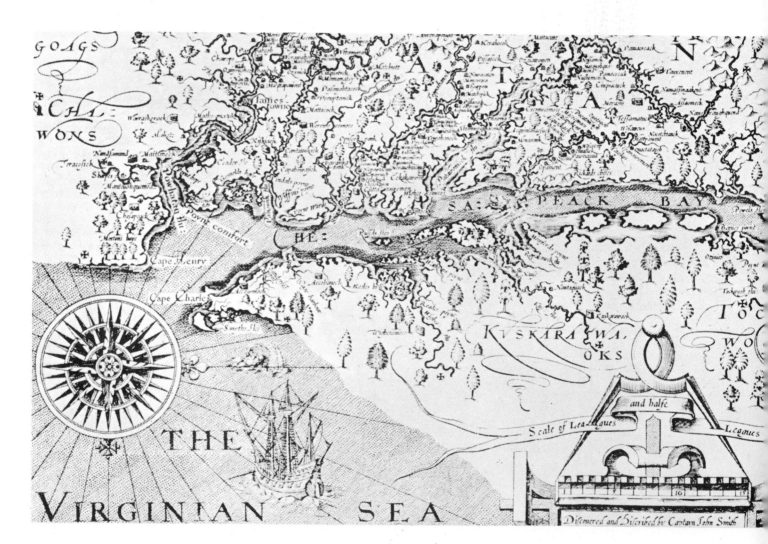

FIG. 168.—Part of Captain John Smith's engraved map of Virginia, 1612.

256

the colony, explored Chesapeake Bay and the rivers flowing into it in fruitless search
for a western passage; and
when Captain Christopher
Newport arrived with the
'second supply', Smith commented satirically: 'How or
why Captaine Newport
obtained such a private Com-
mission, as not to returne
withoute a lumpe of gold, a
certaintie of the South sea, or
one of the lost company sent
out by Sir Walter Raleigh, I
know not.' Henry Hudson,
however, perusing Smith's letters and map at Amsterdam in
1608, conceived the possibility
of a strait in the proximity of
the new Virginia.[6] In 1609,
checked in his attempt on the
North-East Passage, he crossed
the Atlantic to the Carolina
coast, examined Chesapeake
and Delaware Bays, and sailed
150 miles up the Hudson River
(Fig. 169). Five years later
a Dutch fort was built on

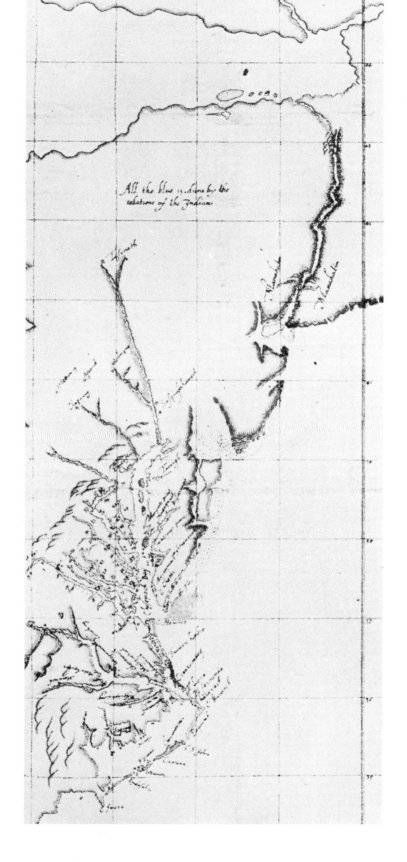

FIG. 169.—The North American
coast from the Hudson River to
Cape Fear, in a map drawn before
1611.

Manhattan Island, and in 1622 the city of New Amsterdam—afterwards New York—was founded there.

These and later colonies planted in New England and along the coasts to the south were still inspired by the old and 'assured hope of a way to be made part ouerland, and part by riuers and lakes, into the South Sea vnto Cathay'. This faith, nourished by Indian reports of 'a great water beyond the mountains', is seen in many maps (Fig. 170). But the riverways probed by the English and Dutch colonists from the Atlantic seaboard gave little promise of the expected passage. The valleys of Virginia led up into the Appalachian Mountains, and the frontier of the British colonies was not pushed into the Ohio valley until the 18th century. The New

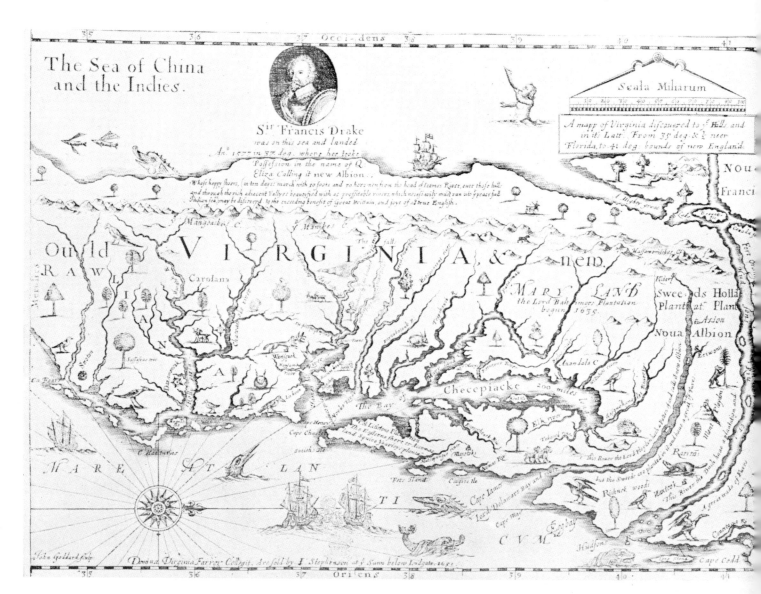

FIG. 170.—Map of Virginia by John Ferrar, published in 1651.

258

England rivers offered routes only into the lower St Lawrence basin, and here the French were already established. From their trading and mission posts in Canada they were, within a century and a half, to penetrate the interior of the continent from the Great Lakes south to the Gulf of Mexico, north to Hudson Bay and west to the Rocky Mountains, following the waterways along rivers and over portages, accompanying the Indians in their wars, proselytizing, and seeking trade.

Samuel de Champlain was the pioneer of this great movement in exploration. An accomplished and zealous cartographer, he recorded in a series of maps the results of his journeys from 1603 to 1616 and of those of the young men whom he sent out. His work in discovery, directed to the search for 'a route to China by the north' within the temperate zone, is displayed in his last map, engraved in 1632 (Fig. 171). New France, in the St Lawrence basin, where Champlain in 1608 founded the town of Quebec, was the base from which the water routes to north, south and west were investigated; and in 1604–7 Champlain charted Nova Scotia and the Bay of Fundy. He discovered the route from the St Lawrence southward up the Richelieu River to Lake Champlain, and he knew of that to the north by the Saguenay River to James Bay, in the south of Hudson Bay; in his map of 1613 this is marked (in English) 'the bay wher hudson did winter'. To the west, in search of the saltwater sea, he had ascended the Ottawa River, reached Lake Huron ('Mer douce', or the Sweetwater Sea), and navigated Lake Ontario. One of his young men, the *coureur de bois* Étienne Brulé, had reached Lake Superior (indicated on Champlain's map of 1632) and had gone up the Susquehannah River and over the divide to Chesapeake Bay. Another, Jean Nicolet, was to go by canoe up Lake Michigan and perhaps over to the Wisconsin River.

After 1663, when New France came under the crown, exploration to the south and west was pursued with renewed vigour. In 1669 Robert de La Salle, from Lake Ontario, discovered the Ohio River and descended it for some distance, although not to its junction with the Mississippi (Fig. 172). Nicolet and other earlier travellers had brought back tales of a great river in the west, 'which must lead to China and Japan'; and in 1672–3 the Jesuit Fr Marquette and Louis Joliet made their way from Lake Michigan by the Fox and Wisconsin rivers to the Mississippi, which they named Rivière Colbert. Following this as far as the junction of the Arkansas, they satisfied themselves that it must flow into the Gulf of Mexico (Fig. 172). In 1681–2 La Salle went to the Mississippi by way of the Illinois and sailed down the great river to its mouth (Figs. 173–4). His last expedition was made by sea to the delta of the Mississippi and ended in his murder in 1687. These great journeys, which revealed the immense prairies of the Mississippi basin and traced the river to the sea, removed all hope that it might lead to California and the Pacific, and made the

FIG. 171.—Champlain's last map of New France, published in 1632, showing his explor

e St Lawrence basin and the routes leading out of it, between 1603 and 1629.

E.M.—S

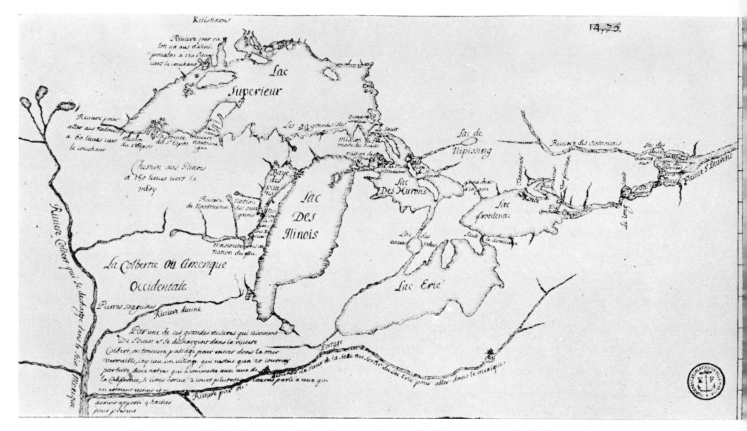

FIG. 172.—Joliet's map of his discoveries, with his route to the Mississippi, 1672–3.

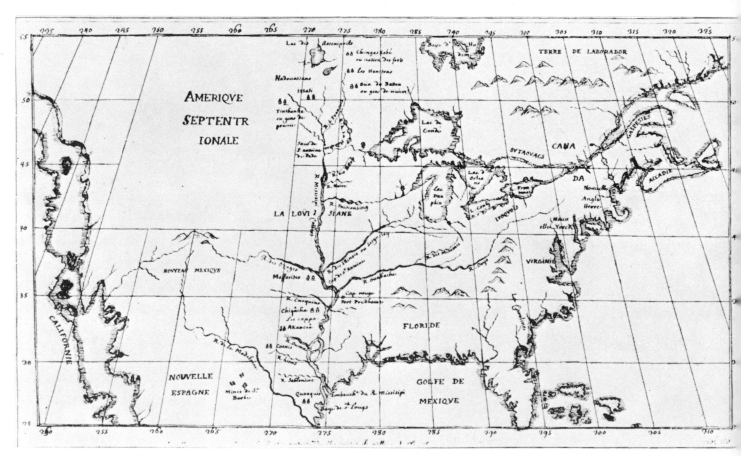

FIG. 173.—Map of North America, showing La Salle's exploration of the Mississippi to its mouth, 1681–7.

Fig. 174.—The earliest view of the Niagara Falls, published in Hennepin's narrative, 1697.

French aware that the vast territory to the west of the Appalachians was pierced by no waterway flowing into the South Sea. The journeys of Marquette and Joliet left a generous cartographic record, for Joliet was an expert surveyor who later became royal hydrographer at Quebec (Fig. 172). The imperfect mapping of La Salle's explorations has however left the routes of his earlier journeys uncertain, and thrown doubt on his discovery of the Ohio and on the question whether he or Joliet can claim that of the Mississippi.

On the other side of the continent, the Spanish missionaries from northern Mexico had clarified the geography of California and the Colorado valley. Correctly mapped as a peninsula in the 16th century, California came to be laid down as an

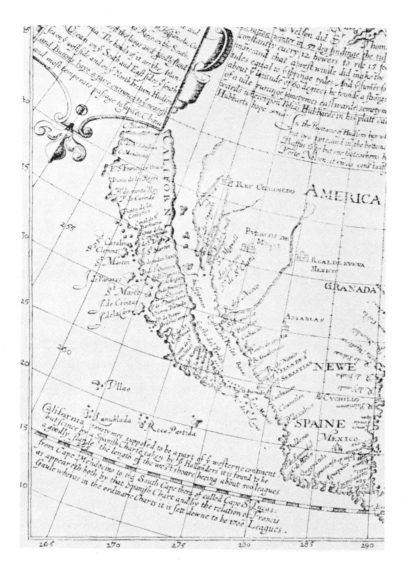

FIG. 175.—California represented as an island in Henry
Briggs's map, 1625.

FIG. 176.—Map of California, from the journeys of
Fr. E. F. Kino, 1697–1701.

island soon after 1600: 'sometymes', as Henry Briggs wrote on his map (Fig. 175), 'supposed to be a part of yᵉ westerne continent but scince by a Spanish Charte . . . it is founde to be a goodly Ilande'.[7] At the end of the 17th century Dampier wrote that the Spanish 'Drafts do not agree about it. Some of them do make California an Island . . . Some . . . newly made do make California to join the Main.' The journeys of the Jesuit Father Kino in the years 1694 to 1702 established the peninsula form of California (Fig. 176); and missionary journeys later in the century reached from Santa Fé as far north as Utah.

Between the Great Lakes and Hudson Bay, and to the north of the French trading posts, lay a region rich in furs and still unexplored when the French were already on the Ohio and the Mississippi. 'We have long known', ran a Jesuit report from Quebec in 1661, 'that in our rear we have the Northern Sea, that it is adjacent to the Sea of China, and that only the gateway has to be found. There is that famous bay, discovered by Hudson.' In 1659 two *coureurs de bois*, Pierre Radisson and Chouart Groseillers, after adventurous wanderings on the upper Mississippi in the course of which they had heard of the Missouri River, found themselves at the west end of Lake Superior. Here Indians brought in rich supplies of furs from the northern region still untapped by French traders. 'We weare Cesars, being nobody to contradict us', wrote Radisson. In the winter Radisson and his companion 'went away with all hast possible to arrive the sooner att the great river. We came to the seaside, where we finde an old howse all demolished and battered with boullets.' The Indians told them 'particularities of the Europeans. We know ourselves, and what Europ is, therefore in vaine they tell us for that.'[8] These details suggest that Radisson reached James Bay, where Hudson had wintered in 1610 and Captain Thomas James in 1631. Radisson and Groseillers entered English service in 1665, and in 1669 an English ship with Groseillers on board brought back to London a cargo of furs from James Bay. In the following year the 'Governor and Company of Adventurers of England trading into Hudson's Bay' received a royal charter 'for the Discovery of a new Passage into the South Sea and for the finding some trade for Furs, Minerals, and other . . . Commodities'.

The French response, designed to curb the trading activity of the posts set up on the Bay by the English company, led to the discovery of Lake Winnipeg and Lake of the Woods and to the remarkable expeditions of the Sieur de la Vérendrye and his sons 'to discover the Western Sea'. In 1728 La Vérendrye had been told by an Indian named Ochagach that from a lake beyond Lake Superior a river flowed westward into a salt tidal sea; and the map drawn by Ochagach (Fig. 177a) showed the water route to Lake Winnipeg and the river which 'must discharge above

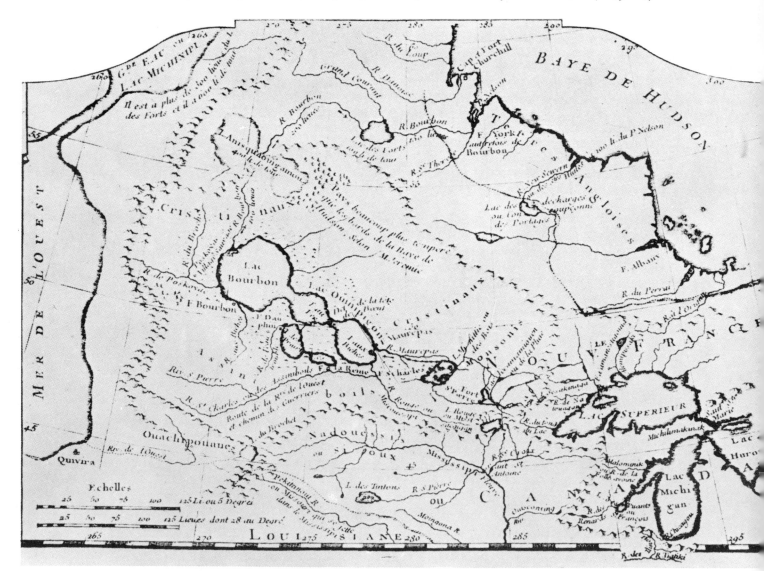

FIG. 177a.—Map drawn by the Indian Ochagach for La Vérendrye in 1728, showing lakes and rivers between Lake Superior and Lake Winnipeg.

FIG. 177b.—Map of the country explored by La Vérendrye and his sons, 1731–49.

California'. The journeys made by La Vérendrye or his sons between 1731 and 1749 extended from Lake Winnipeg to the Missouri River (first believed to flow south-west) and as far west as the Rocky Mountains—'the great mountains which are near the sea'. The 'Mer de l'Ouest', sought by La Vérendrye and drawn on Buache's map of his explorations (Fig. 177b), was a curious feature derived, in the 17th century, from Indian tales of a sea 'ten days' journey westward' from Lake Superior. Geographers of the 18th century adopted it as a device for reconciling the evidently great width of the continent with incessant Indian reports of sea not far to the west of the French posts; it was generally laid down on their maps as communicating with the Pacific Ocean in about 45° N, and sometimes identified with the imaginary Strait of Juan de Fuca.

Like other 'proud and privileged corporations', the Hudson's Bay Company showed less interest in exploration than in trade. The 18th-century searches for a waterway to the west from Hudson Bay[9] were not made under the flag·of the Company, which was sharply attacked 'as being averse from discoveries, and from enlarging their trade'. Competition from two quarters roused it from its sloth. On the Pacific coast, there were the Russians who obtained in Alaska the valuable pelts of the sea-otter, seal, and blue fox; Cook's crews, returning from the North Pacific in 1780, told stories of skins bought for sixpence and sold in China for 100 dollars, and a keen trade in furs from the north-west coast, by American and English ships, quickly developed. Nearer to Canada, the rival North-West Company, based on Montreal, was reaching ever further afield to cut off supplies of furs from the older Company's posts on the Bay. In 1770 Samuel Hearne, a factor of the Hudson's Bay Company, set out from Fort Prince of Wales, on the Churchill River, with orders to seek a coppermine to the north-west and 'to find out . . . whether there is a passage through this continent . . . out of Hudson's Bay into the Western Ocean, as hath lately been represented'. Travelling down the Coppermine River, Hearne reached its mouth on the Arctic Ocean in July 1771 and thus (as he commented) 'put a final end to all disputes concerning a Northwest Passage through Hudson's Bay' (Fig. 209).

Of the North-West Company's traders the most energetic in exploration and in map-making was Peter Pond. Pond moved north to Lake Athabaska in 1778 and to the Great Slave Lake, which he reached in 1787. The river which flowed out of the Great Slave Lake to the west was conjectured by him 'to fall into Cook's River', in Alaska, discovered by Cook in 1778 but not explored to its head. Pond's theory was tested and disproved by the journey made by Alexander Mackenzie in 1789 down the Mackenzie River from the Great Slave Lake to the Arctic Ocean,

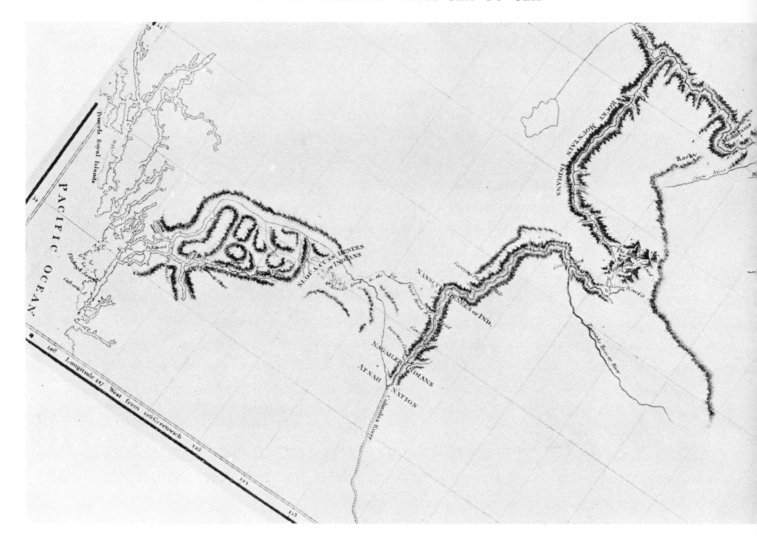

FIG. 178.—Part of Alexander Mackenzie's map of his transcontinental journey in 1793.

3000 miles by canoe in 102 days (Fig. 209). Hearne and Mackenzie had thus traversed the territory across which the 'invisible because imaginary' straits from the Pacific to Hudson Bay were supposed to lie, and their western outlets were effectively removed from the map by the coastal surveys of Cook in 1778 and Vancouver in 1794–4.[10] In 1793 Mackenzie made his second great journey. Ascending the Peace River from Lake Athabaska, he crossed the Rockies and, by way of the Fraser River, reached the Pacific in 52° N (Fig. 178), six weeks after Vancouver had visited the same spot. This completed the first overland journey to the Pacific by a European, and here on a rock he 'inscribed . . . this brief memorial: Alexander Mackenzie, from Canada, by land, the twenty-second of July, one thousand seven hundred and ninety-three'.

Remarks on the Illustrations

Chapter XII

❖◇❖

165 Thomas Hariot's *Briefe and true report of the new found land of Virginia*, with engravings after John White's drawings, was published at Frankfort in 1590, in four languages, as Part I of Theodor de Bry's *America*. 'The arriual of the Englishemen in Virginia' may be based on a now lost map by White, and incorporates details from his drawings of Indian life, e.g. the stockaded villages and the fish-weir. Grenville's fleet, with Raleigh's first colony on board, is seen arriving off the Carolina Outer Banks. The hazards of the North Carolina reefs are shown by wrecked ships. Within the Banks is the island of 'Roanoac', where the colony was planted.

166 This drawing by White represents Pomeioc, a stockaded mainland village of the Algonkians. This and the next illustration are from the only surviving set of White's original drawings, in the Department of Prints and Drawings, British Museum.

167 This detail from White's manuscript map of the North American coast, from Chesapeake Bay to Pamlico Bay, represents the region explored by the Roanoke colonists in 1585-6; the places visited by them are indicated by solid dots (red in the original). This is the first English map of any part of America 'to be based on a survey made on the ground' (Professor D. B. Quinn).

168 The soldier of fortune Captain John Smith played an active part in establishing the Jamestown colony, of which he was Governor in 1608-9; and he did much of the survey work from which the early maps of the region were drawn. The first printed map of the young colony, 'Virginia. Discouered and discribed by Captain John Smith', was engraved by William Hole and published with Smith's pamphlet *A Map of Virginia* (Oxford, 1612). It incorporates the surveys of the James River ('Powhatan flu:') in 1607 and of the York River ('Pamounk flu:') in 1608, with later surveys by Smith. (West is at the top of the map.) Crosses mark the

limit of exploration; 'what beyond is by relation', i.e. from Indian reports. Indian villages are marked by four distinctive symbols. Most of the place-names are those given by Smith; but it is not certain that he himself drew the map. It remained the prototype of maps of Virginia for over half a century.

169   The manuscript map known as the 'Velasco' map, and now in the Spanish archives at Simancas, was drawn by an English surveyor (perhaps John Daniel) and probably sent by Alonso de Velasco, Spanish ambassador in London, to King Philip II in 1611. The Hudson River ('Manahatin') is from Hudson's voyage of 1609; the coast to the south, from Chesapeake Bay to Cape Fear, is from surveys by the colonists of Old and New Virginia.

170   The map of 'old' and 'new' Virginia, with the Atlantic coasts from Cape Cod to Cape Fear, was drawn by John Ferrar, of Little Gidding, Herts., engraved by John Goddard, and published in London in 1651 as 'promotion literature' for the Virginia Company. To later issues of the map (as in the reproduction) Ferrar's daughter Virginia put her name as compiler: 'Domina Virginia Farrer Collegit.' (West is at the top.) Along the rivers flowing into the Atlantic are shown, correctly enough, the plantations of the Dutch on the Hudson River, the Swedes on the Delaware, and the English in Virginia and Maryland, with many charming pictures of native animals and birds. The north and west parts of the map express, in fantastic form, the faith in easy access to the 'Sea of China and the Indies' by land and water. The Hudson River is represented as a waterway connected with the St Lawrence ('Canada flu:') and continued into the Pacific. 'In ten dayes march from the head of Jeames River' lies New Albion, on the coast of California, where Drake had planted the English flag in 1579.

171   Champlain's last map of New France, published with his *Voyages* (Paris, 1632), sums up his exploration of the St Lawrence basin and of the routes leading out of it, from 1603 to 1629. To the south of the river, he had surveyed the maritime region of Acadia (Nova Scotia and New Brunswick), and had discovered the route leading from Quebec and Montreal, through the Iroquois country, by Lake Champlain to the Hudson valley. Northward, he travelled up the Saguenay and St Maurice, having learnt from Indians that it was possible to reach Hudson Bay by these rivers. Of the Great Lakes, Champlain had navigated on Lake Ontario and Lake Huron ('Mer douce'), and heard of Lake Michigan (here wrongly laid down to the north of Lake Huron) and of Lake Superior ('Grand lac').

172   Louis Joliet's manuscript map of the Great Lakes and upper Mississippi basin, in the Bibliothèque Nationale, Paris, shows the route by which he and Marquette in 1672–3 travelled from Lake Michigan ('Lac des Ilinois') over the Fox-Wisconsin portage to reach the Mississippi ('Riuiere Colbert'), from which they hoped to find a river leading to the west. The Ohio, with a legend affirming it to

have been descended by La Salle on his journey from Lake Erie to the Mississippi, is probably a later addition.

173　This engraved map of North America displays La Salle's exploration of the Mississippi from the Illinois River to the Gulf of Mexico in 1681–2.

174　On the Niagara River, in 1678–9, La Salle, accompanied by Fr Louis Hennepin, built a ship for navigation of the Great Lakes. Hennepin's narrative of the expedition, published under the title *Nouvelle découverte d'un très grand pays . . . entre le Nouveau Mexique et la mer glaciale* (Utrecht, 1697), contains the earliest picture of the Falls. These are described (in the English translation of his book) as 'a vast and prodigious Cadence of Water'.

175　The illusion that California was an island persisted throughout the 17th century (cf. Chapter IV). It owed its origin to a report that Vizcaino, on his expedition in 1602, had sailed north out of the Gulf of California into the Pacific. Henry Briggs's map, engraved by Renold Elstrack in 1625 (see Fig. 81), was the second printed map to represent California thus, and he records the source of the concept: 'by a Spanish Charte taken by yᵉ Hollanders it is found to be a goodly Ilande'. This 'chart' is thought to be one by Father Antonio de la Asención, who accompanied Vizcaino as a cartographer; it may have been captured by Spilbergen off Peru in 1615.

176　This printed map shows the results of the journeys made by the German Jesuit Fr E. F. Kino (or Kühn) in 1697–1701. From the Jesuit missions in Sonora, on the mainland, Kino travelled north to the Fila River ('Azul oder Blaufluss') and the mouth of the Colorado. These journeys satisfied him that California was a peninsula connected to the continent.

177　The reproduction shows two sections of the 'physical map' of the 'western part of Canada' published in 1754 by Philippe Buache, in his *Considérations geographiques et physiques*. Above, the map drawn by the Indian Ochagach for La Vérendrye in 1728 depicts a chain of lakes and rivers between Lake Superior and Lake Winnipeg. Flowing westward out of Lake Winnipeg is the 'river of the west', i.e. the Saskatchewan, which (as La Vérendrye and his supporters conjectured) 'must discharge above California'. Below, Buache's map of the country explored by the Sieur de la Vérendrye and his sons, 1731–49, places the 'Mer de l'Ouest' 120 leagues west of Lake Winnipeg, which the La Vérendryes reached on their earlier journeys. Later they travelled south-west through the Sioux country in the valley of the upper Missouri River as far as the foothills of the Rocky Mountains. The 'Mer de l'Ouest', a great gulf in the Pacific coast covering fifteen degrees of longitude and ten of latitude, was first laid down on a map in 1700 by Buache's father-in-law, Guillaume Delisle, from Indian reports. These were thought to confirm an older story, told by an Indian guide to the Spanish in New Mexico in 1541, about Quivira, a city on the sea, visited by great ships with sails; and Delisle (like Humphrey Gilbert 150 years earlier) supposed that these ships came from China or Japan.

178   Alexander Mackenzie's map of his transcontinental journey in 1793 was published in his book, *Voyages from Montreal . . . to the Frozen and Pacific Oceans, in 1789 and 1793* (London, 1801). The section reproduced (in which north-west is at the top) shows his ascent of the Peace River through the Rockies, his portage over the divide ('McKenzie's route to the sea') and his descent of the Bella Coola River to the coast.

Notes

Chapter XII

[1] See Chapters V and VI.

[2] These quotations are from Hakluyt's 'Discourse of Western Planting', prepared in manuscript for Queen Elizabeth in 1584.

[3] The name 'Virginia' was first used by Hakluyt, in his 'Discourse' of 1584, to describe the region between Florida and New England ('Norumbega'); and was adopted by Raleigh, in honour of the Queen, for the colony planted on the coast of North Carolina in 1585.

[4] This identification has been disputed, but the phrases used by John White the governor in 1590 (quoted above), with other evidence of a circumstantial sort, seem to place it beyond doubt.

[5] In the judgment of Professor D. B. Quinn (*The Roanoke Voyages*, Hakluyt Society, 1955).

[6] See Chapter VI.

[7] See Chapter IV.

[8] Radisson's report, written in vigorous but inexpert English for King Charles II in 1665, was preserved by Samuel Pepys.

[9] See Chapter VI.

[10] See Chapter XI.

XIII

THE RIVERS OF AFRICA

16th to 19th centuries

◇—◇

BY THE EARLY YEARS of the 16th century the outline of the African coasts on the chart had been completed by the Portuguese navigations to India round the Cape of Good Hope. For nearly three centuries few European travellers penetrated far inland, and cartographers had little information that was both new and true on the greater part of the interior. It remained a void which they filled on their maps with speculative representations of the river and lake systems, with reported native kingdoms, and (all else failing) with 'Elephants for want of Towns' (Fig. 179). This period of stagnation in discovery may be explained by the forbidding physical character of the continent. The difficulties of travel inland from the sea were formidable. The trade routes southward across the desert from the Mediterranean ports were closed to Christians, and the passage up the Nile led the traveller into the swamps of the Sudan and the broken highlands of Ethiopia. The rivers discharging into the Atlantic and Indian Oceans—unlike those of North America—offered no easy routes into the hinterland. Forcing their way through the mountain ranges which fringe the coasts, they were broken by cataracts which made their navigation dangerous. The complex relief of the interior created no clear hydrographic pattern, and the plan of the watersheds drained by the great rivers of Nile, Congo, and Zambesi remained obscure until the second half of the 19th century; while it was only in 1796 that the direction of the Niger's flow became known by experience. To such obstacles, placed across the traveller's path by the geography of Africa, must be added an unhealthy climate and (in Arab regions) an intolerant religion. In combination, they prevented the spread of a single political power such as that of the Mongols under whose protection Marco Polo explored eastern Asia.[1]

FIG. 179.—Map of the 'Empire of Prester John or of the Abyssinians', published by Ortelius in 1573.

The Portuguese quest of the empire of Prester John was crowned in 1557 by the establishment of a Jesuit mission, from Goa, in Abyssinia. The journeys of the Jesuits in the next three-quarters of a century, notably those of Pedro Páez between 1603 and 1622 and of Antonio Fernandes in 1613–14, made this the best-mapped part of interior Africa before the 18th century. The first European map of Ethiopia from surveys made in the country was that drawn by Fr Manoel de Almeida about 1640 (Fig. 180). 'Delineated by the Fathers of the Society, with the help of the

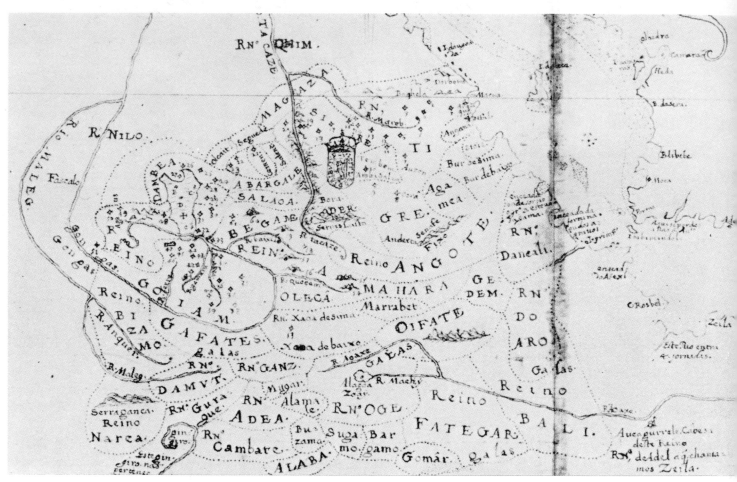

FIG. 180.—Part of the map of Ethiopia, drawn by Manoel de Almeida about 1640.

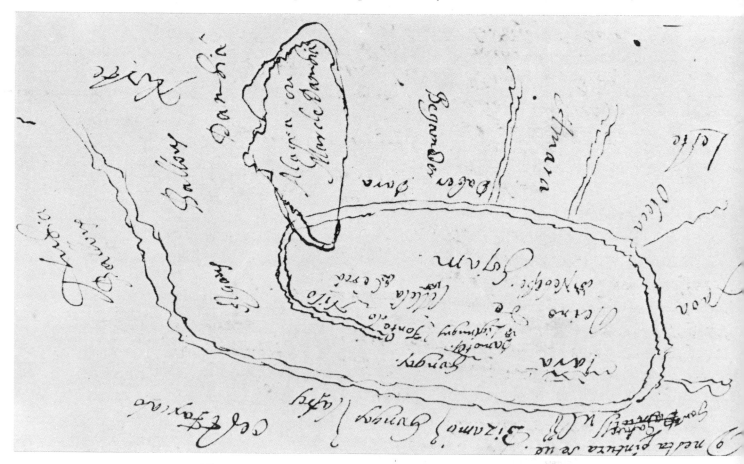

FIG. 181.—Almeida's sketch of the source of the Blue Nile.

Astrolabe [for determining latitudes]',[2] this map and its derivatives were not superseded before the 19th century. Almeida censured earlier maps—'Ptolemy's tables
and the maps of Hortelio and Gerardo Mercator' (Fig. 179)—for their 'numerous
and remarkable mistakes about Abassia'. He criticized in particular the immense
extent attributed to the kingdom by the 16th-century geographers, on whose maps
it stretched from the Red Sea almost to the Atlantic, and south to 'Lake Zaire',
some 10 degrees south of the Equator, where Ptolemy had placed the sources of the
Nile in the Mountains of the Moon. Southward indeed (wrote an English cosmographer in 1555) 'it confineth with the Sea toward Cape de Bona Speranza'.[3] With
characteristic conservatism, however, mapmakers continued to prefer the older
version to the Jesuit cartography of Ethiopia until well into the 18th century, even

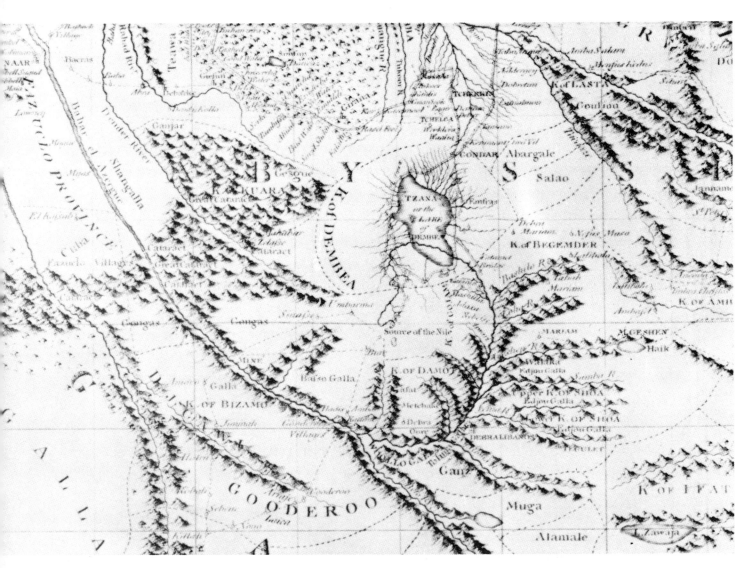

FIG. 182.—Part of James Bruce's map of Ethiopia, from his travels in 1768–72.

warning their readers not to be incautious enough to follow Almeida's representation of the source of the Blue Nile.[1]

Páez had in 1613 reached the source of the Abay or Blue Nile (Fig. 181)—two springs said to be 'unfathomable'. His claim to priority was unjustly disputed by James Bruce who, in the course of his journeys through Abyssinia in 1768–72, was the next European traveller to visit the source (Fig. 182). Bruce described grandiloquently his 'discovery'—'standing in that spot which had baffled the genius, industry, and inquiry of both ancients and moderns, for the course of near three thousand years'; and he determined the latitude of the 'principal fountain' by 35 observations with his astronomical quadrant. Almeida placed it in about 11° 50′ N, Bruce in 10° 59′ 25″.

The coasts of 'Guinea' or West Africa, frequented by English merchant adventurers from 1553, were in the 17th century the scene of commercial rivalry between the Dutch, English, French and other nations. On the Gold Coast, neither the Portuguese nor their successors the Dutch penetrated far inland from their coastal forts; and lack of enterprise in this region delayed the identification of the Niger mouth until the 19th century. English activity was mainly concentrated on the Gambia, which was ascended for over 300 miles by expeditions in 1618 and 1620. In 1661 the Company of Royal Adventurers of England trading into Africa established the 'first permanent English settlement on the West Coast', on James Island in the Gambia estuary (Fig. 185). This became the base for exploratory voyages up the river in search of gold and trade (Fig. 183). The Royal African Company, which succeeded to the rights of the Royal Adventurers, extended its commercial activity upstream; surveys of the river were made by William Smith in 1726 and Captain John Leach in 1732; and Francis Moore, factor at James Island from 1730 to 1734, drew an admirable map from Leach's survey (Fig. 184). In his book *Travels into the Inland Parts of Africa* (1738), Moore printed also the journal of Captain Bartholomew Stibbs, who had in 1723–4 navigated the river by canoe to above the Barrakunda Falls in 14° W. In the first quarter of the 18th century the French, from their trading-posts at the mouth of the Senegal River, had under the direction of André Brue explored up-country to the gold-bearing region of Bambuk, between the Senegal and its tributary the Faleme, where they picked up reports of the River Niger and the renowned city of Timbuktu.

To the geography of the Niger these journeys made only a negative contribution. European mapmakers had no authentic information of the source of this great river, on the direction in which it flowed, or on the waters into which it issued. The Moorish traveller Leo Africanus, whose Description of Africa was published at

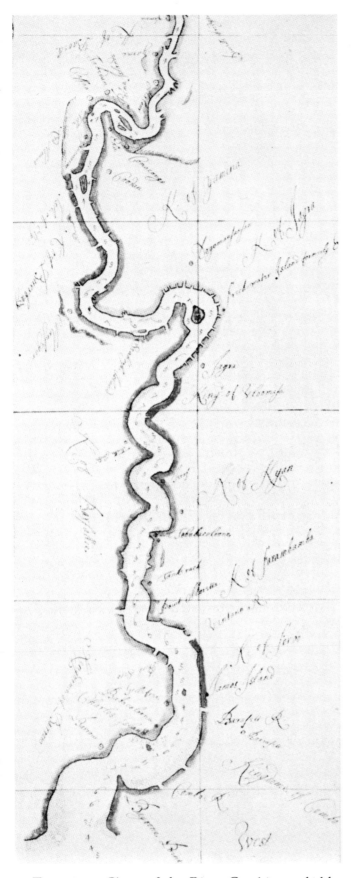

FIG. 183.—Chart of the River Gambia, probably
drawn in connection with Vermuyden's expedition
in 1661.

FIG. 184.—Francis Moore's map of the Gambia,
published in 1738.

FIG. 185.—The English fort on James Island, in the Gambia; a view by William Smith, published in 1727.

Venice in 1550, had indeed seen the Niger, but by a freak of misinterpretation had recorded that it flowed westward.[5] The error led cartographers to give the river a source in an inland lake and a vast delta on the Atlantic, with the Senegal, the Gambia and the Rio Grande as principal mouths. Even those maps which correctly showed its direction of flow as eastward led it into the Nile or a central lake. The nformation obtained by Brue on the Senegal and Stibbs on the Gambia pointed in this direction, for it suggested that neither of these rivers had any connection with the Niger.

This was the next great problem of African geography to be attacked by exploration. The Association for the Discovery of the Interior Parts of Africa—or African Association—was formed in London in 1788, with Sir Joseph Banks as secretary and Major James Rennell (the 'father of English geography') as expert adviser. To the discovery of the Niger and its course the Association first addressed itself. After the failure of its first four expeditions, it sent out the young Scotsman Mungo Park in 1795, with instructions 'to pass on to the river Niger either by way of Bambouk, or by such other route as should be found most convenient [and to] ascertain the course and, if possible, the rise and termination of that river'. Setting out from the Gambia, Park marched east to Bambuk, crossing the Faleme and the Senegal, and on 20 July 1796, he 'saw with infinite pleasure the great object of my mission—the long-sought-for, majestic Niger, glittering to the morning sun, as broad as the Thames at Westminster, and flowing slowly *to the eastward*' (Fig. 186).

Park's journey, from which he returned in 1797, had not revealed the outfall of the Niger, on which conflicting opinions were still maintained. Rennell believed that

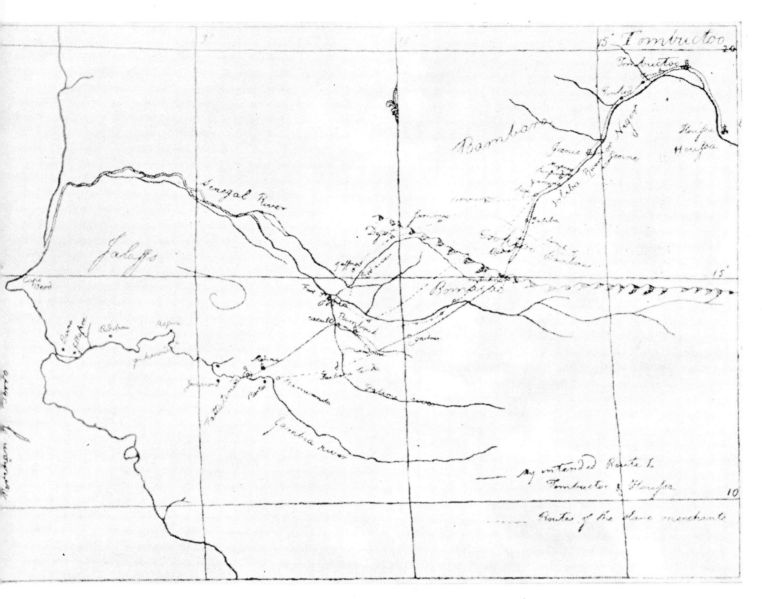

FIG. 186.—Sketch map drawn by Mungo Park in December 1795 to show his 'intended Route'
to Timbuktu on the Niger.

the river discharged into 'lakes in the eastern quarter of Africa'; Park was prepared
to descend it with 'hopes of returning by the Congo'. To test the supposed identity
of the Niger and the Congo, he led a second expedition, promoted by the government, from the Gambia in 1805. After following the Niger for over 1000 miles,
first north-east and then (encouragingly) south-east, he died in a skirmish at the
Bussa rapids.

Park seems to have retained to the end his belief that the Niger issued into the
Congo, for one of his companions wrote from the river on 1 November 1805, that
'Capt Park has made every enquiry concerning the River Niger, and . . . there

281

remains no doubt but it is the Congo'. But theoretical geographers could now demonstrate, by collating all available evidence, that the Niger must fall into the head of the Bight of Benin, and three notable journeys, completing Park's task, placed the whole course of the river on the map. Major Dixon Denham and Captain Hugh Clapperton, travelling over the Sahara from Tripoli, reached Lake Chad in 1823 and showed that it was not the Niger source. In 1825–7 Clapperton and his servant Richard Lander went from Lagos to the Niger at Bussa and on to Sokoto. Finally Lander and his brother, also starting from Lagos, travelled down the Niger from Bussa to the sea in 1830 (Fig. 187).

In the first half of the 18th century the French geographer d'Anville reformed the map of Africa, sweeping from it all data that could not be critically authenticated. His map revealed the poverty of knowledge

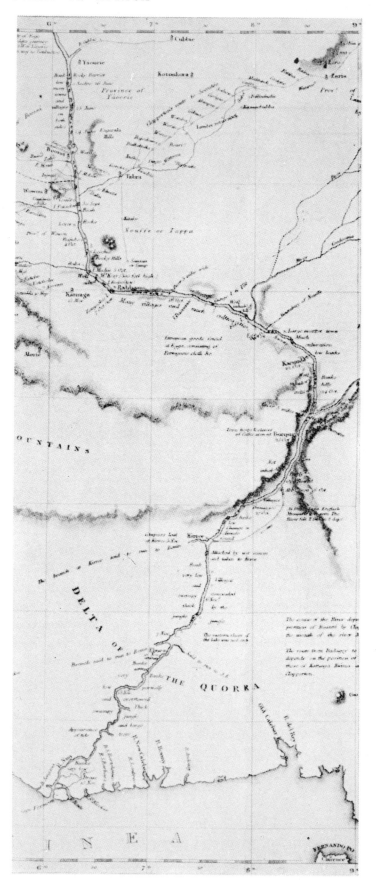

FIG. 187.—The lower course of the Niger, descended to the mouth in 1830 by Richard and John Lander.

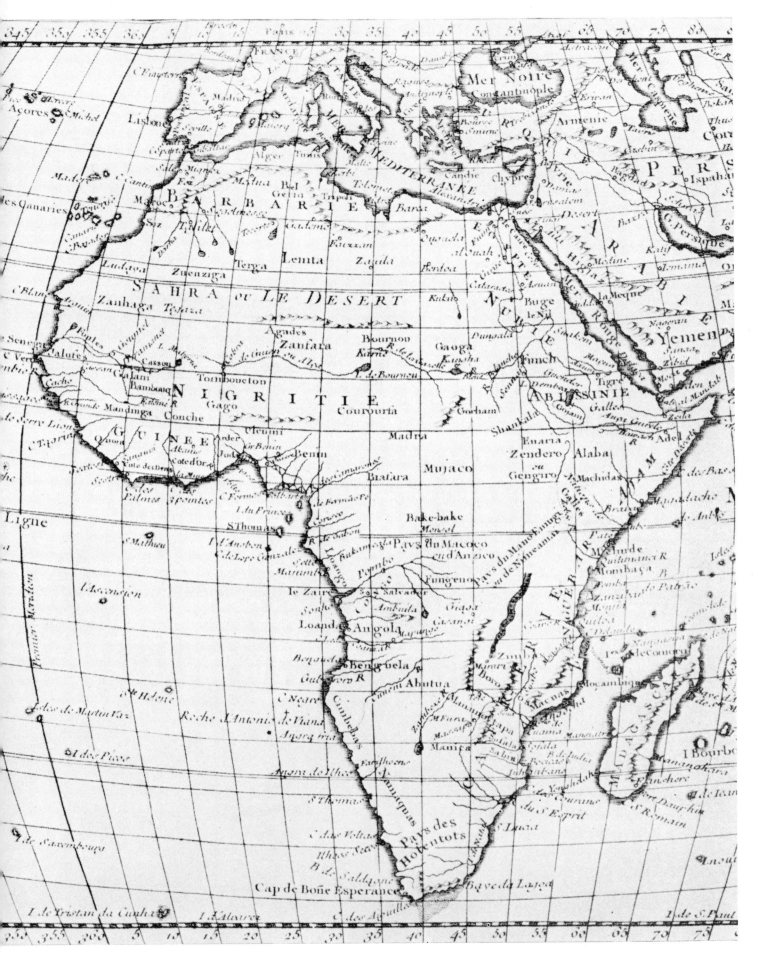

FIG. 188.—D'Anville's map of Africa, published in 1727.

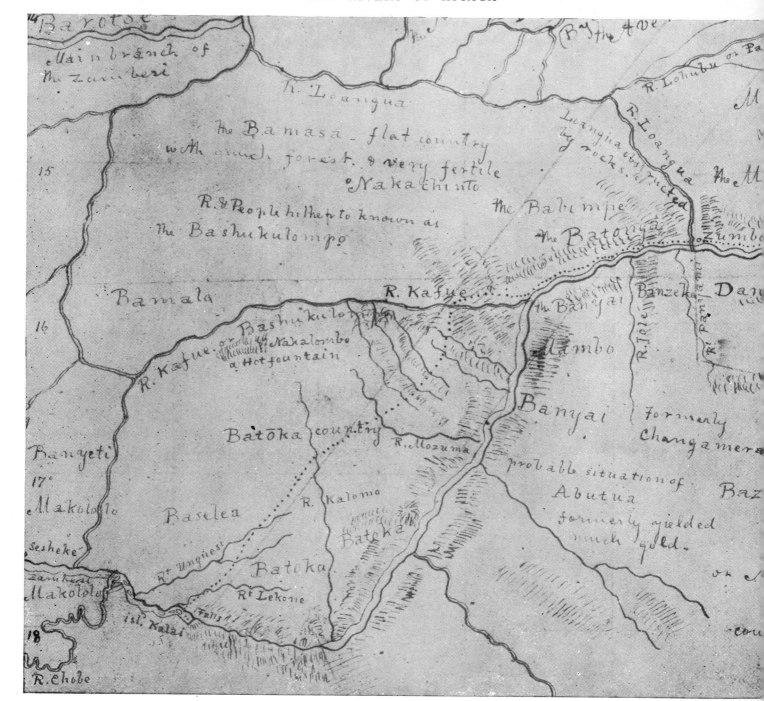

FIG. 189.—Part of Livingstone's MS map of his return journey across Africa in 1855-6.

regarding the great rivers (Fig. 188). Of the Congo and Zambesi only the lower waters were known with any assurance; while on the rise and course of the White Nile no direct information from travellers had reached Europe. Not until the third quarter of the 19th century were the hydrographic systems of these rivers established by navigation along their courses and by exploration of their watersheds and of the great lakes which fed the Nile.

284

David Livingstone's zeal for geographical discovery was fired by his journey across the Kalahari Desert to Lake Ngami in 1849. Two years later he reached the upper reaches of the Zambesi in 25° E, higher than any point reached by the Portuguese: ' . . . that river was not previously known to exist there at all. The Portuguese maps all represent it as rising far to the east of where we now were.' Rivers, as channels of communication to the healthier highlands of the interior, were the routes by which Livingstone hoped to carry European missions and trade inland and so to break the sinister power of the slavers. 'I view', he wrote, 'the end of the geographical feat as the beginning of the missionary enterprise'; his travelling library comprised the Nautical Almanac, logarithm tables, and the Bible. It has been said[6] that 'he loved rivers but abhorred waterfalls', as obstacles to the opening up of Africa; and he compared the country to 'a wide-awake hat, with the crown a little depressed. . . . So long as African rivers remain in what we may call the brim, they present no obstructions, but no sooner do they emerge from the higher lands than their utility is impaired by cataracts.'

FIG. 190.—The Victoria Falls, painted by Thomas Baines in August 1862.

To reveal the river systems of East and Central Africa was the object of all Livingstone's great journeys. By his two expeditions to the Zambesi (1853–6 and 1858–63) he explored the whole basin of the river in search of a navigable route between the interior and the sea (Fig. 189). His crossing of the continent to Luanda,

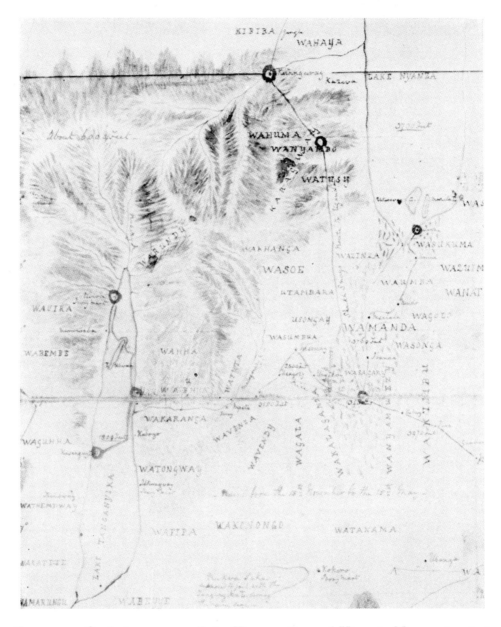

FIG. 191.—Speke's routes to Lake Tanganyika and Victoria Nyanza in 1858, in a map drawn by him.

in Angola, in 1853–4 led him over the Zambesi-Congo divide, and on the return journey to the mouth of the Zambesi he was the first European to see the Victoria Falls (Fig. 190). In 1859, travelling up the Shire River, he discovered Lake Nyasa, which he explored two years later. Disappointed at finding the Zambesi barred to navigation by the 'frightful' rapids of Kebrabasa, Livingstone now turned his mind to a more northerly route by the Rovuma River to the Nyasa region. This was to be the initial object of his last expedition, but in the event it became subordinated to a search for the ultimate sources of the Nile, proposed by Sir Roderick Murchison, President of the Royal Geographical Society.

The principal lakes which supplied the waters of the White Nile had already been discovered. In 1858 Richard Burton, accompanied by John Hanning Speke as 'sole

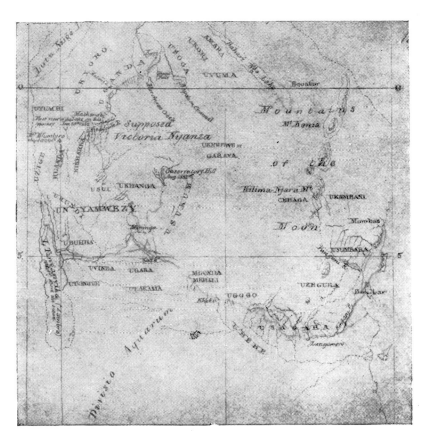

Fig. 192.—Part of a map drawn by Burton in 1864 to show his interpretation of the Nile sources.

surveyor', reached Lake Tanganyika, and Speke, travelling north alone, saw Lake Victoria (Fig. 191). This he apprehended to be '*the* discovery of the source of the Nile'; but Burton refused to accept this interpretation, and on his own map he contrived (as Speke wrote) 'to sever my lake from the Nile by *his* Mountains of the Moon' (Fig. 192).

In 1860–3 Speke, with J. A. Grant, confirmed his discovery by travelling through Uganda, west of Lake Victoria, to the Ripon Falls and down the Nile to Gondokoro, where he was met by Samuel Baker coming up from Egypt. On the map of his journey which Speke drew for Baker (Fig. 193), he marked—to the west of Lake

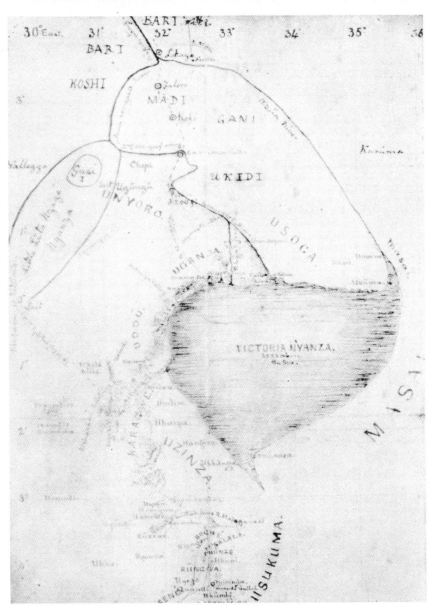

FIG: 193.—Part of Speke's sketch map of the journey made by him and Grant down the Nile to Victoria Nyanza in 1860-3.

FIG. 194.—Albert Nyanza, in a map drawn by Baker to illustrate his discovery of the lake in March 1864.

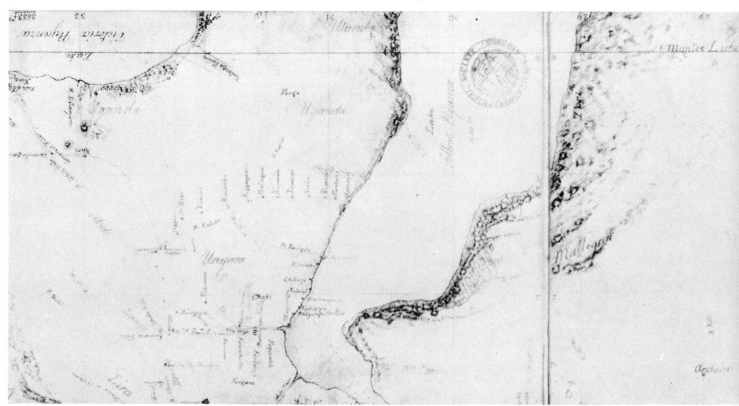

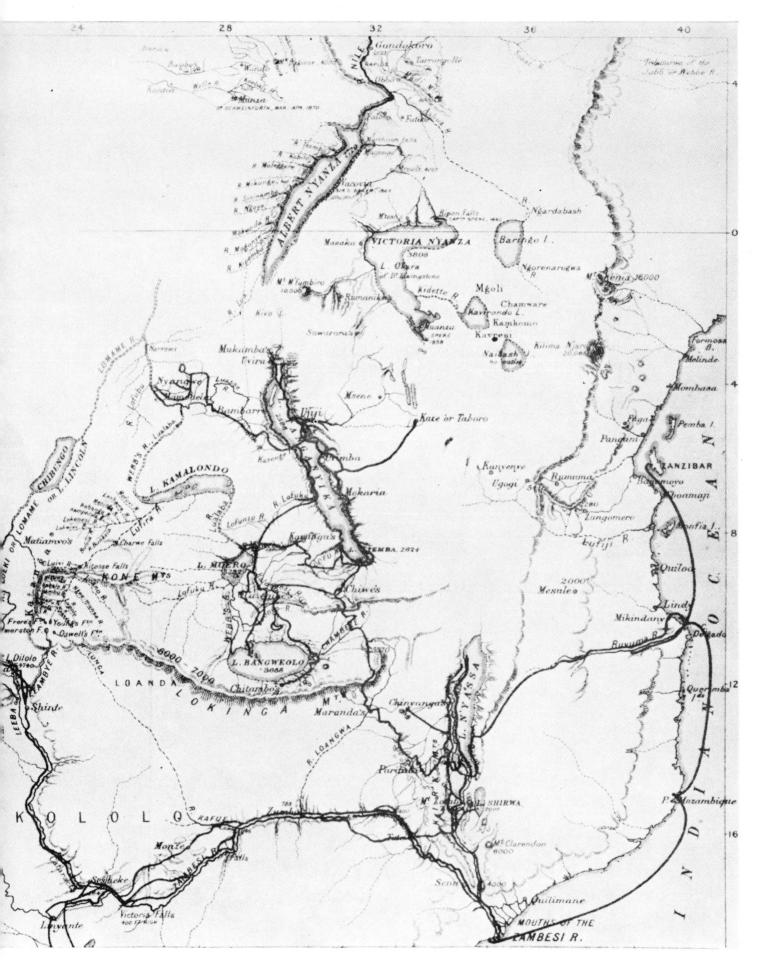

FIG. 195.—'The Forest Plateau of Africa, showing the great rivers and lakes discovered and explored by
Dr Livingstone'; a printed map of his journeys between 1866 and 1873.

Victoria—another large lake called by his native informants 'Luta Nzigé'. Baker's discovery of this lake, which he named Lake Albert, in 1864 led him to claim that 'the Victoria and the Albert lakes are the two Sources of the Nile' (Fig. 194).

Livingstone's last journey took him from the Rovuma and Nyasaland in 1866 to Lake Tanganyika and thence to the discovery of Lake Mweru and Lake Bang-weolo (1868). Here he wrote in his journal: 'If I am not deceived by the information I have received . . . the springs of the Nile rise between 9° and 10° south latitude, or at least 400 or 500 miles south of the south end of Speke's Lake, Victoria Nyanza, which he considered to be the sources of the Nile.' Four years later, after reaching the Lualaba river (1871) and almost traversing Lake Tanganyika, he still remained 'in reference to this Nile Source . . . in perpetual doubt and perplexity. . . . Great Lualaba may turn out to be the Congo and Nile. . . . It would be comfortable to be positive like Baker.' He was haunted by a story told by Herodotus of four springs, the waters of which flowed north to Egypt and south to 'Ethiopia', and from reports which he collected he held it 'all but certain that four full grown gushing fountains

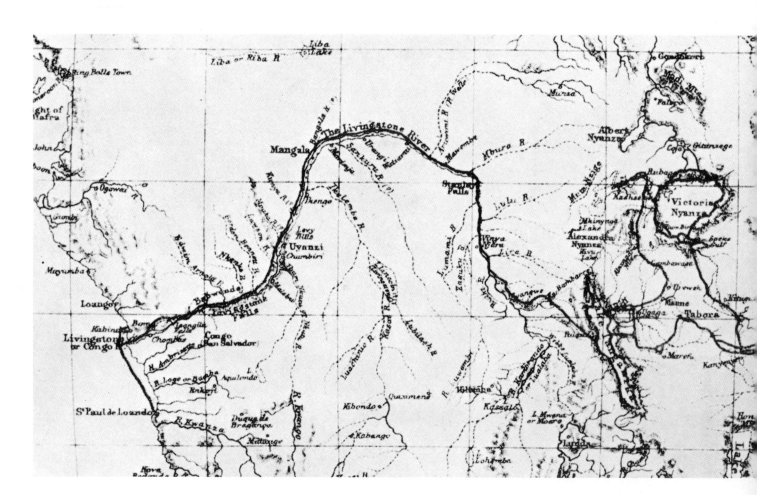

FIG. 196.—Map of Stanley's journeys in the Nile and Congo basins, 1874–7.

rise on the watershed eight days south of Katanga' (i.e. in about 14° S). Working westward in search of the rivers flowing north from these supposed springs, he died on 1 May 1873, to the south of Lake Bangweolo (Fig. 195). He never gave up the geographical quest; a few days before his death, he was questioning some villagers 'whether they knew of a hill on which four rivers took their rise. The spokesman answered that they had no knowledge of it.' Even more moving are the pages of figures in the notebooks in which, despite the utmost physical weakness, he recorded the astronomical observations and the computations by which he determined his latitude and longitude. They remind us that Livingstone was not merely a great traveller; he has been called 'perhaps the most exact surveyor and navigator in Africa at that time'.[7]

The work of Livingstone and Speke was completed by H. M. Stanley, who had in 1871 relieved Livingstone at Ujiji on Lake Tanganyika. In 1875–6 Stanley circumnavigated Lakes Victoria and Tanganyika, paying tribute to Speke's 'geographical genius, that from mere native report sketched with such a masterly hand the bold outlines of the Victoria Nyanza'. Travelling 'down the Livingstone River', as he renamed Livingstone's Lualaba, Stanley traced the Congo to its mouth, reaching the Atlantic in August 1877 (Fig. 196).

Remarks on the Illustrations

Chapter XIII

179   The map published in the 1573 edition of Ortelius' *Theatrum* is derived from Italian maps, engraved at Venice, in which the geography of Africa was pieced together from materials published in the *Navigationi* of Ramusio (Venice, 1557–60). The coastal outline and names follow the Portuguese charts. The provinces and towns of Abyssinia, the realm of Prester John, were known from Alvarez' narrative of the Portuguese embassy in 1520–7, published by Ramusio; but the cartographers, ignorant of their location and area, extended them south of the Equator (e.g. 'Goiame', 'Xoa') and far to the west (e.g. 'Tigrai'). North of 'Xoa' is Mount Amara, 'where the sons of Prester John are held in confinement'—a custom of the royal house of Ethiopia recorded by Alvarez. The White Nile, following Ptolemy, rises from the Mountains of the Moon (in 15° S), 'beyond which, to the south, Africa was unknown to the ancients'. The Niger, issuing from a lake in 5° N, flows north and then west towards the Atlantic, following the course reported by Leo Africanus, whose Description of Africa was first printed by Ramusio.

180   Two copies of Almeida's map are known, one in the British Museum, the other in the School of Oriental and African Studies, London (MS 11966); part of the latter is reproduced here. This shows the source of the Blue Nile or Abay, its course through the southern end of Lake Tana and its loop east, south, and west through Gojjam. Almeida corrected the ludicrous extension attributed to Ethiopia by 16th-century cartographers, and limited it to a range of nine degrees in latitude (8°–17° N).

181   Almeida's sketch of the source of the Blue Nile ('Fonte do Nilo') is in the British Museum manuscript of his history of Ethiopia (Add. MS 9861, fol. 11). It was presumably drawn from a map by Fr Pedro Páez, who reached the source in 1613. (The map has been inverted in reproduction so as to orient it with north at the top.)

182 Bruce's map of Abyssinia was published in his *Travels to discover the Sources of the Nile* (Edinburgh, 1790). This detail shows the source of the Blue Nile which he visited in November 1770. The general similarity to Almeida's representation (Figs. 180, 181) is evident, although Almeida's positions are about a degree too far south and he incorrectly flattened the loop of the river.

183 Colonel John Vermuyden accompanied the expedition sent in 1661 by the Royal Adventurers of England to establish trade on the Gambia. Vermuyden was to prospect for gold, and this manuscript chart (formerly in the Royal Library, now in the British Museum, K. Top. CXVII. 96) appears to record his voyage up the river in 1661, from James Island to 'Diuells bridge', above Baboon Island, 150 miles upstream. (East is at the top.)

184 Francis Moore served in the Gambia as a writer and factor of the Royal African Company from 1730 to 1735. An eager observer, he recorded his experiences in his *Travels into the Inland Parts of Africa* (London, 1738), with his map entitled 'A Draught of the River Gambia, with the soundings; also all the kingdoms, most of the principal towns, and the Royal African Companies factories . . . in a course of 500 miles up the river', i.e. to the Barracunda Falls. Moore's map marks the eight 'out-factories' of the Company, and incorporates information from voyages made upriver in 1723 by Bartholomew Stibbs, whose journal was reprinted in Moore's book, and in 1732 by Captain John Leach. (East is at the top.)

185 'The South-west Prospect of James Island on the River of Gambia', drawn by William Smith in 1727, was published in his *Drafts of Guinea* (London, 1732); Smith had been sent out by the Royal African Company in 1726 to survey its settlements. The fort was built on 'St Andrew's Island' in 1652 by a colony sent out by the Duke of Courland; in 1661 it was captured, and the island re-named, by the Royal Adventurers of England. Although James Island had no water-supply, it remained the centre of trade and government on the Gambia until the establishment of Bathurst on Banjol (St Mary's Island) in 1816.

186 The Gambia was the base from which Mungo Park started on both his expeditions to the Niger. In July 1795 he arrived at the English factory of Fattatenda or Pisania, 'a small village in the King of Yany's dominions' (see Fig. 184). Here, before starting his journey in December, he drew this sketch map, on which he indicated by a dotted line the 'routes of the slave merchants', and by a continuous line his own 'intended Route to Timbuctoo & Houssa', on the Niger, by way of Bambuk, at the junction of the Faleme and Senegal rivers. The Niger is named 'Joliba River or Niger'.

187 This map, 'The Course of the Quorra (the Joliba or Niger of Park) from the Journals of Mess.rs Richard and John Lander', was published in the *Journal of the Royal Geographical Society*, vol. I (1830). It shows the lower waters of the river,

which the Landers descended in 1830, from 'Boossa' (Bussa) rapids, where Park had died, to the mouth.

188 In his map of 1727, the great French geographer J. B. Bourguignon d'Anville suppressed much of the earlier speculative geography of Central Africa and the African rivers. The White Nile ('R. Blanche') is not carried south of 25° N. The rise and course of the Blue Nile are laid down from the Jesuit maps (cf. Figs. 180, 181), by way of the map of Ethiopia by Hiob Ludolf (1683); and Abyssinia is confined within its proper bounds. The Zambesi river is drawn from Portuguese information. North of it (lying in 5°–25° S) is a large lake, recalling the Nile sources in Ortelius' map (Fig. 179), but more probably derived from Arab reports of the great lakes of East Africa. Only the lower reaches of the Congo ('le Zaire') are represented. The Senegal and Gambia are correctly shown; the Niger rises in a central lake, 'L. de Bournou' (cf. Fig. 179), and flows westward, with a conjectured connection (shown by a dotted line) with the Senegal.

189 Livingstone's map of his return journey eastward across Africa in 1855–6 is preserved by the Royal Geographical Society (MS 371/9). This detail shows his route (dotted line) in November–December 1855, with the country north to the Barotse which he had explored earlier from Linyanti, the principal town of the Makololo. Leaving the Makololo country, Livingstone went down the Zambesi to the island of Kalai, and on 17 November 1855 he visited the Victoria Falls, which (as he wrote) 'had never been seen before by European eyes' and to which he 'gave the only English name I have affixed to any part of the country'. Ascending the Lekone river, which he took to be 'the ancient bed of the Zambesi, before the fissure was made', Livingstone crossed the Batoka plateau and descended the Kafue River to rejoin the Zambesi. At Zumbo, the confluence of the Loangwa and the Zambesi, he found the ruins of a Portuguese church (14 December).

190 The oil-painting by Thomas Baines, made from sketches taken at his visit to the Victoria Falls in August 1862, is in the collections of the Royal Geographical Society. In November 1855 Livingstone, standing on this island in mid-stream, 'peered down into a large rent which had been made from bank to bank of the broad Zambesi, and saw that a stream of a thousand yards broad leaped down a hundred feet, and then became suddenly compressed into a space of fifteen or twenty yards'.

191 By 1850 missionaries from Mombasa had discovered Mount Ruwenzori and seen the snow-capped peak of Mount Kenya, which were conjecturally identified with Ptolemy's Mountains of the Moon (cf. Fig. 179); and Arab traders had transmitted native stories of an immense inland lake. The object of Burton and Speke in 1857–8 was 'to penetrate inland . . . to the reputed Lake of Nyasa'. Speke's map (Royal Geographical Society, MS 371/12) shows their discovery of Lake Tanganyika, '1809 feet' above sea-level, and Speke's journey north from Kaze, in Unyam-

wezi, to the southern end of Victoria Nyanza, July 1858. Speke took the plateau east of Lake Tanganyika to be the Mountains of the Moon, and Victoria Nyanza (to which he ascribed a height of 3700 feet above sea level) to be the source of the Nile. The country further north is laid down on the map from Arab reports.

192   The map drawn by Burton in December 1864, with the title 'The Sources of the Nile, adapted from Captn Speke's map' (Royal Geographical Society, MS 371/23), suggests by a dotted line (representing the Rusizi River) that the waters of Lake Tanganyika flowed north into Albert Nyanza ('Luta Nzige'), discovered by Baker in March 1864. The 'Divisio Aquarum', south of Lake Tanganyika, thus represents the Nile watershed. Burton's scepticism about 'Speke's lake' is indicated by the 'supposed Victoria Nyanza', to the east of which he marks the Mountains of the Moon with 'Mt Kenia'.

193   Speke's sketch map of his route (with Grant) down the Nile in 1860–3 (Royal Geographical Society, MS 371/22) was given by him to Baker in Gondokoro, where they met in February 1863. This section of the map, from 4° S to 4° N, depicts the region traversed between February 1861 and February 1863. The height of Victoria Nyanza is given as 3553 feet above sea level. To the north-west Speke marks a large lake, 'Little Luta Nzigé N'yanza', i.e. Albert Nyanza, of which he had heard while in Unyoro but which he was unable to visit.

194   This detail from Baker's map (Royal Geographical Society, MS 371/20) illustrates his discovery of Albert Nyanza ('1988 ft') in March 1864 on his journey from Gondokoro after meeting Speke and Grant. 'This', he concluded, 'was the great reservoir of the Nile.' The representation of Victoria Nyanza is taken from the map drawn by Speke (Fig. 193).

195   The map of 'The Forest Plateau of Africa, shewing the great rivers and lakes discovered and explored by Dr Livingstone', was published in *Livingstone's Last Journals* (London, 1874). In the south are shown his route across Africa and back, 1853–6, and that of his Zambesi–Lake Nyasa expedition, 1858–63. Further north, the map illustrates Livingstone's quest of the Nile sources between 1866 and 1873, with his journey to the Lualaba (the Congo) in 1871 and his final search about Lake Bangweolo in 1872–3.

196   This map in Stanley's book *Through the Dark Continent* (London, 1899) shows the journeys on which Stanley, between 1874 and 1877, circumnavigated Victoria Nyanza and Lake Tanganyika and descended the Congo ('The Livingstone River') to its mouth. This great expedition revealed the hydrography of the Congo headwaters which had perplexed Livingstone.

Notes

Chapter XIII

<><><><><><><><><><><><><><><><><><><><><><><><><><><><><><><><><><><><><><>

[1] See Chapter I.

[2] Almeida's latitudes were generally one or two degrees too far south.

[3] Richard Eden, *The decades of the newe worlde* (London, 1555).

[4] E.g. the legend of J. B. Homann's map of Africa (*c.* 1720) claims that the Jesuit reports have been used; yet the map ignores their discoveries, and readers are warned against their maps!

[5] This error may have sprung from Leo's misreading of the notes of his itinerary on the Upper Niger, above Timbuktu, so that in his final text the order of places visited by him was reversed.

[6] By Professor Frank Debenham.

[7] The estimate is Professor Debenham's.

XIV

THE POLAR REGIONS IN THE NINETEENTH CENTURY

◇-◇

IN EXPLORATION BY SEA the main effort of the 19th century was concentrated on the polar regions. The history of exploration towards the Poles strikingly illustrates the interaction of maps and discovery, of geographical ideas and geographical experience. From the 16th century onward cosmographers, developing mediaeval patterns of the division of the earth's surface between land and water, conceived the Arctic as an ocean (and therefore perhaps navigable), the Antarctic as a continent (and therefore perhaps habitable). Globes and maps on polar projections displayed the distribution of land and water, in high latitudes, in a relationship which encouraged geographical conjecture and commercial enterprise: in the north, a sea almost, but not quite, enclosed by the land masses (the 'Heartland') of the northern hemisphere—in the south, a continent surrounded by the 'embracing ocean' (Fig. 197).[1] These ideas were in essence correct, but the hopes built upon them, and vainly tested by many arduous voyages, were delusions. The 16th-century mapmaker, in the absence of information from experience, could not visualize the physical conditions which controlled navigation within the polar circles, and the sanguine Tudor projector was able to hold 'no land inhabitable, nor Sea innauigable'. The search, lasting 300 years, for northern sea-ways from Europe into the Pacific was disillusioning, for in the age of sail the Arctic could offer no commercially practicable 'waie of the northe'; and Cook, the first European seaman to cross the Antarctic Circle, concluded that the continent which he conjectured to lie behind the ice masses to the south must be of so forbidding a character 'that the world will derive no benefit from it'.[2]

Even if, for want of the means to attain it, the objective came to seem not worth

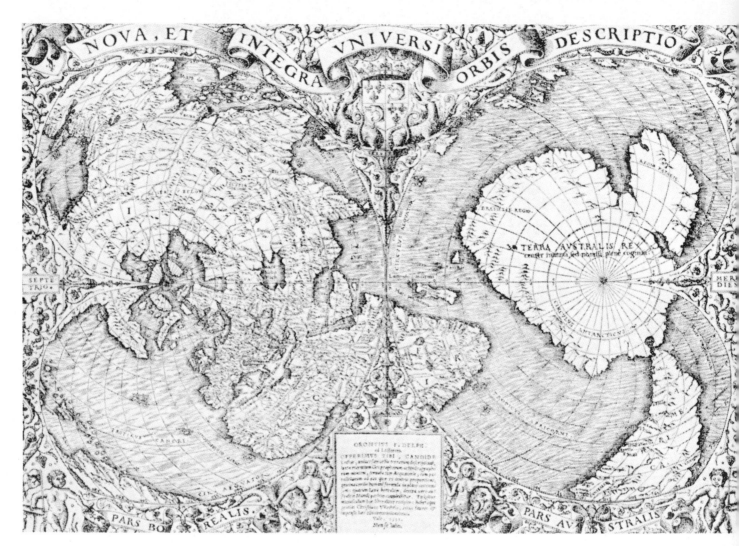

FIG. 197.—Hemispheric world map by Oronce Finé, 1531; reflecting 16th-century ideas on the distribution of land and water.

the toil, the quest itself produced some notable records of human endeavour. The high latitudes reached by navigators in the age of sail testifies to their skill and courage. The furthest north was attained successively by John Davis in 1587 (72° 12′, in Davis Strait), Henry Hudson in 1607 (80° 23′), C. J. Phipps in 1773 (80° 37′), William Scoresby in 1806 (81° 30′), and W. E. Parry in 1827 (82° 45′; the last four all to the north of Spitsbergen). In the south, Cook in 1773 reached the latitude of 71° 10′ S in longitude 106° 54′ W, and in circumnavigating the Antarctic Continent he sailed over 125 degrees of longitude to the south of the 60th parallel.[3] His work was continued by the Russian commander F. G. Bellingshausen who in 1820–1 traversed no less than 242 degrees of longitude south of 60° S (Fig. 199).

FIG. 198.—Chart and view of the South Sandwich Islands, drawn on Cook's second voyage, January 1775.

FIG. 199.—The meeting between Palmer's sealer the *Hero* and Bellingshausen's ships in the South Shetlands, 25 January 1821.

The first authenticated—because correctly charted—discoveries of sub-Antarctic lands were those of South Georgia and the South Sandwich Islands by Cook in January 1775 (Fig. 198). Bellingshausen was the first to sight land (Peter I Island) within the Antarctic Circle, and in January 1820 (in 78° W) he was within thirty miles of the continent, which fog prevented him from seeing. Cook firmly believed in the existence of the Antarctic Continent which he never saw, maintaining 'that there is a tract of land near the pole that is the source of most of the ice that is spread over this vast Southern Ocean'.[4] Since however 'the greatest part of this Southern Continent must lie within the polar circle', he concluded that 'the lands which lie to the south will never be explored' and indeed, 'to judge of the bulk by the sample [South Georgia], would not be worth the discovery'. He could see no other inducement to exploration further south than his own 'ambition not only to go farther than anyone had been before, but as far as it was possible for man to go'.

Yet it was Cook himself who, by his report of the numerous whales in Magellanic waters and of the seal rookeries on the sub-Antarctic islands, drew attention to the chief source of wealth to be found in southern waters. In 1785 the English firm of Enderby sent out its first ships to hunt the sperm whale in the Pacific, and from the first decade of the 19th century sealers from New England were working the beaches of the islands discovered by Cook. The whaling and sealing ships sent out by American and English companies made many chance discoveries in the South Pacific and Antarctic, often incorrectly or imperfectly charted. To the whalers and especially the sealers, constantly searching for new grounds after they had exhausted the old, were due the next important discoveries in Antarctica.

In February 1819 William Smith, skipper of a north-country brig, sailing wide round Cape Horn, sighted land in 62° 40′ S, 60° W. Later, in November of the same year, he revisited 'New South Shetland', observing 'seals in abundance' and assuming it to be part of the Antarctic Continent. Back in Valparaiso, 'with the honest feeling of an Englishman' he reported his discovery to the British naval commander, who chartered his ship and sent it, with Edward Bransfield R.N. as master, to survey the newly found land (Fig. 200). In January 1820 Bransfield and Smith sailed south from the South Shetlands and in 64° S fell in with land which they named Trinity Land, now Trinity Peninsula on Graham Land (Fig. 201). The conjectural easterly extension of Trinity Land ('Supposed Land'), drawn on Bransfield's chart, illustrates the persistent expectation of continental land in this area. This first landfall on the Antarctic Continent was quickly followed by that of the Connecticut sealing captain Nathaniel Palmer, who in November 1820 reached Trinity Land ('Palmer Land') in a latitude of 63° 45′ S and on his return north encountered Bellingshausen's two ships on their way to survey the South Shetlands (Fig. 199).[5] In 1821–2 Palmer

300

FIG. 200.—The brig *Williams* of Blyth, William Smith master, approaching the South Shetlands, February 1819.

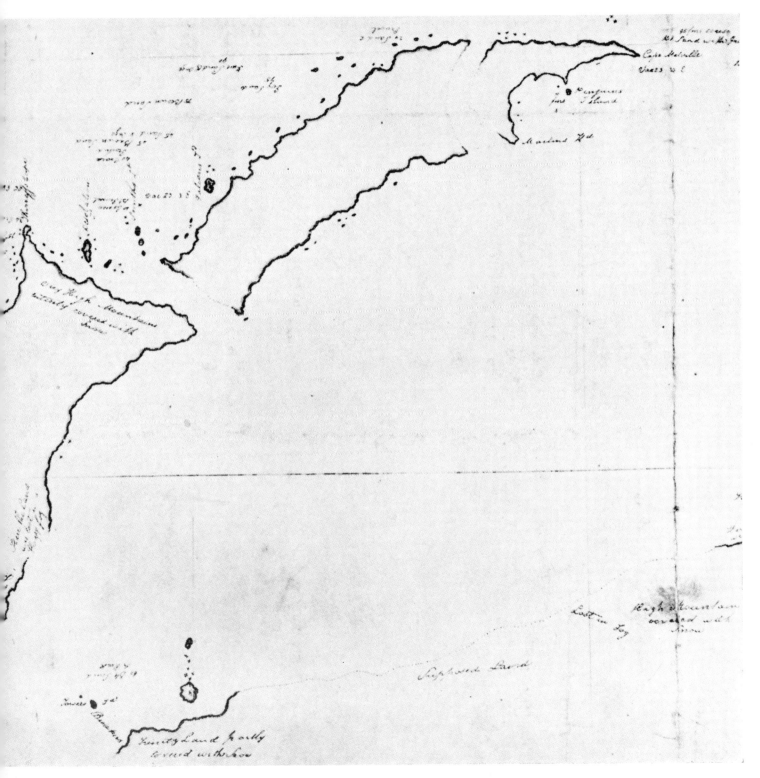

FIG. 201.—Chart of 'New or South Shetland', drawn by Edward Bransfield in the *Williams*.

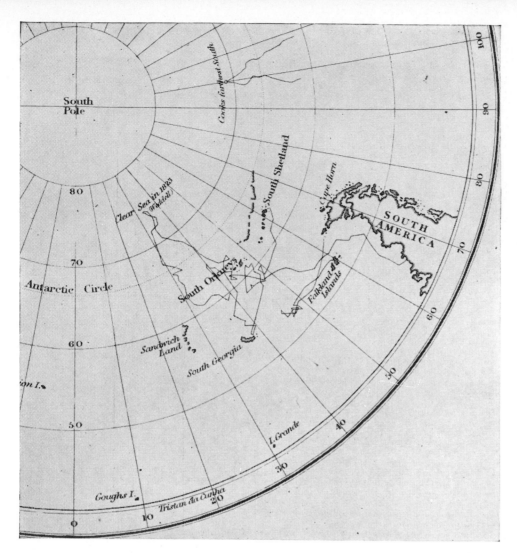

FIG. 202.—Part of Weddell's chart of his voyage to the south in 1823.

FIG. 203.—Weddell's ships at the southernmost point of their voyage, 'in a clear sea', on 20 February 1823.

accompanied the English sealing captain William Powell when he discovered the South Orkneys.

The discovery of further sections of the Antarctic coast and of its two great gulfs was the work of whaling ships and (after 1840) of nationally organized expeditions. Their commanders were experienced surveyors equipped with the best instruments of their day, and the 19th-century voyages were fully and reliably recorded in narrative and chart. In this period the discovery of new lands was subordinated to their intensive survey and scientific study; and even the great journeys for the ultimate discovery—that of the South Pole—were achieved by expeditions equipped for scientific research.

The firm of Enderby Brothers, of London, instructed its captains to seize any opportunity of making discoveries while engaged in their commercial duty of

FIG. 204.—The corvette *Astrolabe*, commanded by Dumont d'Urville, in ice-floes, 1840.

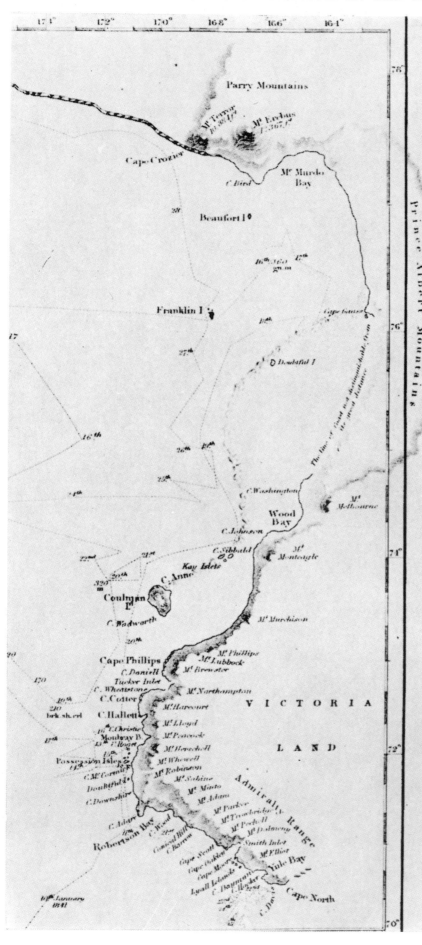

catching whales and seals. Two of the firm's commanders (both retired masters R.N.) made notable contributions to the geography of the Antarctic Continent. In 1822 James Weddell, on his second sealing voyage, charted the South Orkneys (which he had touched in the previous year, six days after their discovery by Powell), and stood south and east in search of land. In 72° S 'not a particle of ice of any description was to be seen', and on 20 February 1823, Weddell's two ships reached 74° 15′ S—'214 geographical miles farther south than Captain Cook' (Figs. 202, 203). Weddell was no doubt lucky, 'for no later explorer has found the Weddell Sea so clear of ice'. He himself concluded 'that the conjecture of Captain Cook, that field ice is formed and proceeds from land, and is not formed in the open sea, is true'; and he suggested that the 'sea perfectly clear of field ice', which he found at his farthest south, might well extend to the Pole itself. Weddell's views on

FIG. 205.—Part of James Clark Ross's chart, with the tracks of his ships in the Ross Sea, 10–28 January 1841.

the formation of sea ice were disputed by another Enderby skipper, John Biscoe, who believed all Antarctic field-ice to be frozen sea-water 'accumulating with time'. In 1830–2 Biscoe, under instructions to search for land to the south of the Indian Ocean, discovered Enderby Land (in 66° 25′ S, 49° 18′ E), which was not revisited for a hundred years, and circumnavigated the continent, sailing over 160 degrees of longitude above 60° S and nearly 50 degrees of longitude within the Antarctic Circle.

The running was now taken up by elaborately organized scientific expeditions sponsored by the French, United States and British governments. In January 1840 the French expedition of Dumont d'Urville discovered Terre Adélie, to the south of Australia, in 66° 30′ S (Fig. 204). In the same month the American expedition under Charles Wilkes fell in with land, which was named Wilkes Land, in the same sector and, following his instructions, coasted it westward.

The first Admiralty expedition to the Antarctic since that of Cook was led by

FIG. 206.—Beaufort Island and Mount Erebus, with Ross's ships, January 1841.

Captain James Clark Ross. Ross, who had served with Parry in the Arctic and had in 1829 discovered the North Magnetic Pole, sailed in 1839, in command of the two robustly built bomb ketches *Erebus* and *Terror*.[6] The voyage was designed to serve 'the science of magnetism . . . by an extensive series of observations made in high southern latitudes'; Ross was 'to determine the position of the magnetic pole, and even to attain to it if possible', and his search was to be made to the south of Tasmania. In January 1841 Ross (in 69° 15′ S, 176° 15′ E) passed through the pack ice into open sea and soon after sighted land which he followed southward. Naming the two volcanoes which he sighted after his two ships, he reached 78° 4′ S before being checked by the great ice-barrier which blocks the head of the Ross Sea (Figs. 205–7). On his second cruise from Tasmania he penetrated the Ross Sea further east to his highest latitude of 78° 9′. His third attempt to reach the Pole, this time by the Weddell Sea, took him to 71° 30′ S, and he rightly concluded that 'Weddell was favoured by an unusually fine season'.

FIG. 207.—The *Erebus* and *Terror* in collision on the weather side of two icebergs, 12 March 1842.

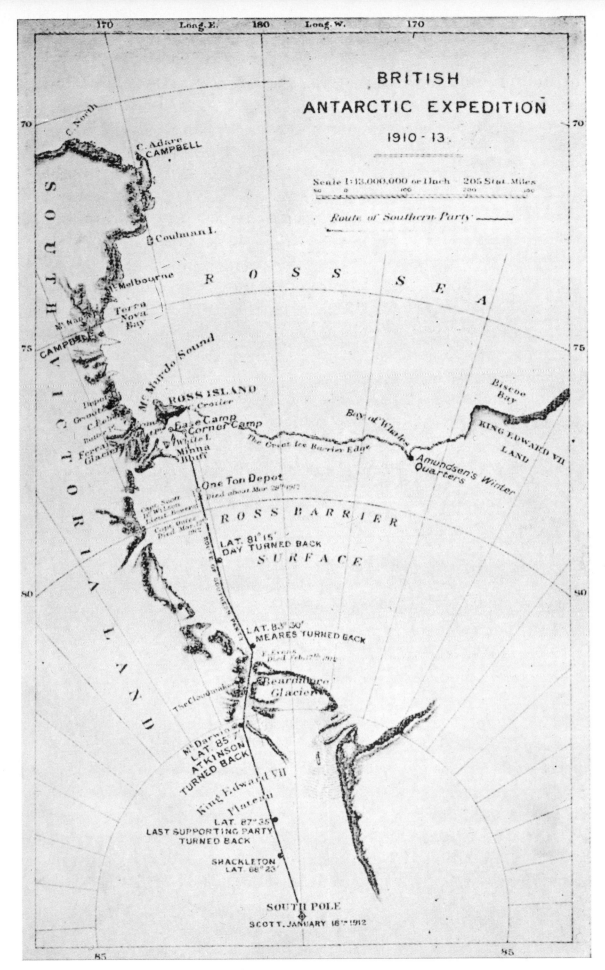

FIG. 208.—Map showing attempts on the South Pole from the Ross Sea in the early
20th century: Shackleton's furthest south in 1909, Amundsen's base for his journey to the
Pole in 1911–12, and the course of Scott's southern party to the Pole, 1911–12.

After Ross, no other important ventures were made to the Antarctic for a quarter of a century; but the two great indentations pointing to the Pole—the Weddell and Ross Seas—had already been laid down on the map. These were to furnish the bases from which the 20th-century expeditions, culminating in the heroic enterprises of Shackleton, Scott and Amundsen, were to spring (Fig. 208).

In the Arctic, as in the Antarctic, speculation and promotion turned on the possibility of open sea as far as the Pole, which had been tested by Phipps in 1773. High latitudes were attained by Greenland whalers, like Captain William Scoresby of Whitby, taking advantage of open seasons in which the sea to the north was ice-free. In 1818 John Barrow, Second Secretary of the Admiralty, conjectured that 'if the great polar basin should be free of land, the probability is, that it will also be free of ice'.[7] This hypothesis inspired a remarkable attempt to reach the North Pole made in 1827 by Captain W. E. Parry, Hydrographer of the Navy, who had four earlier Arctic voyages behind him. In boats fitted with sledge runners, Parry reached the latitude of 82° 45′ N (the furthest north for forty-eight years) before being turned back by the southerly drift.

During the first half of the 19th century, however, the mainspring of Arctic exploration was to be the search for 'a practicable passage from the Northern Atlantic into the Northern Pacific', which had been the motive of Cook's last voyage. To Barrow, 'the discovery of a north-west passage to India and China has always been considered an object peculiarly British'; and, while he wrote, a British expedition under Captain John Ross in a Hull whaler was already at sea in pursuit of this 'object'. Most of the ensuing ventures were promoted by the Admiralty, at the instigation of Barrow, and they are recorded in numerous original charts preserved in the Hydrographic Department.

The known or conceivable ends of the passage were marked, in the east, by the discoveries of William Baffin in 1616; in the west, by those of Cook in 1778 (Fig. 209). Baffin had pronounced Davis Strait and its northerly extension 'to be no other then a great Bay'; Cook had been stopped by ice at Icy Cape, in 70° 44′ N. The explorers of the 19th century had three geographical problems to solve before the passage could be established (Fig. 209): first, the discovery of a westward lead out of Davis Strait or Baffin Bay; second, the traverse of the coast of the continent eastward from Cook's *ne plus ultra* to and beyond the mouths of the Mackenzie and Copper-mine Rivers (reached by Alexander Mackenzie and Samuel Hearne in 1789 and 1771 respectively); and third, the tracing of channels through the archipelago to link the first two routes.

Unlike former theorists, Barrow could soberly assess the difficulties of navigation

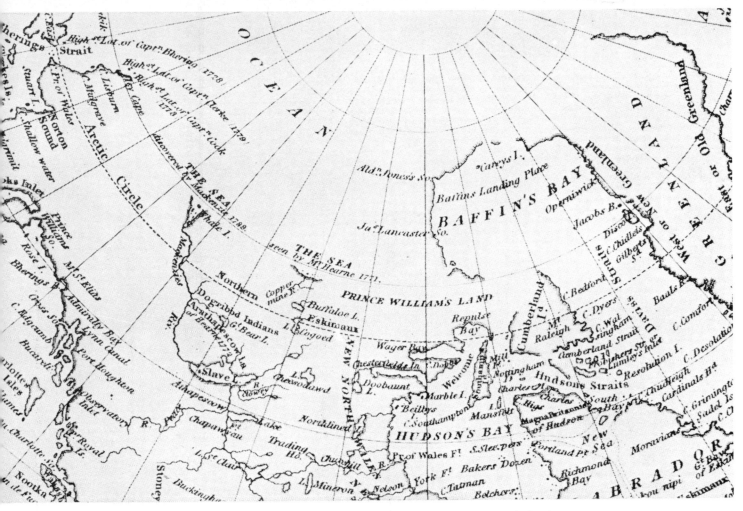

FIG. 209.—'Map of the Countries round the North Pole', published in 1818.

FIG. 210.—The *Hecla*, Lieutenant W. E. Parry, in Baffin Bay, July 1819.

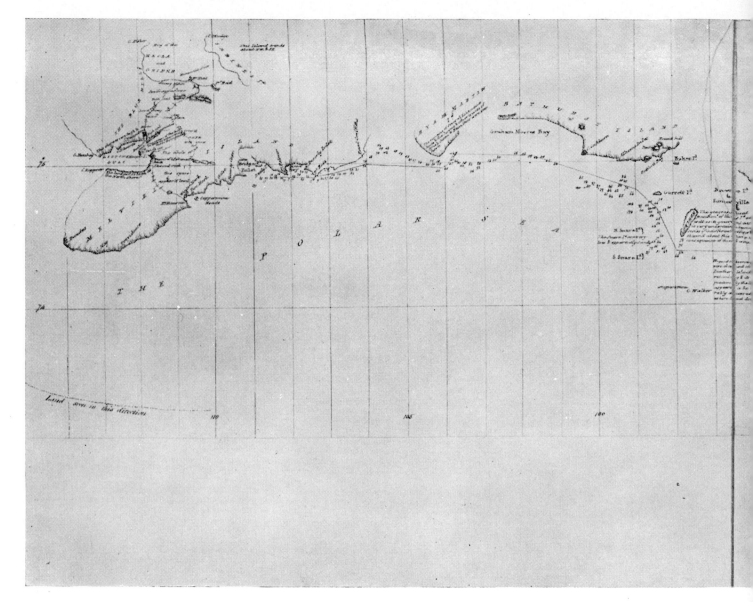

FIG. 211.—MS map by Parry, with his track in 1819 wes

in Arctic waters; he criticized earlier navigators for clinging to shores where they could be caught in pack-ice, and advocated open sea passages. His doctrine was exemplified by Parry, who in 1819–20 took his ships, the Hull-built bomb *Hecla* and the gun-brig *Griper*, through Lancaster and Barrow Sounds to winter on Melville Island (Figs. 210, 211). The 'heavy and extensive fields' of ice which he found to the west, blocking McClure Strait ('Banks Strait'), convinced him that there was 'little or nothing to be hoped for from any further attempts to prosecute the main object of the voyage in this place'; but he had in fact opened up the eastern entrance of the North-West Passage. His chart shows ice-free openings to the north from Barrow Strait, which might confirm Barrow's view of navigable sea towards

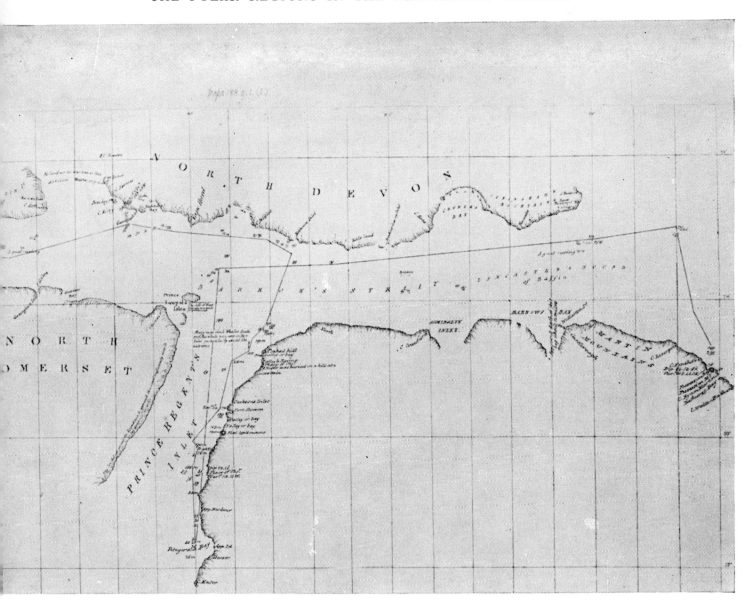

n Baffin Bay to winter quarters on Melville Island.

the Pole. Parry's voyage answered the outstanding question posed by Barrow, whether Greenland were an island or had a land connection with America which would close the North-West Passage. Southward out of Lancaster Strait, Prince Regent Inlet was explored, between 1822 and 1832, by naval expeditions under Parry and Captain John Ross.

The north coast of America was surveyed by a number of expeditions between 1821 and 1839. From the Pacific Captain F. W. Beechey had sailed beyond Cook's furthest point to Point Barrow, in 156° 20′ W. Naval land-based parties, led by Captain John Franklin in 1821–2 and 1825–7, descended the Mackenzie and Copper-mine Rivers and mapped their deltas and the adjacent coasts. In 1834 Captain George

Back went down the Back (or Great Fish) River to its mouth. In 1837–9 Thomas Simpson linked up these discoveries by navigating the coast of the continent by boat between Boothia Peninsula in the east and Point Barrow in the west.

The navigable passage would be continuously traced as soon as an open channel had been found through the unexplored area between Lancaster and Barrow Straits, in the north, and any point of the continental coast. Here the bomb *Terror* comes into the story again. She had had her first polar service under the command of Captain George Back in 1836–7. Caught in the pack-ice at the entrance of the Fox Channel, to the west of Baffin Island (Fig. 212), and stranded for 118 days on a great ice floe, on which she drifted for 200 miles, she took a severe battering from which she emerged 'crazy, broken, and leaky'; and only her robust construction enabled her to limp home with chain cables passed under her keel to frap her together until she was beached on the Irish coast to prevent her from sinking. The *Terror* was repaired in time to be commissioned, with the *Erebus*, for Captain J. C. Ross's Antarctic

Fig. 212.—The *Terror* frozen up at the entrance of Hudson Bay, 20 February 1837.

voyage of 1839–43. Two years after their return the two bombs were selected for the expedition of Sir John Franklin for the North-West Passage; for this duty the ships were fitted with auxiliary steam engines, of 20 horsepower, converted from railway locomotives. He sailed in May 1845, with instructions to penetrate south and west from Barrow Strait 'towards Bhering's Strait'; and his ships were last sighted by an English whaler off the Greenland coast in July of that year. Franklin, sailing south through Peel Sound, unhappily chose to attempt the passage to the west of King William Island (Victoria Strait), where in September 1846 his ships became ice-locked (Fig. 217). The crews, untrained in polar travel, attempted to make their way overland to the Back River and perished to a man. The only surviving written record of the last days of the expedition, found in the north of King William Island and dated 25 April 1848, reported that 'H.M. ships *Terror* and *Erebus* were deserted on the 22nd April, 5 leagues NNW of this, having been beset since 12th Septr 1846 . . .' The two ships are believed to have drifted through Victoria Strait to the south-west of King William Island before foundering; but it is a possibility which cannot be excluded that they suffered a similar experience to that of the *Terror* under Back in 1836–7 and drifted out into Baffin Bay and south through Davis Strait into the Atlantic.[8]

Seldom in the annals of exploration has a disaster been more fruitful of further discovery. By the summer of 1847 it was realized that Franklin's venture must have miscarried, and during the next ten years immense efforts were made, both by government and by private persons, to recover evidence of his fate. In the autumn of 1850 no fewer than fifteen vessels were engaged in the search (Fig. 213).[9] Two

FELIX   RESOLUTE   PIONEER   ASSISTANCE   SOPHIA   LADY FRANKLIN   P. ALBERT   INTREPID

FIG. 213.—Ships engaged in the search for Franklin lying off Cape Dudley Digges, in the north of Baffin Bay, August 1850.

FIG. 214.—H.M.S. *Enterprise*, Captain R. Collinson, entering Dolphin and Union Strait, September 1852.

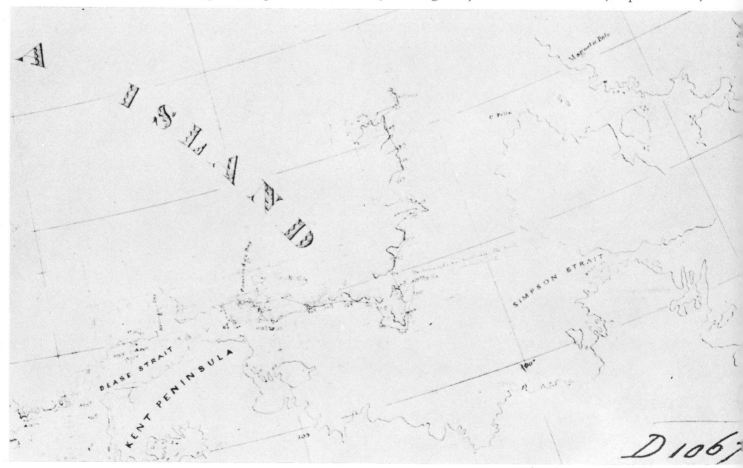

FIG. 215.—Collinson's chart of the track of his ship into Dease Strait and of his sledging parties along the west side of Victoria Strait.

large expeditions were dispatched by the Admiralty. Four ships under Austin went to Barrow Strait; and two ships—the *Enterprise* under Collinson and the *Investigator* under McClure—were to search eastward from Bering Strait. Collinson, who after five years at sea brought his ship safely home, penetrated Coronation Gulf as far as Cambridge Bay, in the south-east of Victoria Island (Figs. 214, 215). His sledging parties, travelling over the ice along the south and east coasts of Victoria Island, narrowly failed to discover the wreck of one of Franklin's abandoned ships, which had drifted southward through Victoria Strait; but he pointed the way to the navigable passage. McClure's ship had to be abandoned in 1853 in Mercy Bay, on the north coast of Banks Island, and he sledged across the ice of McClure Strait to Melville Island, where he was picked up, near Parry's 'Winter Harbour', by two ships of Austin's expedition (now commanded by Belcher). Thus McClure completed the North-West Passage from west to east, although in three different ships and (over one section) by sledge (Fig. 216).

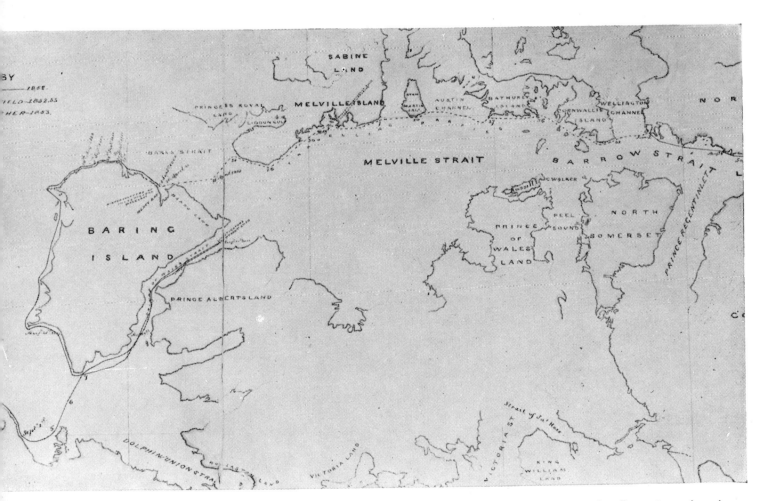

FIG. 216.—Chart showing McClure's completion of the North-West Passage by sledge from the *Investigator's* winter quarters (1852–3) on Banks ('Baring') Island.

In 1853 Dr John Rae, of the Hudson's Bay Company, picked up relics and reports of the death of Franklin's men from the Eskimos in the neighbourhood of King William Island, the channels round which had been explored by Rae. Six years later Captain F. L. McClintock in the steam yacht *Fox*, fitted out by Lady Franklin, sailed south into Prince Regent Inlet, and made sledge journeys along the coasts of King William Island, where he found the two written records and many other relics of the expedition (Fig. 217).[10]

The search for Franklin had revealed the navigable channels by which the North-West Passage could be made. Amundsen, making the first continuous navigation of the passage in 1903–6 in the motor herring-boat *Gjöa*, of only 47 tons, followed Franklin's route through Peel Sound and the east—and so far unnavigated—coast of King William Island to Collinson's furthest east in Cambridge Bay. Thus the achievement of the passage was built upon Franklin's expedition and its sequel. It was in this sector again, from Ellesmere Island in the north of the Canadian archipelago, that the Pole itself was reached by R. E. Peary in 1907.

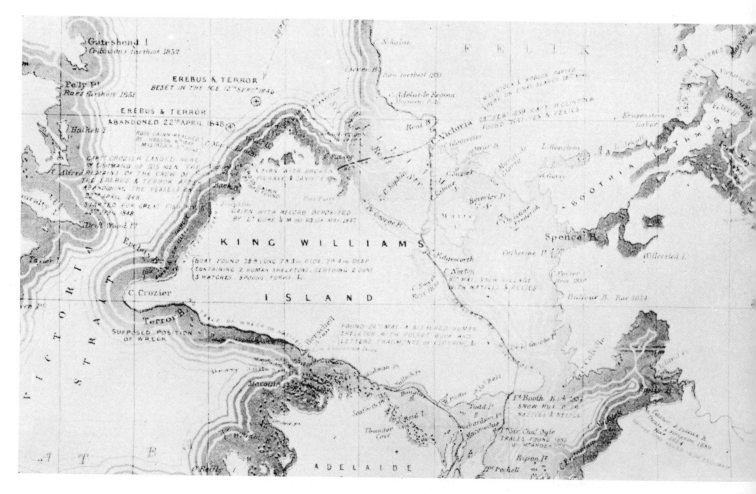

Fig. 217.—Map showing the final stages of the search for Franklin.

FIG. 218.—The *Fram* in the ice in 1895.

In October 1892 the most remarkable vessel ever designed and built for polar navigation was launched in Christiania Fjord. This was the *Fram*, in which Fridtjof Nansen had conceived the plan of drifting in the ice across the Pole from the mouth of the Lena River to Greenland. In thus reviving the project attempted by Phipps and Parry, Nansen proposed to use the ice as a vehicle instead of a barrier. His ship was to be 'as small and strong as possible', so as to 'withstand the pressure of the ice'; and was to carry five years' stores for twelve men. She was constructed with sloping sides, to the end that 'instead of nipping the ship, the ice must raise it out of the water'; and she was fitted with an auxiliary steam engine of 220 h.p. Nansen's project was generally condemned as 'ignoring the accepted canons of ice-navigation, of avoiding besetment, and of following the protected lee of land-masses'; yet the *Fram* proved all these criticisms to be unfounded. In September 1893 she was frozen up near the New Siberian Islands (Fig. 218) and after reaching the latitude of 85° 57′ she drifted west and south until she freed herself north of Spitsbergen in June 1896. The *Fram* made a second voyage to the Arctic under Otto Sverdrup; and she was

317

lent to Roald Amundsen for the voyage to the Ross Sea, from which in 1909 he made his journey to the South Pole.

Of the northern passages proposed by Thorne,[11] that by the north-east was, at the beginning of the 19th century, considered to be the most discouraging; yet it was the first to be navigated throughout in a single vessel. A century after Cook, the experience of Russian and Scandinavian expeditions by sea and land had convinced the Swedish scientist A. E. Nordenskiöld 'that the open navigable water which two years in succession [1875 and 1876] had carried me across the Kara Sea . . . to the mouth of the Yenisei, extended in all probability as far as Behring's Straits, and that a circumnavigation of the old world was thus within the bounds of possibility'. Nordenskiöld's ship, the whaler *Vega*, sailed from Tromsö on 21 July 1878 and, passing through the Yugor Strait, rounded Cape Chelyuskin on 19 August and wintered in 173° E longitude, 120 miles from East Cape. In the summer of 1879 she passed through Bering Strait into the Pacific Ocean (Fig. 219).

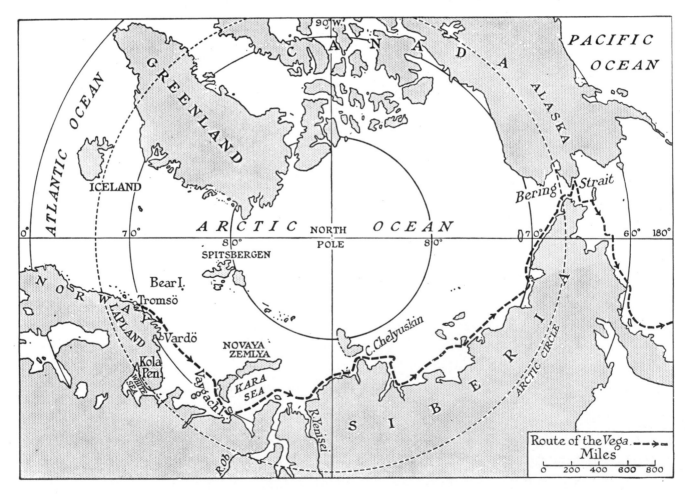

FIG. 219.—The North-East Passage traversed by Nordenskiöld in the *Vega*, 1878–9.

In 1932 a Soviet ice-breaker made the first passage in a single season between the White Sea and the Pacific. In 1939 eleven vessels completed the passage which for over three centuries defied the efforts of European voyagers. Today the ice-breakers of the Soviet Union keep the sea lanes open for the summer convoys between the harbours of Northern Russia, the river estuaries giving access to the interior of Asia, and the Pacific ports. Thus the 16th-century dream of a commercial 'waie of the northe' to the Far East has been realized.

Remarks on the Illustrations

Chapter XIV

<><><><><><><><><><><><><><><><><><><><><><><><><><><><><><><><><><><><><><><><><><><><><><><>

197   The woodcut world map by Oronce Finé, on a double cordiform (heart-shaped) projection, is dated 1531 and is found in the *Novus orbis* of Simon Grynaeus (Paris, 1532). The northern and southern hemispheres are divided at the Equator. In the Arctic, the four islands set round a polar sea derive from records of older voyages to the north (see Chapter V, and Figs. 61, 62); but Asia and North America are laid down as a single land mass. In the Antarctic the southern continent, already figured by Schöner in 1515 and Franciscus Monachus in 1529 (Figs. 42, 45), is extended by Finé to the tropic. Its geography is adapted to the results of Magellan's voyage (cf. 'mare magellanicum' and the Strait), and the continent is here first named Terra Australis, with the cautious comment 'recently discovered, but not yet fully known'. The map of Finé was the prototype for representations of Terra Australis, including that of Mercator, throughout the 16th century (cf. Figs. 8, 125–7).

198   This chart of the South Sandwich Islands, perhaps drawn by Henry Roberts (British Museum, Add. MS 15500.13), marks the *Resolution's* track off them, from west to east, 31 January–3 February 1775. (South is at the top.) Although he made no landings, Cook correctly divined that this was an island chain, and not a continuous coast; and to his first landfall he gave the name Southern Thule, 'the most southern land . . . yet . . . discovered'. Below is a view of Cape Bristol.

199   This lithograph in Fanning's book (see note 5) illustrates his description of the meeting between Palmer's whaler, the *Hero*, and Bellingshausen's two ships, the *Vostock* and *Mirni*, on 25 January 1821. When the fog lifted, they were 'in sight of the Shetland Islands, but nearest to Deception Island . . . Far off to the south, the icy tops of two or three of the mountains on Palmer's Land could be faintly seen'.

200   This representation of Smith's discovery of the South Shetlands in February

1819 is an inset of a manuscript 'Chart of New South Britain' forwarded by Smith to the Admiralty in 1821 and now in the Hydrographic Department (S 91).

201   Bransfield's chart of 'New or South Shetland' (Hydrographic Department, S 92), part of which is reproduced, was drawn from surveys made on his voyage in the *Williams*, January–February 1820. After taking possession of the South Shetlands he sailed south and discovered, in 64° S, 'Trinity Land partly covered with snow'.

202   The chart printed in Weddell's *A Voyage towards the South Pole* (London, 1825) lays down the tracks of his ships from the South Orkneys (which he surveyed) east and then south-east into the Weddell Sea to 74° 15' south latitude—over three degrees beyond Cook, whose furthest south in 1773 (in 106° 54' W) is also marked. Both Cook and Weddell were favoured by unusual ice conditions: no other ship has reached Cook's position in his longitude, and no later expedition has found the Weddell Sea so clear of ice. The suspicion that the South Sandwich group sighted by Cook might be part of the continent is indicated by the name 'Sandwich Land' given to it.

203   The illustration, engraved 'from a sketch by Cap. Weddell' for his book, shows his ships—the 160-ton brig *Jane* of Dundee and the 65-ton cutter *Beaufoy*— at the southernmost point of their voyage 'in a clear sea' on 20 February 1823. Here, as 'nothing like land was to be seen' and his crews began to grumble at the failure to find seals, Weddell decided to return northward to South Georgia and the Falklands. The small brigs, schooners and cutters used by the sealers were handy craft for manœuvring among icebergs or along the edges of the pack; but an Antarctic cruise in them was 'no picnic', and many were lost in this service.

204   The illustration, in the Atlas accompanying Captain Dumont d'Urville's *Voyage au Pôle Sud et dans l'Océanie* (Paris, 1841–5), shows the *Astrolabe* forcing her way through ice-floes under courses and topsails, with her consort the *Zélée* in the distance. This was in the Weddell Sea, in January 1838. These warships were not well adapted for polar navigation; unfortified against the ice, they had large gun-ports which made it impossible to keep them dry between decks.

205   This detail from the engraved Admiralty chart of 'Victoria Land, discovered in H.M.S. Erebus & Terror . . . Jany 1841' shows Captain James Clark Ross's tracks along the west coast of the Ross Sea as far as the 'great icy barrier' (29 January) which he found to extend across the head of the Sea. (South is at the top.)

206   Ross's ships gave their names to the two volcanoes discovered by him. Here, in January 1841, an eruption of Mount Erebus was seen. This is a lithograph, from a drawing by J. E. Davis, in Ross's book, *A Voyage of Discovery and Research in the Southern and Antarctic Regions* (London, 1847). The volcanoes in fact lie on an island, not on the mainland as supposed by Ross (see Fig. 205).

207   The collision shown in another illustration from Ross's book took place in a gale which was driving the ships down on the berg on the left. Although 'entangled by the rigging', they were skilfully disengaged and navigated through the narrow channel between the two bergs.

208   This map was published in *The Geographical Journal*, vol. XLI (1913).

209   The map of 1818, the year in which Barrow's book was published (see note 7) and the first two British expeditions sailed, illustrates the problems of the North-West Passage at the opening of the Admiralty's attempts on it. It was still uncertain whether Greenland had not a land connection with North America, which would close any sea lead to the north and west. The relationship between the points on the north coast of America reached by Cook, Mackenzie and Hearne was unknown.

210   This engraving, from a sketch by Lieutenant F. W. Beechey, was published in Parry's *Journal of a Voyage for the Discovery of a North-West Passage from the Atlantic to the Pacific* (London, 1821). The *Hecla* was barque-rigged, enabling the crew to be set at three (instead of two) watches, and she made three further voyages to the Arctic under Parry's command, ending in his expedition towards the Pole in 1827.

211   Parry's map (British Museum, Maps 188. o. 1 (3)) illustrates his discovery of the westerly lead from Baffin Bay. It shows his track in 1819 westward from Baffin Bay, through Lancaster Sound and Barrow Strait, to his winter quarters on Melville Island, in 111° W, from which he could see the land of Banks Island across the ice which blocked Banks (McClure) Strait. From Barrow Strait Parry had penetrated Prince Regent Inlet southward for about 120 miles before being turned back by ice. To the north he observed that Wellington Channel, in which 'no land nor ice was seen', seemed to offer a navigable passage into the open sea supposed to lie nearer the Pole; and he recognized that Melville Sound ('The Polar Sea') and Banks Strait also opened to the north and west.

212   This engraving from Back's *Narrative of an Expedition in H.M.S. Terror* (London, 1838) depicts the temporary 'disruption of the ice' round the *Terror*, frozen up at the entrance of Hudson Bay, 20 February 1837. The force with which she was nipped, wrote Back, 'would have crushed a less strengthened vessel to atoms'.

213   This lithographed view appeared in *Illustrated Arctic News*, a magazine prepared on board H.M.S. *Resolute*. The *Resolute* and *Assistance*, with their steam tenders *Pioneer* and *Intrepid*, were under the command of Captain H. T. Austin. In 1853 all four ships, when commanded by Sir Edward Belcher, were abandoned in Barrow Sound.

214   The lithograph, 'drawn by F. Bedwell Esq. R.N. from original sketches', in

Collinson's *Journal of H.M.S. Enterprise* (London, 1889) shows his ship at the western entrance of Dolphin and Union Strait, in the south of Victoria Island, September 1852.

215   Collinson's manuscript chart is in the Hydrographic Department of the Admiralty (D 1067). The detail reproduced marks, by a dotted line, his ship's track eastward from Dolphin and Union Strait into Cambridge Bay, on Dease Strait, in 1852; and, by a continuous line, the sledge journeys of his 'travelling parties' along the south-east and east coasts of Victoria Island in 1853. At this time one of Franklin's wrecked ships still lay on the west side of Victoria Strait (see Fig. 217).

216   The chart drawn by W. H. Fawkner, second master *Investigator*, and now in the Hydrographic Department (L 9311), marks the tracks of McClure's ship and of other vessels engaged in the Franklin search, 1848–53. The detail reproduced shows McClure's exploration of Prince of Wales Strait to the east of 'Baring Island' (Banks Island), in 1850–1, and his route up the west coast of the island to winter quarters (1851 2) in Mercy Bay. Here he was forced to abandon his ship and sledged across Banks Strait to Parry's Winter Harbour, on Melville Island, where he was picked up by ships of Austin's squadron.

217   The detail reproduced from a map published in 1860 records the final phases of Franklin's expedition in 1846–8, with the 'supposed position' of one of his wrecked ships; the search along the straits round King William's Island; and the discovery of relics by Rae and other explorers (1851–5) and by McClintock (1858–9).

218   This photograph of the *Fram* in the ice was published in Nansen's *Farthest North* (London, 1897). The windmill shown generated electricity.

Notes

Chapter XIV

◇◇◇

[1] See Chapters V and XI.

[2] At the end of his second voyage, in January 1775, Cook was even 'bold enough to say . . . that the lands which may lie to the south will never be explored'. This was, for him, an unusually unsuccessful forecast.

[3] See Chapter XI.

[4] He was led to this inference by observing 'the breaking up of the ice-cliffs' of South Georgia.

[5] The story of this meeting is told, with somewhat different emphasis, in Bellingshausen's narrative and in Captain Edmund Fanning's *Voyages round the World* (New York, 1833). According to Fanning, Palmer offered to pilot the Russian ships into harbour and reported 'the existence of an immense extent of land to the south, whose mountains might be seen from the mast-head'; Bellingshausen 'was so forcibly struck with the circumstances of the case, that he named the coast then to the south, Palmer's Land'. None of this finds any confirmation in Bellingshausen's account of the meeting.

[6] Bombs, like the later monitors, were specially designed for carrying heavy mortars. They rolled heavily in a sea, but drew little water; and they were considered suitable for long voyages, being 'of large scantling, and having a capacious hold'.

[7] This and subsequent quotations are from Barrow's *A Chronological History of Voyages into the Arctic Regions; undertaken chiefly for the purpose of discovering a . . . polar passage between the Atlantic and Pacific* (London, 1818).

[8] In April 1851, off the Newfoundland Banks, an English brig bound for Quebec sighted two three-masted ships stranded on a large ice-floe and corresponding to the *Erebus* and *Terror* in appearance.

[9] Austin's squadron in Barrow Strait had two steam tenders (seen in Fig. 213). This was 'practically the first occasion on which full-powered steamers were employed in ice navigation'.

[10] The relics of the Franklin expedition brought home by McClintock are exhibited at the National Maritime Museum, with the steering wheel, binnacle and bell of the *Fox*.

[11] See Chapter V.

AFTERWORD

THE MAPS REPRODUCED in this book reflect, in varying degree, the knowledge with which the early explorer set out, his hopes and expectations, and the discoveries which he made. The chart or map was originally developed as a guide to travellers along frequented routes. As the limits of the world known to Europeans were extended, the critical effort of cartographers came to be concentrated at its periphery, on the uncertain boundary between knowledge and ignorance. From the 15th century the map has been a powerful instrument in the communication of geographical ideas and experience. As a graphic document employing visual symbols it has made a more immediate impact on men's minds than the written word. This may be partly explained by the positiveness with which it presents geographical facts. The statements which it makes—on position, direction, distance, or extent—have an absolute character, in comparison with those of written texts which can more easily be qualified. At the same time, and perhaps for similar reasons, the influence of mapmakers on geographical thought has tended to be conservative rather than progressive, and maps alone are no true index to the state of knowledge in their time.

These general considerations are exemplified time and again in the history of exploration and in the maps associated with it. Many important discoveries have been made by expeditions in quest of illusory objectives laid down on their maps. 'The fictions', wrote Sir Walter Raleigh, '(or let them be called coniectures) painted in Maps, doe serue only to mis-lead such discouerers as rashly beleiue them.' In the longitudes in which he thought to find Cipangu and Cathay, Columbus made his landfalls in the West Indies and South America. French, Spanish and English explorers, seeking a waterway from the Atlantic seaboard to the Pacific, revealed the great extent of the American continent 'from sea to sea'. The west coast of Australia was 'unexpectedly and accidentally' discovered by Dutch ships eastward bound and out in their reckoning. Tasman, in search of a Southern Continent, fell in with New

Zealand. The concepts which inspired these and many other venturers are recorded in the maps which they carried with them; and the maps which they brought home often reveal the pertinacity with which they held to their original hypothesis and sought to reconcile it with their new discoveries. Raleigh defended conjecture in History, 'as Geographers in their Maps describe those Countries, whereof as yet there is made no true discouery, that is, either by leauing some part blanke, or by inserting . . . Head-lands, Bayes, great Riuers, and other particularities, agreeable to common report, though many times controlled by following experience, and found contrary to truth.'

Thus a chronological sequence of early maps will not necessarily show continuous progress in representation. Running through it, and defying experience, may sometimes be found a constant and dominant feature: a strait or sea-way connecting two oceans, a land bridge between two territories, a stretch of continental coast. These are the great geographical myths—navigable passages within the Arctic Circle, a Strait of Anian or of Juan de Fuca, a Terra Australis ranging from the South Pole to the Tropics, a southward extension of New Guinea linking it to Australia.

Such myths were not merely the creation of armchair geographers like Herrick's brother:

> . . . thou at home without or tyde or gale,
> Canst in thy Map securely sail:
> Seeing those painted Countries; and so guesse
> By those fine Shades, their Substances.

An *a priori* theory, born in the study and resting on arguments from analogy and symmetry, might indeed lie behind the cartographer's representation of a Southern Continent; and it was erroneous estimates of the size of the earth, and so of the length of a degree, that deluded the early discoverers of America and in the Pacific. But into his pattern, extending or completing it, the mapmaker wove also many imperfectly correlated travellers' tales. The explorers themselves, seeking illusory lands and the wealth which they too willingly located in them, made their contribution to the myths and furnished corroborative evidence for them. Landfalls on scattered islands, seabirds and floating weed, the absence of ocean swell—such reports could be pieced together into the outline of a continuous continental coast. An estuary or gulf, barred to a pilot by reefs or adverse winds, could be interpreted as an open strait.

Until the 18th century the explorer's map must in general be considered an imperfect record of his achievement. Before the day of light precision instruments, notably the reflecting sextant and chronometer, his technique for laying down his position and track admitted a wide margin of error, and the uncertainty with which his discoveries were mapped often broke the thread of continuity for centuries.

The want of exact data gave scope, in Bougainville's phrase, to 'that spirit of system-making . . . so incompatible with true philosophy' and to the 'haughty writers who confine nature within the limits of their own invention'. His retort was in tune with the new age that was opening—'Geography is a science of facts'; and Dalrymple, when the dust of the Terra Australis controversy had long settled, was to write: 'Precision is not to be expected in Geographical Combinations; Surveys and Astronomical Observations only can give Precision.' But the early explorer was no slayer of myths: he sought in the expectation of finding, and few of the predecessors of Cook and Bougainville, or of Park and Mackenzie, approached their task in the sceptical spirit of the scientific traveller.

Nevertheless these reservations do but increase the value of early maps as documents in the history of human thought and enterprise. They testify to the slender resources with which the early traveller boldly measured his skill against unknown hazards by sea and land 'in searching the most opposite corners and quarters of the worlde, and . . . in compassing the vast globe of the earth'.

BIBLIOGRAPHICAL NOTE

Some collections of voyages and travels, published before 1700
(in chronological order of publication)

MONTALBODDO, Fracanzano. *Paesi nouamente retrouati*. Vicenza, 1507.

RAMUSIO, Giambattista. *Delle nauigationi e viaggi*. Venice, 1550-9. 3 vols.

BARROS, João de. *Decadas da India*. Lisbon, Madrid, 1552-1615. (A chronicle of Portuguese voyages to 1538.)

EDEN, Richard. *The Decades of the New Worlde, or West India*. London, 1555.

GALVÃO, Antonio. *Livro dos descobrimentos das Antilhas e India*. Lisbon, 1563. (A summary of Portuguese voyages to 1555.)

WILLES, Richard. *The History of Travayle in the West and East Indies*. London, 1577. (An enlarged edition of Eden's collection of 1555.)

HAKLUYT, Richard. *The Principall Nauigations, Voiages, and Discoueries of the English Nation*. London, 1589. Enlarged edition, in 3 vols., London, 1598-1600.

DE BRY, Theodor. 'Grands Voyages' [to the West]. Frankfort, 1590-1634. 13 pt.

—— 'Petits Voyages' [to the East]. Frankfort, 1598-1628. 12 pt.

PURCHAS, Samuel. *Hakluytus Posthumus, or Purchas his Pilgrimes*. London, 1625. 4 vols.

COMMELIN, Isaac. *Begin ende voortgangh van de Vereenighde Nederlandsche Geoctroyeerde Oost-Indische Compagnie*. Amsterdam, 1646.

THÉVENOT, Melchisedech. *Relation de divers voyages curieux*. Paris, 1663. Enlarged edition, 1696.

Some histories of exploration

BAKER, J. N. L. *A History of Geographical Discovery and Exploration*. London, 1937.

CARY, Martin, and WARMINGTON, E. H. *The Ancient Explorers*. London, 1929.

BEAZLEY, Raymond. *The Dawn of Modern Geography*. Oxford, 1897-1906. 3 vols.

PENROSE, Boies. *Travel and Discovery in the Renaissance, 1420-1620*. Cambridge, Mass., 1952.

HEAWOOD, Edward. *A History of Geographical Discovery in the Seventeenth and Eighteenth Centuries*. Cambridge, 1912.

INDEX